D0455179

# *More* Classics to Read Aloud to Your Children

*Also by William F. Russell*

The Gramma Game
The Parents' Handbook of Grammar and Usage
Classics to Read Aloud to Your Children

WILLIAM F. RUSSELL, Ed.D.

# *More* Classics to Read Aloud to Your Children

Crown Publishers, Inc.
New York

Grateful acknowledgment is given for the following excerpts:

"The Lottery" from *The Lottery,* copyright 1948, 1949 by Shirley Jackson, copyright renewed © 1976, 1977 by Lawrence Hyman, Barry Hyman, Sarah Webster, and Joanne Schnurer. "The Lottery" originally appeared in *The New Yorker.* Reprinted by permission of Farrar, Straus and Giroux, Inc.

Chapter One of *The Yearling,* copyright 1938 by Marjorie Kinnan Rawlings, copyright renewed © 1966 by Norton Baskin. Reprinted by permission of Charles Scribner's Sons.

"Birches" and "Stopping by Woods on a Snowy Evening" from *The Poetry of Robert Frost,* edited by Edward Connery Lathem, copyright 1916, 1923, © 1969 by Holt, Rinehart and Winston. Copyright 1944, 1951 by Robert Frost. Reprinted by permission of Holt, Rinehart and Winston, Publishers.

"A Miserable, Merry Christmas" from *The Autobiography of Lincoln Steffens,* copyright 1931 by Harcourt Brace Jovanovich, Inc., copyright renewed © 1959 by Peter Steffens. Reprinted by permission of the publisher.

"Arithmetic" from *The Complete Poems of Carl Sandburg,* copyright 1950 by Carl Sandburg, copyright renewed © 1978 by Margaret Sandburg, Helga Sandburg Crile, and Janet Sandburg. Reprinted by permission of Harcourt Brace Jovanovich, Inc.

Published by Crown Publishers, Inc., 225 Park Avenue South, New York, New York 10003, and represented in Canada by the Canadian MANDA Group

More classics to read aloud to your children.

CROWN is a trademark of Crown Publishers, Inc.

Manufactured in the United States of America

**Library of Congress Cataloging-in-Publication Data**
More classics to read aloud to your children.
     Summary: Selections for reading aloud from poems, novels, and plays by Blake, Longfellow, O. Henry, Twain, Shakespeare, Poe, and other well-known authors.
     1. Children's literature. 2. Oral reading.
[1. Literature—Collections] I. Russell, William F., 1945-
PZ5.M834 1986     808.8'99282     86–4201
ISBN 0-517-56108-5

10   9   8   7   6   5   4   3   2   1

First Edition

# *Contents*

# Reading Aloud and the Teachable Moment

**"Read the best books first,
or you may not have a chance to read them at all."
—HENRY DAVID THOREAU**

Reading aloud is the cornerstone of family learning, and family learning may very well be our best hope for revitalizing public education in America. For decades now, educators and policymakers have ignored the clear and consistent research that shows the powerful impact a family can have on the education of its children. This impact is not dependent upon race, income, the parents' education, or any of the other conditions that "everyone knows" differentiate parents who want their children to succeed in school from those who don't really care. What the research shows is that it is not what a family *is* or what a family *has* that affects—and perhaps determines—the academic achievement of its children; the differences can be traced, instead, to what a family *does* to encourage learning in the home.

Reading aloud to and with children encourages learning in the home. Hearing a well-crafted work of literature not only accustoms a child (or an adult) to the use of precise vocabulary and the sound of standard English usage, but it also provides inspiration for future learning and action. Hearing a story or a poem about travel to the stars, for example, can excite young minds to learn more about the wonders of the night sky, perhaps to study aviation, perhaps to read or write about space and time. Hearing a tale of human frailty can alert youngsters early on that all humans have strengths and weaknesses and that they can find similar examples throughout the species, perhaps by studying the lives of historic heroes or the struggles of ancient civilizations, perhaps by looking at the behaviors of people around them, perhaps by focusing on their own behaviors—past, present, and future.

Read-alouds create these "teachable moments": sparks of interest in learning about where or when or how an event in the story occurred; moments at which a child practically demands to be taught a piece of geography or history or science. These sparks are not the learnings themselves, but they are the necessary beginnings for all learning. They must be cared for and attended to right away, or else they will likely die. They are teachable *moments* only, and they will not wait patiently until a certified teacher and a classroom and a curriculum are all in place and prepared to nurture a specific spark.

It is for this reason that ignoring the educational power of the home has become so intolerable. In a very real sense, our society simply can no longer afford to maintain its narrow and restrictive insistence upon equating learning and schooling. There are millions of parents throughout the land—parents on whom we have already spent billions of dollars providing for their own education—who are eager to use that education in igniting and nourishing fires of learning in their children. All they ask is to be given some guidance and training in the proper methods and materials that will enhance learning in their homes.

Here, then, is a wonderfully exciting and productive new area of opportunity for teachers and for teachers of teachers. Family learning, you see, should not be conducted in competition with the schools, but in cooperation with them.

Since reading aloud has such educational benefit in the home, one would think that it should have some merit within the schools as well. And so it does. In fact, its benefits—for *all* grade levels and for *all* ability levels—are now becoming so apparent to educators that read-alouds are beginning to occupy their rightful place as regular and scheduled parts of the classroom day. No longer do teachers have to close their doors lest the principal catch them employing the practice too frequently. It is clear now that reading aloud to students is directly and positively related to their reading performance, to their language development, and to the development of their reading interests. It creates teachable moments in the classroom just as surely as it does in the home. In short, it is every bit as important in the cognitive development of children, every bit as justifiable as a regular classroom activity, as any other subject or practice in the curriculum. I hope that we have finally seen the last of the withdrawing of read-aloud time as a punishment for a class that has misbehaved. Would any teacher ever consider —let alone try to justify—punishing a class by taking away its math or science time?

Classroom read-alouds, like those in the home, create the opportunity for teaching and learning in some areas that the schools no longer include or do not emphasize in the curriculum. The study of geography, for example—so ideally suited to a listener's need to know about where an adventure occurred—has been removed altogether from some schools and confined in others to a specific semester of a specific grade. But placing the scenes from *Treasure Island* or "To Build a Fire" on a map helps students fix these stories in their minds; an appreciation for both geography and history can be a part of the benefits of hearing Lincoln's "Gettysburg Address."

The development of character and moral values has been unnecessarily confused by many educators with the teaching of religion, and so our teenagers are all too often consigned to an education that tries to be "value-free" or "value-neutral"— a policy that conforms quite well to the "anything goes" philosophy they hear professed on the street or in rock videos. Yet the moral struggles that have provided the focus for the greatest works ever written can now provide a learning opportunity for adolescents who are themselves struggling with questions of conscience and character. Macbeth's belief that "the end justifies the means" and the power of group pressure in "The Lottery" provide examples by which listening teens can test and develop their own character.

Even the study of oral language itself—the development of a child's ability to present ideas to others in a clear and polished way—has evaporated, in many cases, from our school work. Memorizing and presenting poems or speeches is now thought to be old-fashioned and, therefore, poor pedagogy. A course in public speaking is rarely required, and even in-class responses are allowed to be grunted in whatever argot is currently in vogue. What a shame, for there is now abundant evidence to show that adolescent competence in oral language is essential for their satisfactory performance in reading, writing, and spelling. Having students prepare, practice, and present a read-aloud to their classmates encourages the development of their confidence and competence in using spoken English.

Most read-alouds, however, will still be conducted in the home, and that is as it should be. Reading aloud in the home has myriad language benefits as well as emotional benefits for children—pre-schoolers and adolescents alike. But home read-alouds also benefit the parents, especially when the chosen selections are "classics." I don't know how many times during the past year I have had parents (and some teachers, too) come up to me after a speech or a workshop and say, "Dr. Russell, I just wanted you to know how much I enjoyed 'The Ransom of Red Chief' (or *A Christmas Carol* or 'The Legend of Sleepy Hollow'). You know, I never actually read some of the works I was supposed to when I was in school, and now I find I'm reading them as much for my own enjoyment as for my children's." Wonderful! Here is adult education at its finest.

Indeed, the defining characteristic of "classic" works may not be their age or their critical acclaim; instead, the great works seem able to be fully comprehended only when one has some experience with living. Yes, they have meaning to children, but it is at a different level, and that meaning will grow and change as those children grow and change.

This is especially true with great poetry, and a special mention should be made here concerning the best method for reading these poems aloud. The sonnets of Shakespeare ("When, in disgrace with fortune and men's eyes" and "Let me not to the marriage of true minds" are included in this volume), for example, do not yield up their treasure quickly or easily. Poems like these must be read silently first, mulled over, then set aside and allowed to steep or ferment in one's mind and memory. On the next reading, new images appear and new messages as well. More fermentation. Now a return, and magically, more ideas, different thoughts come to mind. Each re-reading gives new appreciation for the beauty, the grace, and the perfection of the language: just the right words in just the right places. You didn't see these ideas or this beauty when you read the poem earlier; I didn't either; no one does or can. That is the nature of well-written poetry in general and time-less poetry in particular.

But now that your eyes have been opened to the insights in the poem, and the lines come easily to the tongue, now is the time to read it aloud to someone. Don't expect the listener to be able to taste all the delicacies of the poem after hearing it but once, either. Let it steep and ferment, then try it again, and so on.

Children from families in which reading aloud is a common activity in the home make better listeners in the classroom. But all classes can become—and rather quickly, too—eager and considerate audiences if their teachers will be eager in their reading and considerate of the interests of their students. One cannot begin a school read-aloud program by edict and then merely expect the students' appreciation. We teachers must remember that our audience belongs to a television generation: These children have grown up seeing and hearing performances by professional actors and actresses, and they will expect a similar polish in their teacher's presentation. Two points are in your favor, however. First, keep in mind that, the quality of television being what it is, your audience's taste in performing skill and its experience in hearing mastery of the mother tongue are not very extensive or highly refined. Second, if you choose to read masterpieces of the language—such as those contained in this book and in the previous collection—your material will far eclipse that of your competition. In fact, an effective read-aloud does not require accomplished acting as much as it does accomplished *reading*. The three most important words to remember are PRACTICE, PRACTICE, PRACTICE.

No teacher should ever think that a story—any story—can be just trotted out and read without rehearsal. Research into oral reading in the classroom shows that eye contact with the audience is among the most important characteristics of an effective read-aloud. This eye contact comes from being familiar with the story: having an unshakable knowledge of the words and the events, and using the text merely for momentary refreshment. Practice can also lengthen the span of words that your eyes take in with a single glance; it can allow you to discover new pitches and "characters" in your voice, as well as actions that will enhance a particular passage.

Eye contact is not as important in a parent/child read-aloud because the reader is not as commonly the sole focus of attention, but experience with the story is still requisite, if only to make the pronunciation of unfamiliar words seem so smooth that the child will accept these words as being familiar. Pre-reading allows the parent an opportunity to introduce beforehand some of the words that will be new to the child by weaving them into casual conversation, so that when those words come up later in the presentation of the story, the child will hear them in context and will be better prepared and better able to understand their meaning and to store them for later use.

The educational value of reading aloud in the home is not a new discovery—far from it. E. B. Huey, in a text entitled *The Psychology and Pedagogy of Reading,* summed it up quite well: "The secret of it all lies in the parents' reading aloud to and with the child." That book was published in 1908! We in the business of education may have ignored this piece of wisdom for the past few generations, but, fortunately, ignorance is a correctable condition, and I think we would do well to begin demonstrating that fact right away. There is so much learning potential—both for home learning and for classroom learning —in reading aloud, especially in reading classics aloud, that perhaps this educational practice will help unite our homes and schools, our parents and teachers, into a working partnership for the benefit of children.

Someday our children's schools and our schools of education will begin to see parents as legitimate clients for the skills of classroom teachers. Someday parents will realize that the tools for learning—both for their own learning and for that of their children—are all around them and have only to be summoned up when the need—the spark—appears. And someday children will grow up thinking that the world is a thoroughly knowable place, that they can learn about it from everything and from everybody, and they'll wonder what all this fuss was ever about. Oh, I'm looking forward to that.

# Listening Level I

## (Ages 5 and up)

*Although reading aloud should be an important part of every stage in a child's growth, it is most critical to this one. When children approach the age of five, they are ready to be weaned from picture books; they have the creative ability and the attention span necessary to hear a tale and see it only in their mind's eye. And it is at this stage that children have the greatest need to experience more than they can read for themselves.*

*Here are some classics that will be most appealing to this young and varied group, whether your aim is to fire their imagination or usher them to sleep. The simpler selections are presented first and the more challenging ones later, but keep in mind that no child is too young or too old for any of these stories and poems.*

*As I remarked in the previous collection, the majority of parents* stop *reading aloud when their children reach this stage, and that one omission in good parenting creates repercussions that can be seen in their children's reading ability and reading enjoyment forever after.*

*But we read aloud out of self-interest, too. We get a feeling of warmth and a pride in widening the horizons of our children when we share any reading with them, but when that reading is a classic, we can find food for our own thoughts as well. In this section you will encounter poetic language to charm adult tastes, too, and you will read deeper meanings in the accounts of naked emperors, materialistic toads, and overly curious goddesses. Enjoy!*

# The Brave Tin Soldier

by
## HANS CHRISTIAN ANDERSEN

**About the story:**

*Few would have guessed that the tall and awkward boy who stayed away from school to avoid the taunts and the ridicule of his classmates would grow to become a world-famous author and the outstanding literary figure in his homeland of Denmark. Hans Christian Andersen, himself, always knew he would be famous, and he tried his hand at almost every art form in order to secure that fame; he tried dancing, singing, acting, writing plays and poetry—all without success. Indeed, most of his young life was mired in poverty and failure.*

*He didn't try writing fairy tales until he was thirty years old, but by then he had acquired the kind of worldly knowledge that would allow him to root his imaginary tales in the happenings of real life. "The Ugly Duckling" (which appears in the previous collection), tells of the loneliness and rejection he experienced in his own childhood; "The Emperor's New Clothes," beginning on page 17, is a commentary on the behavior of humans, both in Andersen's time and in our own.*

*And then there are the tales like the one presented here, the pure fantasies that Andersen intended for his youngest listeners—those charming and exciting stories that have no moral, just magic.*

**Approximate reading time:** 10 minutes
**Vocabulary and pronunciation guide:**
    **muslin** [MUZZ-lin]: a fabric of woven cotton, used especially for sheets
    **gnash** [NASH]: to grind one's teeth together
    **steadfast** [STED-fast]: unchanging; constant, especially in loyalty or bravery

——— 11 ———

Some years ago, there were twenty-five tin soldiers, who were all brothers, for they had been made out of the tin of the same old tin spoon. They all carried rifles on their shoulders; they all looked straight ahead; and they all wore splendid red and blue uniforms. The first thing in the world they ever heard were the words, "Tin soldiers!" uttered by a little boy, who clapped his hands with delight when the lid of the box in which they lay was taken off. They were given to him for a birthday present, and he stood at the table to set them up. The soldiers were all exactly alike, except one, who had only one leg. He had been the last one to be made, and then there was not enough of the melted tin to finish him. But he stood just as firmly on one leg as the others did on two, and because of that, he was very noticeable.

The table on which the soldiers stood was covered with other toys, but the most attractive one was a pretty little paper castle. You could even look through the small windows in the castle to see the rooms inside. In front of the castle, a number of little trees surrounded a piece of mirror, which was intended to represent a transparent lake. Swans, made of wax, swam on the lake and were reflected in it. All this was very pretty, but the prettiest of all was a tiny little lady, who stood at the open door of the castle. She, also, was made of paper, and she wore a dress of the thinnest muslin [MUZZ-lin], with a narrow blue ribbon over her shoulders just like a scarf. In the middle of this ribbon was fixed a glittering tinsel rose, as large as her whole face.

The lady was a dancer, and she stretched out both her arms and raised one of her legs so high that the tin soldier could not see it at all, and he thought that she, like himself, had only one leg. "That is the wife for me," he thought; "yet she is too grand, and she lives in a castle, while I have only a box to live in, twenty-five of us all together; that is surely no place to make a home for her. Still, I must try to meet her." Then he laid himself full length on the table behind a bookend, so that he could peek out unseen at the delicate little lady who continued to stand on one leg without losing her balance.

When evening came, the other tin soldiers were all placed in the box, and the people of the house all went to bed. Then the toys began to talk to each other, to have their own games together, to engage in make-believe battles, and to dance at their own festive parties. The tin soldiers rattled in their box; they wanted to get out and join the amusements, but they could not open the lid. The nutcracker bounded about noisily playing leapfrog, and the pencil clattered as it jumped around on the table. There was such a racket that the canary woke up and began to talk, and in poetry too. Only the tin soldier, who was still behind the bookend, and the dancer remained in their place. She stood on the tip of one toe, with her arms stretched out, and he lay motionless, never taking his eyes off her for a moment.

The clock struck twelve, and, by some magic, the figure that was carved in the bookend became a little black goblin who jumped out and spoke to the tin soldier saying, "Tin soldier, don't wish for what does not belong to you and what you cannot ever have." But the tin soldier pretended not to hear. "Very well," said the goblin, "just wait till tomorrow, then you'll see."

When the children came into the room on the next morning, they found the tin soldier, but instead of placing him back in the box with the others, they stood him up in the window sill. Now, whether it was the goblin that did it, or a sudden draft, or whatever, I don't know, but in any event the window flew open, and out fell the tin soldier, head over heels, down and down from the third story window to the street below. It was a terrible fall, for he landed head downwards, his helmet and his bayonet stuck in between the sidewalk stones, and his one leg straight up in the air. The maid and one of the children went immediately downstairs to look for him, but although they nearly stepped on him at one point in their search, they could not locate him. They had been so close that if he had only called out, "Here I am," they would surely have heard him and taken him back upstairs. But, being the true soldier, he was too proud to cry out for help while he was wearing a uniform.

Presently it began to rain, and the drops fell faster and faster until it was a heavy shower. When it was over, two boys happened to pass by, and one of them said, "Look, there is a tin soldier! He ought to have a boat to sail in."

So they made a boat out of a newspaper they found lying nearby. They placed the tin soldier in the boat and sent him sailing down the gutter, which was swollen from the fresh rainfall, while the boys ran alongside clapping their hands. Good gracious, what large waves arose in that gutter! And how fast the stream rolled on, for the rain had been very heavy!

The paper boat rocked up and down, and turned itself round sometimes so quickly that the tin soldier trembled. Yet he remained firm; his appearance did not change; he looked straight before him and kept his rifle at his shoulder. Suddenly the boat shot under a bridge and through the openings of a sewer cover and into a drainage tunnel, and then it was as dark as it was in the box where the tin soldier slept with his twenty-four comrades in arms.

"Where am I going now?" thought he. "This is the black goblin's fault, I am sure. Oh, but if the little dancing lady were only here with me in the boat, I wouldn't care no matter how dark it was."

Suddenly there appeared a large water rat, who lived in the drain.

"Have you a passport?" asked the rat. "Give it to me at once." But the tin soldier remained silent and held his musket tighter than ever.

The boat sailed on, and the rat followed it. How he did gnash [NASH] his teeth and cry out to the bits of wood and straw that bobbed in the rushing stream, "Stop him, stop him! He has not paid his toll, and has not shown his passport!"

But the stream rushed on stronger and stronger. The tin soldier could already see daylight where the tunnel ended. Then he heard a roaring sound quite terrible enough to frighten anyone. It was only that, at the end of the tunnel, the gutter spilled out and splashed down into a large river. The fall was only a few feet, but that was as dangerous to him as a high waterfall would be to us.

He was too close to it to stop. The boat rushed on, and the poor tin soldier could only hold himself as stiffly as possible, without moving an eyelid, to show that he was not afraid. The boat whirled round three or four times, and then filled with water to the very edge; nothing could save it from sinking. He now stood up to his neck in water, while deeper and deeper sank the boat, and as the paper soaked quite through, it became soft and loose. At last the water closed over the soldier's head. He thought of the pretty little dancer whom he would never see again, and the words of a song sounded in his ears—

> "Farewell warrior! ever brave,
> Drifting onward to thy grave."

Then the paper boat fell to pieces, and the soldier sank into the water and was immediately swallowed by a huge fish.

Oh, how dark it was inside the fish! A great deal darker than in the drainage tunnel, and narrower too, but the tin soldier remained steadfast [STED-fast] and brave, lying down full length with his musket still shouldered. The fish swam to and fro, making the most fearful movements, but at last he became quite still. Presently a flash of lightning seemed to pass through him, and then the daylight appeared, and a voice cried out, "I declare, look here; it's a tin soldier!" The fish had been caught, taken to the market, and sold to the cook, who took it into the kitchen and cut it open with a knife. She picked up the soldier and held him by the waist between her finger and thumb. Then she carried him into another room, where the people were all anxious to see this wonderful soldier who had traveled about inside a fish, but he was not at all proud. They placed him on the table, and—wonder of wonders, miracle of miracles!—there he was in the very same room with the very same window from which he had fallen. There were the same children, the same toys standing on the table, and the fine castle with the little dancer at the door. She still balanced herself on one leg and held up the other: She was as steadfast as he was himself. It touched the tin soldier so much to see her that he almost wept tin tears, but he kept them back. He looked at her, but she said nothing.

Presently one of the little boys picked up the tin soldier and threw him into the fire, which was roaring in the fireplace. He had no reason for doing this, and so it must have been the evil magic of the black goblin in the bookend that caused the boy to be so wicked. The flames lighted up the tin soldier as he stood. The heat was terrible, but whether it came from the real fire or from the fire of his love for the dancer, he could not tell. The bright colors of his uniform were faded, but whether they had been washed off during his journey or from the effects of his sorrow, no one could say. He looked out at the little lady, and she looked at him. He felt himself melting away, but he still remained firm and brave, and his gun remained on his shoulder.

Suddenly the door of the room flew open, and the draft of air caught up the little dancer. She fluttered like a sprite right into the fireplace by the side of the tin soldier, was instantly engulfed in flames, and was gone. The tin soldier melted down into a lump, and the next morning when the maid took the ashes out of the fireplace, she found him in the shape of a little tin heart. Of the little dancer, nothing remained but the tinsel rose, which was burned black as a cinder.

# The Emperor's New Clothes

by
## HANS CHRISTIAN ANDERSEN

**About the story:**

*Hans Christian Andersen's tales for children were, at first, denounced by critics in his native Denmark for not teaching or preaching historical and cultural values, as fairy tales up to that time had done. It was not long, however, before everyone realized that in these allegorical tales there were more lessons about life and values than had ever been taught to children before. Indeed, Andersen tried to write stories that would appeal to children and adults alike. "I seize an idea for older people," he said, "and then tell it to the young ones, while remembering that father and mother are listening and must have something to think about."*

*One frequent Andersen subject and one that parents can think about along with their children is the pretension and humbug that commonly parade as wisdom in society. The self-interest displayed in "The Emperor's New Clothes" has many parallels in modern politics, and all of us can benefit from a reminder that fear of being different from the crowd keeps people from seeing or speaking the truth. Still, this story does not depend entirely upon these lessons for its value. You may, quite properly, decide to let your youngsters enjoy it as a story first, and then draw upon it for lessons years later.*

**Approximate reading time:** 10 minutes

**Vocabulary and pronunciation guide:**

    **courtiers** [CORE-tee-erz]: members of the king's court
    **mantle:** a loose, sleeveless cloak
    **train:** the part of a gown that trails behind the wearer
    **writhed** [RYEthd]: twisted or squirmed

MMany years ago there was an Emperor who was so excessively fond of new clothes that he spent all his money on them. He cared nothing about his soldiers, nor for the theater, nor for driving in the woods except for the sake of showing off his new clothes. He had a costume for every hour in the day. Instead of saying, as one does about any other king or emperor, "He is in his council chamber," the people here always said, "The Emperor is in his dressing room."

Life was merry in the great town where he lived. Hosts of strangers came to visit it every day, and among them one day were two swindlers. They made themselves out to be weavers and said that they knew how to weave the most beautiful fabrics imaginable. Not only were the colors and the patterns unusually fine, but the clothes that were made of this cloth had the peculiar quality of becoming invisible to every person who was not fit for the office he held, or who was impossibly dull.

"Those must be splendid clothes," thought the Emperor. "By wearing them I should be able to discover which men in my kingdom are unfit for their jobs. I shall distinguish the wise men from the fools. Yes, I certainly must order some of that fabric to be woven for me."

The Emperor paid the two swindlers a lot of money in advance, so that they might begin their work at once.

They did put up two looms, and they pretended to weave, but they had nothing whatever upon their shuttles. At the outset they asked for a quantity of the finest silk and the purest gold thread, all of which they put into their own bags while they worked away at the empty looms far into the night.

"I should like to know how those weavers are getting on with their cloth," thought the Emperor, but he felt a little queer when he reflected that anyone who was stupid or unfit for his post would not be able to see it. He certainly thought that he need have no fears for himself, but still he thought he would send somebody else first to see how it was getting on. Everybody in the town knew what wonderful power the cloth possessed, and everyone was anxious to see how stupid his neighbor was.

"I will send my faithful old minister to the weavers," thought the Emperor. "He will be best able to see how the pattern looks, for he is a clever man and no one fulfills his duties better than he does."

So the good old minister went into the room where the two swindlers sat working at the empty loom.

"Heaven help us," thought the old minister, opening his eyes very wide. "Why, I can't see a thing!" But he took care not to say so.

Both the swindlers begged him to be good enough to step a little nearer, and asked if he did not think it a good pattern and beautiful coloring. They pointed to the empty loom. The poor old minister stared as hard as he could, but he could not see anything, for, of course, there was nothing to see.

"Good heavens," thought he. "Is it possible that I am a fool? I have never thought so, and nobody must know it. Am I not fit for my position? It will never do to say that I cannot see the goods."

"Well, sir, you don't say anything about the cloth," said the one who pretending to weave.

"Oh, it is beautiful—quite charming," said the minister, looking through his spectacles. "Such a pattern and such colors! I will certainly tell the Emperor that the marvelous fabric pleases me very much."

"We are delighted to hear you say so," said the swindlers, and then they named all the colors and described the peculiar pattern. The old minister paid great attention to what they said, so as to be able to repeat it when he got home to the Emperor.

Then the swindlers went on to demand more money, more silk, and more gold, to be able to proceed with the weaving. But they put it all into their own pockets. Not a single strand was ever put into the loom, but they went on as before, weaving at the empty loom.

The Emperor soon sent another faithful official to see how the weaving was getting on and if it would soon be finished. The same thing happened to him as to the minister. He looked and looked, but as there was only the empty loom, he could see nothing at all.

"Is not this a beautiful piece of fabric?" said both the swindlers, showing and explaining the beautiful pattern and colors, which were not there to be seen.

"I know I am no fool," thought the man, "so it must be that I am unfit for my high office. It is very strange, though. However, one must not let it appear." So he praised the cloth he did not see, and assured them of his delight in the beautiful colors and the originality of the design.

"It is absolutely charming," he said to the Emperor. Everybody in the town was talking about this splendid weave.

Now the Emperor thought he would like to see it while it was still on the loom. So, accompanied by a number of selected courtiers [CORE-tee-erz], among whom were the two faithful officials who had already seen the imaginary cloth, he went to visit the crafty impostors, who were working away as hard as ever they could at the empty loom.

"It is magnificent," said both the honest officials. "Only see, Your Majesty, what a design! What colors!" And they pointed to the empty loom, for they each thought, no doubt, the others could see what they could not.

"What?" thought the Emperor. "I see nothing at all. This is terrible! Am I a fool? Am I not fit to be Emperor? Why, nothing worse could happen to me!"

"Oh, it is beautiful," said the Emperor. "It has my highest approval." And he nodded his satisfaction as he gazed at the empty loom. Nothing would induce him to say that he could not see anything.

The whole group gazed and gazed, but saw nothing more than all the others. However, they all exclaimed with His Majesty, "It is very beautiful." And they advised him to wear a suit made of this wonderful cloth on the occasion of a great procession that was just about to take place. "Magnificent! Gorgeous! Excellent!" went from mouth to mouth. They were all equally delighted with it. The Emperor gave the rogues a medal of knighthood to be worn in their buttonholes and the title "Gentleman Weaver."

The swindlers sat up the whole night before the day on which the procession was to take place, burning sixteen candles, so that people might see how anxious they were to get the Emperor's new clothes ready. They pretended to take the cloth off the loom. They cut it out in the air with a huge pair of scissors, and they stitched away with needles without any thread in them.

At last they said, "Now the Emperor's new clothes are ready."

The Emperor, with his grandest courtiers, went to them himself, and both swindlers raised one arm in the air, as if they were holding something. They said, "See, these are the trousers. This is the coat. Here is the mantle," and so on. Beaming with pride, they announced, "It is as light as a spider's web. One might think one had nothing on, but that is the very beauty of it."

"Yes," said all the courtiers, but they could not see anything, for there was nothing to see.

"Will Your Imperial Majesty be graciously pleased to take off your clothes?" said the impostors. "Then we may put on the new ones, over here before the great mirror."

The Emperor took off all his clothes, and the impostors pretended to give him each article of dress, one at a time, which they had pretended to make. They pretended to fasten something around his waist and to tie on something. This was the train, he was told, and the Emperor turned round and round in front of the mirror.

"How well His Majesty looks in the new clothes! How becoming they are!" cried all the people round. "What a design, and what colors! They are most gorgeous robes!"

"The canopy is waiting outside which is to be carried over Your Majesty in the procession," said the master of the ceremonies.

"Well, I am quite ready," said the Emperor. "Don't the clothes fit well?" Then he turned round again in front of the mirror, so that he should seem to be looking at his grand new outfit.

The chamberlains who were to carry the train stooped and pretended to lift it from the ground with both hands, and they walked along with their hands in the air. They dared not let it appear that they could not see anything.

Then the Emperor walked along in the procession under the

gorgeous canopy, and everybody in the streets and at the windows exclaimed, "How beautiful the Emperor's new clothes are! What a splendid train! And they fit to perfection!" Nobody would let it appear that he could see nothing, for then he would not be fit for his post, or else he was a fool.

None of the Emperor's clothes had been so successful before.

"But he has got nothing on," said a little child in the crowd standing along the side of the street.

"Oh, listen to the innocent," said the child's father. And one person whispered to the other what the child had said. "He has nothing on—a child says he has nothing on!"

"But he has nothing on!" at last cried all the people.

The Emperor writhed [RYEthd], for he knew it was true. But he thought, "The procession must go on now." So he held himself stiffer than ever, and the chamberlains held up the invisible train.

# The Kitten at Play

by
## WILLIAM WORDSWORTH

**Vocabulary and pronunciation guide:**
**conjurer:** a magician or sorcerer

See the kitten on the wall,
Sporting with the leaves that fall,
Withered leaves—one—two—and three—
Falling from the elder tree,
Through the calm and frosty air
Of this morning bright and fair.

See the kitten, how she starts,
Crouches, stretches, paws, and darts!
First at one, and then its fellow,
Just as light and just as yellow;
There are many now—now one—
Now they stop and there are none.

What intenseness of desire
In her upward eye of fire,
With a tiger-leap half-way
Now she meets her coming prey,
Lets it go as fast, and then
Has it in her power again.

Now she works with three and four,
Like an Indian conjurer;
Quick as he in feats of art,
Far beyond in joy of heart.
Yet were gazing thousands there,
What would little Tabby care?

# The Lamb

### by
### WILLIAM BLAKE

**Vocabulary and pronunciation guide:**
    **mead** [MEED]: meadow
    **vales:** valleys

    Little Lamb, who made thee?
    Dost thou know who made thee?
Gave thee life, and bid thee feed
By the stream and o'er the mead;
Gave thee clothing of delight,
Softest clothing, wooly, bright;
Gave thee such a tender voice,
Making all the vales rejoice?
    Little Lamb, who made thee?
    Dost thou know who made thee?

    Little Lamb, I'll tell thee;
    Little Lamb, I'll tell thee;
He is called by thy name,
For He calls Himself a Lamb.
He is meek, and He is mild,
He became a little child.
I a child, and thou a lamb,
We are called by His name.
    Little Lamb, God bless thee!
    Little Lamb, God bless thee!

# Aladdin and the Wonderful Lamp

from *The Thousand and One Nights*

**About the story:**

> The story of Aladdin, like the stories of Sindbad and Ali Baba, comes to us through a collection known as **The Thousand and One Nights** *or* **The Arabian Nights' Entertainments.** *No one knows who created these tales or when they were first told, but they are thought to be of Persian or Indian origin and have been around for at least a thousand years.*
>
> *Each adventure is part of a larger story (called a "frame story") in which a king—whose unfaithful wife had caused him to hate all women—vowed to defile and then slay every maiden in his kingdom, one each night. The beautiful Scheherazade [sha-HAIR-is-odd], however, foiled his plan by telling him exciting stories, but withholding the end of each adventure until the following night. The king became so enthralled with these tales that he kept her alive to finish each story, and Scheherazade was able to stretch her stay of execution for a thousand nights, until the king professed his love for her, and they were wed.*

**Approximate reading time:** 21 minutes
**Vocabulary and pronunciation guide:**

> **bade** [BAD]: ordered; commanded
> **beguiled** [be-GILED]: charmed; diverted his attention
> **niche** [rhymes with ITCH]: a recessed space; a hollow
> **whence:** from where
> **Grand Vizier** [vih-ZEER]: the prime minister in Moslem lands
> **to the dregs:** to the very bottom

*I*n Persia, there once lived a poor tailor, who had a son called Aladdin. Aladdin was a careless, idle boy who would do nothing but play all day long in the streets with little idle boys like himself. This so grieved his father that he died; yet, in spite of his mother's tears and prayers, Aladdin did not mend his ways.

One day, when Aladdin was playing in the streets as usual, a stranger asked him his age and if he was not the son of Mustapha the tailor. "I am, sir," replied Aladdin, "but he died a long while ago."

On this the stranger, who was a famous African magician, hugged the boy and kissed him, saying, "I am your uncle, and I knew you from your likeness to my brother. Go to your mother and tell her I am coming."

Aladdin ran home and told his mother of his newly found uncle. "Indeed, child," she said, "your father had a brother, but I always thought he was dead." She prepared supper, and bade [BAD] Aladdin go to meet his uncle, who came laden with wine and fruit.

Presently the uncle fell down and kissed the place where Mustapha used to sit, bidding Aladdin's mother not to be surprised at not having seen him before, as he had been forty years out of the country. He then turned to Aladdin, and asked him his trade, at which the boy hung his head, while his mother burst into tears.

On learning that Aladdin was idle and would learn no trade, he offered to rent a shop for him and stock it with merchandise. On the next day, he bought Aladdin a fine suit of clothes and took him all over the city, showing him the sights, and brought him home at nightfall to his mother, who was overjoyed to see her son dressed so fine.

On the following day the magician led Aladdin into some beautiful gardens a long way outside the city gates. They sat down by a fountain, and the magician pulled a cake from his sash, which he divided between them. They then journeyed onwards till they almost reached the mountains. Aladdin was so tired that he begged to go back, but the magician beguiled [be-GILED] him with pleasant stories, and led him on in spite of himself.

At last they came to two mountains divided by a narrow valley. "We will go no farther," said the uncle. "I will show you something wonderful; you need only gather up some sticks while I kindle a fire."

When the fire was lit, the magician threw on it a powder he had with him, at the same time saying some magical words. The earth trembled a little and opened in front of them, disclosing a square flat stone with a brass ring in the middle to raise it by. Aladdin tried to run away, but the magician caught him and gave him a blow that knocked him down.

"What have I done, Uncle?" Aladdin said piteously.

Whereupon the magician said more kindly, "Fear nothing, but obey me. Beneath this stone lies a treasure that is to be yours, and no one else may touch it; so you must do exactly as I tell you."

At the word "treasure" Aladdin forgot his fears, and grasped the ring as he was told, saying the names of his father and grandfather. The stone came up quite easily, and some steps appeared.

"Go down," said the magician. "At the foot of those steps you will find an open door leading into three large halls. Tuck up your robe and go through them without touching anything, or you will die instantly. These halls lead into a garden of fine fruit trees. Walk on, till you come to a niche [rhymes with ITCH] in a terrace where stands a lighted lamp. Pour out the oil it contains, and bring the lamp to me." He drew a ring from his finger and gave it to Aladdin, wishing him well.

Aladdin, finding everything as the magician had said, gathered some fruit from the trees, and having got the lamp, arrived at the mouth of the cave. The magician cried out in a great hurry, "Make haste and give me the lamp!"

This Aladdin refused to do until he was out of the cave. The magician flew into a terrible rage, and, throwing some more powder on the fire, he said something, and the stone rolled back into its place, sealing Aladdin inside!

This man was surely no uncle of Aladdin's, but, instead, a cunning magician who had read in his magic books of a wonderful lamp which would make him the most powerful man in the world. Though he alone had discovered where to find it, he could only receive it from the hand of another, and so he had picked out the foolish and idle Aladdin for this purpose, intending to get the lamp and kill the boy afterwards. Now, since he could not force the boy to give him the lamp, he returned to Africa, whence he had come.

For two days Aladdin remained in the dark, crying and lamenting. At last he clasped his hands in prayer, and in so doing, rubbed the ring, which the magician had forgotten to take from him.

Immediately an enormous and frightful genie rose out of the earth, saying, "What wouldst thou with me? I am the slave of the ring and will obey thee in all things."

Aladdin fearlessly replied, "Deliver me from this place!" whereupon the earth opened, and he found himself outside. As soon as his eyes adjusted to the bright daylight, he made his way home. He told his mother what had happened, and showed her the lamp and the fruits he had gathered in the garden, which were in reality precious stones. He then asked for some food. "Alas, child!" she said, "I have nothing in the house, but I have spun a little cotton and will go and sell it."

Aladdin bade his mother keep her cotton, for he would sell the lamp instead. As it was very dirty, she began to rub it, so that it might fetch a higher price. Instantly a hideous genie appeared and asked what she would have. She fainted straight away, but Aladdin snatched the lamp and said boldly, "Fetch me something to eat!"

The genie returned with a silver bowl, twelve silver plates containing rich meats, two silver cups, and two bottles of wine.

Aladdin's mother, when she came to her senses, said, "Whence comes this splendid feast?"

"Ask not, but eat," replied Aladdin. So they sat at breakfast till it was dinnertime, and Aladdin told his mother about the lamp. She begged him to sell it and have nothing to do with magic. "No," said Aladdin, "since fate has brought this lamp to us, we will use it. It is rightfully ours, and the ring likewise, which I shall always wear on my finger."

When they had eaten all the genie had brought, Aladdin sold one of the silver plates, and then another, and so on until none were left. He then summoned the genie again, who gave him another set of plates; and in this way they lived for many years.

One day the Sultan sent out a proclamation ordering all people in the city to stay at home and close their shutters while the Princess, his daughter, went to and from the bath. When Aladdin heard this, he was seized by a desire to see her face, which was very difficult for she always wore a veil. But soon Aladdin was hidden behind the door of the bath, peeping out through a small crack. The Princess lifted her veil as she went in, and looked so beautiful that Aladdin fell in love with her at first sight. He went home in a trance, and he told his mother that he loved the Princess so deeply that he could not live without her, and meant to ask her father for her hand in marriage.

His mother, on hearing this, burst out laughing; but Aladdin at last prevailed upon her to go before the Sultan and carry his request. As gifts to please the Sultan, she took with her the magic fruits from the enchanted garden, wrapped in a napkin. They sparkled and shone like the most beautiful jewels, as indeed they were.

The Grand Vizier [vih-ZEER] and the lords of the council had just gone in as she entered the hall and placed herself in front of the Sultan. He took no notice of her. She went every day for a week, and stood in the same place, each day with the same result. On the sixth day, when the council meeting ended, the Sultan said to the Vizier, "I see a certain woman in the audience chamber every day. She is carrying something in a napkin. Call her next time, that I may find out what she wants."

On the following day, at a sign from the Vizier, she went up to the foot of the throne and remained kneeling till the Sultan said to her, "Rise, good woman, and tell me what you want."

She hesitated, so the Sultan sent away everyone but the Vizier. He bade her to speak freely, promising to forgive her beforehand for anything she might say. She then told him of her son's passionate love for the Princess.

"I begged him to forget her," she said, "but in vain; he threatened to do some desperate deed if I refused to go and ask Your Majesty for the hand of the Princess. Now I pray you to forgive not me alone, but my son Aladdin."

The Sultan asked her kindly what she had in the napkin, whereupon she unfolded the jewels and presented them. He was thunderstuck and, turning to the Vizier, said, "What sayest thou? Ought I not to bestow the Princess on one who values her at such a price?"

The Vizier, who wanted his own son to marry the Princess, begged the Sultan to withhold her for three months, in the course of which time he hoped his son would manage to make an even richer present. The Sultan granted the Vizier's request, and told Aladdin's mother that, though he consented to the marriage, she must not appear before him again for three months.

Aladdin waited patiently for two months, but then his mother, on going into the city to buy oil, found everyone rejoicing and asked what was going on. "Do you not know," was the answer, "that the son of the Grand Vizier is to marry the Sultan's daughter tonight?"

Breathless, she ran and told Aladdin, who was overwhelmed at first, but soon decided it best to send his mother to remind the Sultan of his promise. She stood in the same place as before, and the Sultan, who (with the help of the Vizier) had forgotten all about Aladdin, now recognized her and called her to speak. This she did, but the Sultan, seeing her impoverished state, felt less inclined than ever to keep his word. The Vizier, too, saw her shabby clothes and advised the Sultan to set so high a value on the Princess that no man living could come up with it. "Good woman," the Sultan said to her, "I will remember my promise, but your son must first send me forty basins of gold, brimful of jewels, carried by forty slaves and led by forty more, all splendidly dressed. Tell him I await his answer."

Aladdin's mother bowed low and went home, thinking all was lost. She gave Aladdin the message, and was astounded to hear him reply, "I would do a great deal more than that for the Princess." He summoned the genie, and in a few moments the eighty slaves arrived, and filled up the small house and garden. Aladdin made them set out to the palace, two by two, followed by his mother. They were so richly dressed, with splendid jewels in their sashes, that everyone along the way crowded to see them and the golden basins of jewels they carried on their heads.

They entered the palace and, after kneeling before the Sultan, stood in a half-circle round the throne with their arms crossed, while Aladdin's mother presented them to the Sultan. He hesitated no longer, but said, "Good woman, return and tell your son that I wait for him with open arms."

She lost no time in telling Aladdin, bidding him make haste. But Aladdin first called the genie.

"I want a scented bath," he said, "a richly embroidered gown, a horse more magnificent than the Sultan's, and twenty slaves to attend me. Besides this, six slaves, beautifully dressed, to wait on my mother; and lastly, ten thousand pieces of gold in ten purses." No sooner was it said than done.

Aladdin mounted his horse and passed through the streets, the slaves strewing gold as they went. When the Sultan saw him, he came down from his throne, embraced him, and led him into a hall where a feast was spread, intending to marry him to the Princess that very day. But Aladdin refused, saying, "I must build a palace fit for her," and took his leave.

Once home, he said to the genie, "Build me a palace of the finest marble, set with jasper, agate, and other precious stones. In the middle you shall build me a large hall with a dome, its four walls of heavy gold and silver, each side having six windows. There must be stables and horses and grooms and slaves; attend to this at once!"

The palace was finished the next day, and the genie carried him there and showed him how all his orders had been faithfully carried out, even to the laying of a velvet carpet from Aladdin's new palace to the Sultan's. Aladdin's mother then dressed herself in her new finery and walked to the palace with her slaves. The Sultan sent musicians with trumpets and cymbals to meet them, so that the air resounded with music and cheers.

At night the Princess said good-bye to her father, and set out on the carpet for Aladdin's palace, with his mother at her side, and followed by the hundred slaves. After the wedding had taken place, Aladdin led her into the hall where a feast was spread, and she dined with him, after which they danced till midnight.

Aladdin had won the hearts of all the people with his gentle ways. He was made captain of the Sultan's armies, winning several battles, but he remained modest and courteous as before and lived thus in peace and contentment for several years.

But far away in Africa, the magician remembered Aladdin, and by his magic arts discovered that Aladdin, instead of perishing miserably in the cave, had escaped and had married a princess, with whom he was living in honor and wealth. He knew that the poor tailor's son could only have accomplished this by means of the magic lamp, and so he traveled night and day till he reached the capital of Persia, determined to ruin Aladdin and have the lamp for himself. As he passed through the town he heard people talking everywhere about a marvelous palace.

"Forgive my ignorance," he said. "What is this palace you speak of?"

"Have you not heard of Prince Aladdin's palace," was the reply, "the greatest wonder of the world? I will direct you if you have a mind to see it."

Upon seeing the magnificent palace for himself, the magician knew that it could have been raised only by the genie of the lamp, and he became even more determined to have the lamp for his own.

Unluckily, Aladdin had gone hunting for eight days, which gave the magician plenty of time. He bought a dozen copper lamps, put them into a basket, and went to the palace crying, "New lamps for old!" followed by a jeering crowd.

The Princess, sitting in the hall of twenty-four windows, sent a slave to find out what the noise was all about. The slave came back, laughing so, that the Princess scolded her.

"Madam," replied the slave, "who could help laughing to see an old fool offering to exchange fine new lamps for old ones?"

Another slave, hearing this, said, "There is an old one on the mantelpiece there that he can have." Now, this was the magic lamp which Aladdin had left there, for he could not take it out hunting with him. But the Princess, not knowing its value, laughingly agreed to the exchange. The slave then went and said to the magician, "Give me a new lamp for this."

He snatched it and bade the slave take her choice from all his shiny new lamps, amid the jeers of the crowd. Little he cared about their jeers, for he knew that he had the magic lamp at last!

He left the city for a lonely place, and at nightfall he pulled out the lamp and rubbed it. The genie appeared, and at the magician's command carried him, together with the entire palace, and the Princess in it, to a secluded spot in far-off Africa.

On the next morning, the Sultan looked out of his window toward Aladdin's palace and rubbed his eyes, for it was gone! He sent thirty men on horseback to fetch Aladdin and bind him in chains. They met Aladdin riding home, bound him, and forced him to follow them on foot.

Aladdin was brought before the Sultan, who ordered the executioner to cut off his head. Aladdin begged to know what he had done.

"False wretch!" cried the Sultan. "Come hither," and he showed him from the window the place where his palace had stood. Aladdin was so amazed that he could not say a word.

"Where is the palace, and where is my daughter?" demanded the Sultan. For the first I am not so deeply concerned, but my daughter I must have, and you must find her or lose your head!"

Aladdin begged to be given forty days in which to find her, promising that if he failed, he would return and suffer death at the Sultan's pleasure. His wish was granted, and he went forth sadly from the Sultan's presence.

For three days he wandered about like a madman, asking everyone what had become of his palace, but they only laughed and pitied him. He came to the banks of a river, and knelt down to say his prayers before throwing himself in. In so doing, he rubbed the magic ring he still wore. The genie he had seen in the cave appeared and asked his will.

"Save my life, genie," begged Aladdin, "and bring my palace back."

"That is not in my power," said the genie. "I am only the Slave of the Ring; you must ask him of the lamp."

"Even so," said Aladdin, "but thou canst take me to the palace, and set me down under my dear wife's window." He at once found himself in Africa, under the window of the Princess, and fell asleep out of sheer weariness.

That morning the Princess rose earlier than usual, and opened her bedroom window to find Aladdin sleeping below. She called to him to come to her, and great was the joy of these lovers at seeing each other again.

After he had kissed her, Aladdin said, "I beg of you, Princess, before we speak of anything else, for your own sake and mine, tell me what has become of an old lamp I left on the mantelpiece in the room of twenty-four windows."

"Alas!" she said, "I am the innocent cause of our sorrows," and she told him of the exchange of the lamp.

"Now I know," cried Aladdin, "that we have the evil magician to thank for this. Where is the lamp?"

"He carries it about with him at all times," said the Princess. "I know, for he pulled it out of his robe to show me. He wants me to break my faith with you and marry him, saying that you were beheaded by my father's command. I have replied to him only with my tears."

Aladdin comforted her and left her for a while. He made haste to the nearest town, where he bought a certain powder; then he returned to the Princess, who let him in by a little side door.

"Put on your most beautiful dress," he said, "and receive the magician with smiles, leading him to believe that you have forgotten me. Invite him to dine with you and say you wish to taste the wine of his country. He will go to the wine cellar, and while he is away, you will do what I am about to say."

She listened carefully as Aladdin told her what to do, and when he left, she arrayed herself in her finest and most beautiful clothes. She then called for the magician, saying, to his great amazement, "I have made up my mind that Aladdin is dead, and that all my tears will not bring him back to me, so I am resolved to mourn no more, and I have invited you to dine with me. But I am tired of the wines of Persia, and would like to taste those of Africa."

The magician fairly flew to his wine cellar, and the Princess put the powder Aladdin had given her in her cup. When he returned she asked him to drink a toast to her health, handing him her cup in exchange for his, as a sign that she was giving herself to him. She set her cup to her lips and kept it there, while the magician drained his to the dregs and fell over backwards in a deep sleep.

The Princess then opened the door to Aladdin, and flung her arms around his neck. Aladdin took the lamp out of the sleeping magician's robe and bade the genie to dispose of the magician, and then carry the palace and all in it back to Persia. This was done in a flash, and the Princess could hardly believe that she was home again.

The Sultan, who was sitting in his hall, mourning for his lost daughter, happened to look up, and rubbed his eyes, for there stood the palace as before! He hastened there, and Aladdin received him in the hall of the four and twenty windows, with the Princess at his side. Aladdin told him what had happened, and the Sultan proclaimed a ten-day feast to celebrate their return.

After this, Aladdin and his wife lived in peace. He succeeded the Sultan when he died, and reigned for many years, leaving behind a long line of kings.

# The Pied Piper of Hamelin Town

adapted from the poem
by
ROBERT BROWNING

**About the story:**

> *This legend dates from the thirteenth or fourteenth cen-*
> *tury and has many variations. The poem by Robert*
> *Browning is perhaps the best known and is here pre-*
> *sented in short-story form.*
>
> *After your children are familiar with the events of the*
> *tale, you might give the original poem a try—though be*
> *prepared for some difficult and dated vocabulary. The*
> *"pied" in Pied Piper, by the way, refers to the character's*
> *clothes, and means "splotched or patched in colors."*

**Approximate reading time:** 11 minutes
**Vocabulary and pronunciation guide:**

> **Hamelin** [HAM-lin]
> **sprats:** young herring
> **kith and kin:** friends and relatives (therefore, one's
> hometown)
> **guilders** [GILL-durs]: a unit of money in old Germany;
> like a dollar
> **ere** [AIR]: before

O nce a long, long time ago, in Germany in a region
called Brunswick, there was a pleasant little town
known as Hamelin [HAM-lin]. It was, in fact, quite
pleasant in every single aspect—save one: Hamelin, you see,
was dreadfully plagued with rats! The houses were full of
them; they were *everywhere*.

Rats!
They fought the dogs and killed the cats,
And bit the babies in the cradles,

And ate the cheeses out of the vats,
And licked the soup from the cooks' own ladles,
Split open the kegs of salted sprats,
Made nests inside men's Sunday hats,
And even spoiled the women's chats
By drowning their speaking
With shrieking and squeaking
In fifty different sharps and flats!

At last it got so bad that the people simply couldn't stand it any longer, and so they all gathered at the town hall and demanded that the Mayor and the city council of Hamelin town put an end to these rats at once. "See here," the outraged citizens cried, "what do we pay your salaries for, anyway? What good are you if you can't do a little thing like rid us of these rats? You had better think of something soon!" they threatened.

"Rouse up, sirs! Give your brains a racking
To find the remedy we're lacking,
Or, sure as fate, we'll send you packing!"

Well, the poor Mayor was in a terrible way, for he could think of no solution whatever. Indeed, he wished that he had never been made Mayor in the first place. He sat in his office with his head in his hands, and he thought, and thought, and thought.

Suddenly there came a little *tap-tap* at his door. Oh! how the Mayor jumped! His poor heart went racing pit-a-pat at anything like the sound of a rat. But this was just the scraping of some shoes on the mat. And so, relieved, the Mayor said, "Come in!"

And in came the strangest figure!

His queer long coat from heel to head
Was half of yellow and half of red,
And he himself was tall and thin,
With sharp blue eyes, each like a pin,
And light loose hair, yet swarthy skin,

No tuft on cheek no beard on chin,
But lips where smiles went out and in;
There was no guessing his kith and kin:
And nobody could enough admire
The tall man and his quaint attire.

He really was the strangest fellow! And round his neck he had a long red and yellow ribbon, and on it was hung a flute, or something like a flute anyway, and his fingers went straying up and down it as if he wanted to be playing.

He approached the Mayor and said, "I hear you are troubled with rats in this town."

"I should say we are," groaned the Mayor.

"If you'd like to get rid of them," said the stranger, "I can do it for you."

"You can?" cried the Mayor. "How? Who are you, anyway?"

"I am known as the Pied Piper," said the man, "and I have a way to draw after me everything that walks or flies or swims. Will you give me a thousand guilders [GILL-durs] if I rid your town of rats?"

"A thousand?" exclaimed the Mayor. "Why, it would be worth *fifty thousand* guilders to me if you could do what you say. But I don't believe you can."

"All right," said the Piper, "it is a bargain."

And then he went to the door and stepped out into the street and stood; and he put his musical pipe to his lips and began to play a strange, high, little tune.

And ere [AIR] three shrill notes the pipe uttered,
You heard as if an army muttered;
And the muttering grew to a grumbling;
And the grumbling grew to a mighty rumbling;
And out of the houses the rats came tumbling!
Great rats, small rats, lean rats, brawny rats,
Brown rats, black rats, gray rats, tawny rats,
Grave old plodders, gay young friskers,
Fathers, mothers, uncles, cousins,
Cocking tails and pricking whiskers,

> Families by tens and dozens,
> Brothers, sisters, husbands, wives—
> Followed the Piper for their lives!

From street to street he piped, advancing, from street to street they followed, dancing. Up one street and down another, till they came right down to the edge of the big river, and there the Piper turned sharply about and stepped aside, and all those rats tumbled hurry-scurry, head over heels, down the bank into the river *and—were—drowned*. Every single last rat, except one big old fat rat, who managed to swim across the river and carry the story of what happened back home to Rat Land.

Well, the town erupted with joy, now that it was finally rid of all the dreaded rats. The people, old and young alike, waved their hats and jumped up and down with glee.

> You should have heard the Hamelin people
> Ringing the bells till they rocked the steeple.
> "Go," cried the Mayor, "and get long poles,
> Poke out the nests and block up the holes!
> Consult with carpenters and builders,
> And leave in our town not even a trace
> Of the rats!"—when suddenly, up the face
> Of the Piper perked in the marketplace,
> With a, "First, if you please, my thousand guilders!"

"H'm—er—a thousand guilders—well," said the Mayor. "Oh, you mean that little joke I made a while ago. Of course that was all a joke, don't you see?"

"I do not joke," said the Piper in a quiet but stern manner. "So I'll have my thousand guilders now, if you please."

"Oh, come now," said the Mayor, "you know very well that it isn't worth a single guilder to play a simple tune like that. But, just to show you how generous we are, here, take fifty and be done with it."

"A bargain is a bargain," said the Piper. "For the last time— will you give me my thousand guilders?"

"I'll give you a pipe of tobacco, something good to eat, and call you lucky at that!" snapped the Mayor, tossing his head back.

Then the Piper's mouth grew strange and thin, and sharp blue and green lights began dancing in his eyes, and he said to the Mayor very softly, "I know another tune than that which I played; I play it to those who play me false."

"Play what you please!" replied the Mayor. "You can't frighten me! Go ahead, do your worst!"

Once more the Piper stepped into the street, put the pipe to his lips, and began to play a little tune. It was quite a different little tune this time, soft and sweet and very, very strange. And before he played three little notes,

> There was a rustling that seemed like a bustling
> Of merry crowds justling at pitching and hustling;
> Small feet were pattering, wooden shoes clattering,
> And, like fowls in a farmyard when barley is scattering,
> Out came the children running,
> All the little boys and girls,
> With rosy cheeks and flaxen curls,
> And sparkling eyes and teeth like pearls,
> Tripping and skipping, ran merrily after
> The wonderful music with shouting and laughter.

"Stop, stop!" cried the people. "He is taking our children! Stop him, Mayor!"

"I will give you your money; I promise I will!" cried the Mayor, and he tried to run after the Piper.

But the very same music that made the children dance made the grown-up people stand stock-still; it was as if their feet had been tied to the ground; they could not move a muscle. There they stood and saw the Piper move slowly down the street, playing his little tune, with the children dancing at his heels. On and on he went; on and on the children danced, till he came to the bank of the river.

"Oh, no!" the people cried, "he's going to drown our children in the river!" But the Piper turned and went along by the riverbank, and all the children followed after. Up, and up, and up the hill they went, straight toward the mountain that over-looks the city. When suddenly, the mountainside *opened*—just like two great doors, and the Piper went through the opening, still playing the little tune, and the children danced after him —and—just as they got through—the great doors slid together again and shut them all in! Every last one of them, except one little lame child, who couldn't keep up with the rest and didn't get there in time. And the children were never seen again, never.

But years and years afterwards, when the fat old rat who swam across the river was a grandfather, his children would ask him, "What made you follow the music, Grandfather?" and he would tell them, "My dears, when I heard that tune, I thought I heard the moving aside of pickle-crate covers, and the leaving ajar of pantry doors, and I smelled the most delicious old cheese in the world, and I saw sugar barrels ahead of me; and then, just as a great yellow cheese seemed to be say-ing, 'Come on, bore into me'—I felt the river rolling over me!"

And, in the same way, the people asked the little lame child, "What made you follow the music?"

"I do not know what the others heard," he said, "but I, when the Piper began to play, I heard a voice that told of a wonderful country just ahead, where the bees had no stings, and the horses had wings, and the trees bore wonderful fruits, where no one was tired or lame, and children played all day; and just as the beautiful country was one step away—the mountain closed on my playmates, and I was left alone."

That was all the people ever knew. The children never came back. All that was left of the Piper and the rats was just the big street that led to the river, which they renamed Pied Piper Street, and a town full of people who had learned never to go back on a promise.

# The Owl and the Pussycat

by
**EDWARD LEAR**

**Vocabulary and pronunciation guide:**
**five-pound note:** English paper money
**quince** [KWINS]: a yellow, applelike fruit
**runcible spoon** [RUN-suh-bull]: a three-pronged fork
curved like a spoon and having a cutting edge

The Owl and the Pussycat went to sea
In a beautiful pea-green boat:
They took some honey, and plenty of money
Wrapped up in a five-pound note.
The Owl looked up to the stars above,
And sang to a small guitar,
"O lovely Pussy, O Pussy, my love,
What a beautiful Pussy you are,
You are,
You are!
What a beautiful Pussy you are!"

Pussy said to the Owl, "You elegant fowl,
How charmingly sweet you sing!
Oh! let us be married; too long we have tarried:
But what shall we do for a ring?"
They sailed away, for a year and a day,
To the land where the bong tree grows;
And there in a wood a Piggy-wig stood,
With a ring at the end of his nose,
His nose,
His nose,
With a ring at the end of his nose.

"Dear Pig, are you willing to sell for one shilling
Your ring?" Said the Piggy, "I will."
So they took it away, and were married next day
By the Turkey who lives on the hill.

They dined on mince and slices of quince [KWINS],
 Which they ate with a runcible [RUN-suh-bull] spoon;
And hand in hand, on the edge of the sand,
 They danced by the light of the moon,
     The moon,
     The moon,
 They danced by the light of the moon.

# The Open Road

from *The Wind in the Willows*
by
KENNETH GRAHAME

**About the story:**

*Like Lewis Carroll's* Alice *adventures,* The Wind in the Willows *was written for an audience of one: Kenneth Grahame's four-year-old son, Alastair. These imaginative adventures of Rat, Toad, and Mole began as bedtime stories; today they are a favorite with children throughout the world.*

*The entire novel is an excellent read-aloud for youngsters because each chapter is a separate episode and fits neatly into a child's attention span. Although the story was not intended to be an allegory about the society of Grahame's day, there are lessons here just the same. Children quickly come to see Toad's arrogance and foolishness for what they are, and they see how senseless he is for refusing to learn from his experiences.*

*In this, the second chapter from the novel, we are witness to the beginning of Toad's fascination with cars—an unbridled passion that will later lead him into joyriding, and then into prison.*

# Part One

**Approximate reading time for Part One:** 13 minutes
**Vocabulary and pronunciation guide:**
> **larder:** a place where food is stored
> **sculls:** oars used for rowing a boat

**shipped his sculls:** put his oars in the boat
**amiable** [AA-me-uh-bull]: pleasant, good-natured
**gypsy caravan:** a covered horse-drawn cart in which an
    entire family could live during its travels
**paddock:** a fenced-in area near a stable

Ratty," said the Mole suddenly, one bright summer morning, "if you please, I want to ask you a favor."

The Rat was sitting on the river bank, singing a little song. He had just composed it himself, so he was very taken up with it, and would not pay proper attention to Mole or anything else. Since early morning he had been swimming in the river in company with his friends the ducks. And when the ducks stood on their heads suddenly, as ducks will, he would dive down and tickle their necks just under where their chins would be if ducks had chins, till they were forced to come to the surface again in a hurry, spluttering and angry and shaking their feathers at him, for it is impossible to say quite *all* you feel when your head is under water. At last they implored him to go away and attend to his own affairs and leave them to mind theirs. So the Rat went away, and sat on the river bank in the sun, and made up a song about them, which he called

### DUCKS' DITTY

All along the backwater,
Through the rushes tall,
Ducks are a-dabbling,
Up tails all!

Ducks' tails, drakes' tails,
Yellow feet a-quiver,
Yellow bills all out of sight
Busy in the river!

Slushy green undergrowth
Where the roach swim—

Here we keep our larder,
Cool and full and dim.

Every one for what he likes!
*We* like to be
Heads down, tails up,
Dabbling free!

High in the blue above
Swifts whirl and call—
*We* are down a-dabbling
Up tails all!

"I don't know that I think so *very* much of that little song,
Rat" observed the Mole cautiously. He was no poet himself
and didn't care who knew it; and he had a candid nature.

"Nor don't the ducks neither," replied the Rat cheerfully.
"They say, '*Why* can't fellows be allowed to do what they like
*when* they like and *as* they like, instead of other fellows sitting
on banks and watching them all the time and making remarks
and poetry and things about them? What *nonsense* it all is!'
That's what the ducks say."

"So it is, so it is," said the Mole, with great heartiness.

"No, it isn't!" cried the Rat indignantly.

"Well then, it isn't, it isn't," replied the Mole soothingly.
"But what I wanted to ask you was, won't you take me to call
on Mr. Toad? I've heard so much about him, and I do so want
to make his acquaintance."

"Why, certainly," said the good-natured Rat, jumping to his
feet and dismissing poetry from his mind for the day. "Get the
boat out, and we'll paddle up there at once. It's never the
wrong time to call on Toad. Early or late he's always the same
fellow. Always good-tempered, always glad to see you, always
sorry when you go!"

"He must be a very nice animal," observed the Mole, as he
got into the boat and took the sculls, while the Rat settled
himself comfortably in the stern.

"He is indeed the best of animals," replied Rat. "So simple, so good-natured, and so affectionate. Perhaps he's not very clever—we can't all be geniuses; and it may be that he is both boastful and conceited. But he has got some great qualities, has Toady."

Rounding a bend in the river, they came in sight of a handsome, dignified old house of mellowed red brick, with well-kept lawns reaching down to the water's edge.

"There's Toad Hall," said the Rat; "and that creek on the left, where the sign says, 'Private. No Landing Allowed,' leads to his boathouse, where we'll leave the boat. The stables are over there to the right. That's the banqueting hall you're looking at now—very old, that is. Toad is rather rich, you know, and this is really one of the nicest houses in these parts, though we never admit as much to Toad."

They glided up the creek, and the Mole shipped his sculls as they passed into the shadow of a large boathouse. Here they saw many handsome boats, slung from the crossbeams or hauled up on a slip, but none in the water; and the place had an unused and a deserted air.

The Rat looked around him. "I understand," said he. "Boating is played out. He's tired of it, and done with it. I wonder what new fad he has taken up now? Come along and let's look him up. We shall hear all about it quite soon enough."

They disembarked, and strolled across the gay flower-decked lawns in search of Toad, whom they presently happened upon resting in a wicker garden chair, with a preoccupied expression of face, and a large map spread out on his knees.

"Hooray!" he cried, jumping up on seeing them, "this is splendid!" He shook the paws of both of them warmly, never waiting for an introduction to the Mole. "How *kind* of you!" he went on, dancing round them. "I was just going to send a boat down the river for you, Ratty, with strict orders that you were to be fetched up here at once, whatever you were doing. I want you badly—both of you. Now what will you take? Come inside and have something! You don't know how lucky it is, your turning up just now!"

"Let's sit quiet a bit, Toady!" said the Rat, throwing himself into an easy chair, while the Mole took another by the side of him and made some civil remark about Toad's "delightful residence."

"Finest house on the whole river," cried Toad boisterously. "Or anywhere else, for that matter," he could not help adding.

Here the Rat nudged the Mole. Unfortunately the Toad saw him do it, and turned very red. There was a moment's painful silence. Then Toad burst out laughing. "All right, Ratty," he said. "It's only my way, you know. And it's not such a very bad house, is it? You know you rather like it yourself. Now, look here. Let's be sensible. You are the very animals I wanted. You've got to help me. It's most important!"

"It's about your rowing, I suppose," said the Rat, with an innocent air. "You're getting on fairly well, though you splash a good bit still. With a great deal of patience, and any quantity of coaching, you may—"

"O, pooh! boating!" interrupted the Toad, in great disgust. "Silly boyish amusement. I've given that up *long* ago. Sheer waste of time, that's what it is. It makes me downright sorry to see you fellows, who ought to know better, spending all your energies in that aimless manner. No, I've discovered the real thing, the only genuine occupation for a lifetime. I propose to devote the remainder of mine to it, and can only regret the wasted years that lie behind me, squandered in trivialities. Come with me, dear Ratty, and your amiable [AA-me-uh-bull] friend also, if he will be so very good, just as far as the stable yard, and you shall see what you shall see!"

He led the way to the stable yard accordingly, the Rat following with a most mistrustful expression; and there, drawn out of the coach house into the open, they saw a gypsy caravan, shining with newness, painted a canary-yellow trimmed with green, and red wheels.

"There you are!" cried the Toad, straddling and expanding himself. "There's real life for you, embodied in that little cart. The open road, the dusty highway, the heath, the hedgerows, the rolling hills! Camps, villages, towns, cities! Here today, up and off to somewhere else tomorrow! Travel, change, interest, excitement! The whole world before you, and a horizon that's always changing. And mind, this is the very finest cart of its sort that was ever built, without any exception. Come inside and look at the arrangements. Planned 'em all myself, I did!"

The Mole was tremendously interested and excited, and followed him eagerly up the steps and into the interior of the caravan. The Rat only snorted and thrust his hands deep into his pockets, remaining where he was.

It was indeed very compact and comfortable. Little sleeping bunks—a little table that folded up against the wall—a cooking stove, lockers, bookshelves, a birdcage with a bird in it; and pots, pans, jugs, and kettles of every size and variety.

"All complete!" said the Toad triumphantly, pulling open a locker. "You see—biscuits, potted lobster, sardines—everything you can possibly want. Soda water here—juice there—writing paper, bacon, jam, cards, and dominoes—you'll find," he continued, as they descended the steps again, "you'll find that nothing whatever has been forgotten, when we make our start this afternoon."

"I beg your pardon," said the Rat slowly, as he chewed a straw, "but did I overhear you say something about *'we,'* and *'start,'* and *'this afternoon'?"*

"Now, you dear good old Ratty," said Toad imploringly, "don't begin talking in that stiff and sniffy sort of way, because you know you've *got* to come. I can't possibly manage without you, so please consider it settled, and don't argue—it's the one thing I can't stand. You surely don't mean to stick to your dull fusty old river all your life, and just live in a hole in a bank, and *boat*? I want to show you the world! I'm going to make an *animal* of you, my boy!"

"I don't care," said the Rat doggedly. "I'm not coming, and that's flat. And I *am* going to stick to my old river, *and* live in a hole, *and* boat, as I've always done. And what's more, Mole's going to stick to me and do as I do, aren't you, Mole?"

"Of course I am," said the Mole loyally. "I'll always stick to you, Rat, and what you say is to be—has got to be. All the same, it sounds as if it might have been—well, rather fun, you know!" he added wistfully. Poor Mole! The Life Adventurous was so new a thing to him, and so thrilling; and this fresh aspect of it was so tempting; and he had fallen in love at first sight with the canary-colored cart and all its little fixtures.

The Rat saw what was passing in his mind, and wavered. He hated disappointing people, and he was fond of the Mole, and would do almost anything to oblige him. Toad was watching both of them closely.

"Come along in and have some lunch," he said diplomatically, "and we'll talk it over. We needn't decide anything in a hurry. Of course, *I* don't really care. I only want to give pleasure to you fellows. 'Live for others!' That's my motto in life."

During luncheon—which was excellent, of course, as everything at Toad Hall always was—the Toad simply let himself go. Disregarding the Rat, he proceeded to play upon the inexperienced Mole as on a harp. Naturally a talkative animal, and always mastered by his imagination, he painted the prospects of the trip and the joys of the open life and the roadside in such glowing colors that the Mole could hardly sit in his chair for excitement. Somehow, it soon seemed taken for granted by all three of them that the trip was a settled thing; and the Rat, though still unconvinced in his mind, allowed his good nature to override his personal objections. He could not bear to disappoint his two friends, who were already deep in schemes and anticipations, planning out what they would do on each day for several weeks ahead.

When they were quite ready, the now-triumphant Toad led his companions to the paddock and set them to capture the old grey horse, who, without having been consulted, and to his own extreme annoyance, had been appointed by Toad for the dustiest job in this dusty expedition. He frankly preferred the paddock, and took a deal of catching. Meantime Toad packed the lockers still tighter with provisions, and hung nose bags, nets of onions, bundles of hay, and baskets from the bottom of the cart. At last the horse was caught and harnessed, and they set off, all talking at once, each animal either trudging by the side of the cart or sitting on the shaft, whatever his pleasure.

# Part Two

**Approximate reading time for Part Two:** 12 minutes
**Vocabulary and pronunciation guide:**
   **placid** [PLASS-id]: calm; composed
   **twopence** [TUP-ens]: an English coin once valued at two
   pennies

*I*t was a golden afternoon. The smell of the dust they kicked up was rich and satisfying; out of thick orchards on either side of the road, birds called and whistled to them cheerily; good-natured wayfarers, passing them, gave them "Good day," or stopped to say nice things about their beautiful cart; and rabbits, sitting at their front doors in the hedgerows, held up their forepaws, and said, "O my! O my! O my!"

Late in the evening, tired and happy and miles from home, they came to a remote field far from habitations, turned the horse loose to graze, and ate their simple supper sitting on the grass by the side of the cart. Toad talked big about all he was going to do in the days to come, while stars grew fuller and larger all around them, and a yellow moon, appearing suddenly and silently from nowhere in particular, came to keep them company and listen to their talk. At last they turned into their little bunks in the cart; and Toad, kicking out his legs, sleepily said, "Well, good night, you fellows! This is the real life for a gentleman! Talk about your old river!"

"I *don't* talk about my river," replied the patient Rat. "You *know* I don't, Toad. But I *think* about it," he added pathetically, in a lower tone: "I think about it—all the time!"

The Mole reached out from under his blanket, felt for the Rat's paw in the darkness, and gave it a squeeze. "I'll do whatever you like, Ratty," he whispered. "Shall we run away tomorrow morning, quite early—*very* early—and go back to our dear old hole on the river?"

"No, no, we'll see it out," whispered back the Rat. "Thanks awfully, but I ought to stick by Toad till this trip is ended. It wouldn't be safe for him to be left to himself. It won't take very long. His fads never do. Good night!"

The end was indeed nearer than even the Rat suspected.

After so much open air and excitement, the Toad slept very soundly, and no amount of shaking could rouse him out of bed next morning. So the Mole and Rat went to it, quietly and manfully, and while the Rat saw to the horse, and lit a fire, and cleaned last night's cups and platters, and got things ready for breakfast, the Mole trudged off to the nearest village, a long way off, for milk and eggs and various necessities the Toad had, of course, forgotten to provide. The hard work had all been done, and the two animals were resting, thoroughly exhausted, by the time Toad appeared on the scene, fresh and gay, remarking what a pleasant easy life it was they were all leading now, compared with the cares and worries and fatigues of housekeeping at home.

They had a pleasant ramble that day over grassy hills and along narrow trails, and camped, as before, in a field, only this time the two guests took care that Toad should do his share of work. In consequence, when the time came for starting next morning, Toad was by no means so rapturous about the simplicity of the primitive life, and indeed attempted to resume his place in his bunk, from which he was hauled by force. Their way lay, as before, across country following narrow trails, and it was not till the afternoon that they came out on the main road, their first main road; and there disaster, fleet and unforeseen, sprang out on them—disaster momentous indeed to their expedition, but simply overwhelming in its effect on the later life of Toad.

They were strolling along the roadway easily, the Mole by the horse's head, talking to him, since the horse had complained that he was being frightfully left out of it, and nobody considered him in the least; the Toad and the Water Rat walking behind the cart talking together—at least Toad was talking, and Rat was saying at intervals, "Yes, precisely, and what did *you* say to *him?"*—and thinking all the time of something very different, when far behind them they heard a faint warning hum, like the drone of a distant bee. Glancing back, they saw a small cloud of dust, with a dark center of energy, advancing on them at incredible speed, while from out of the dust a faint "Poop-poop!" wailed like an uneasy animal in pain. Hardly regarding it, they turned to resume their conversation, when in an instant (as it seemed) the peaceful scene was changed, and with a blast of wind and a whirl of sound that made them jump for the nearest ditch, it was on them! The "poop-poop" rang with a brazen shout in their ears, they had a moment's glimpse of an interior of glittering plate glass and rich leather, and the magnificent motorcar, immense, breath-snatching, passionate, with its pilot tense and hugging his wheel, possessed all earth and air for the fraction of a second, flung an enveloping cloud of dust that blinded and enwrapped them utterly, and then dwindled to a speck in the far distance, changed back into a droning bee once more.

The old grey horse, dreaming, as he plodded along, of his quiet paddock, in a new raw situation such as this simply abandoned himself to his natural emotions. Rearing, plunging, backing steadily, in spite of all the Mole's efforts at his head, and all the Mole's lively language directed at his better feelings, he drove the cart backward toward the deep ditch at the side of the road. It wavered an instant—then there was a heart-rending crash—and the canary-colored cart, their pride and their joy, lay on its side in the ditch, an irredeemable wreck.

The Rat danced up and down in the road, simply transported with passion. "You villains!" he shouted, shaking both fists at the motorcar. "You scoundrels, you highwaymen, you —you—road hogs!—I'll have the law on you! I'll report you! I'll take you through all the Courts!" His homesickness had quite slipped away from him, and for the moment he was the skipper of the canary-colored vessel driven on a shoal by the reckless jockeying of rival mariners, and he was trying to recollect all the fine and biting things he used to say to captains of steamboats when their wake, as they drove too near the bank, used to flood his parlor carpet at home.

Toad sat straight down in the middle of the dusty road, his

legs stretched out before him, and stared fixedly in the direction of the disappearing motorcar. He breathed short, his face wore a placid [PLASS-id], satisfied expression, and at intervals he faintly murmured, "Poop-poop!"

The Mole was busy trying to quiet the horse, which he succeeded in doing after a time. Then he went to look at the cart, on its side in the ditch. It was indeed a sorry sight. Panels and windows smashed, axles hopelessly bent, one wheel off, sardine tins scattered over the wide world, and the bird in the birdcage sobbing pitifully and calling to be let out.

The Rat came to help him, but their united efforts were not sufficient to right the cart. "Hey! Toad!" they cried. "Come and lend a hand, won't you!"

The Toad never answered a word, nor budged from his seat in the road; so they went to see what was the matter with him. They found him in a sort of trance, a happy smile on his face, his eyes still fixed on the dusty wake of their destroyer. At intervals he was still heard to murmur "Poop-poop!"

The Rat shook him by the shoulder. "Are you coming to help us, Toad?" he demanded sternly.

"Glorious, stirring sight!" murmured Toad, never offering to move. "The poetry of motion! The *real* way to travel! The *only* way to travel! Here today—in next week tomorrow! Villages skipped, towns and cities jumped—always somebody else's horizon! O bliss! O poop-poop! O my! O my!"

"O *stop* being an ass, Toad!" cried the Mole despairingly.

"And to think I never *knew*!" went on the Toad in a dreamy monotone. "All those wasted years that lie behind me, I never knew, never even *dreamt*! But *now*—but now that I know, now that I fully realize! O what a flowery track lies spread before me, henceforth! What dust clouds shall spring up behind me as I speed on my reckless way! What carts I shall fling carelessly into the ditch in the wake of my magnificent onset! Horrid little carts—common carts—canary-colored carts!"

"What are we to do with him?" asked the Mole of the Water Rat.

"Nothing at all," replied the Rat firmly. "Because there is really nothing to be done. You see, I know him from way back. He is now possessed. He has got a new craze, and it always takes him that way, in its first stage. He'll continue like that for days now, like an animal walking in a happy dream, quite useless for all practical purposes. Never mind him. Let's go and see what there is to be done about the cart."

A careful inspection showed them that, even if they succeeded in righting it by themselves, the cart would travel no longer. The axles were in a hopeless state, and the missing wheel was shattered into pieces.

The Rat knotted the horse's reins over his back and led him by the head, carrying the birdcage and its hysterical occupant in the other hand. "Come on!" he said grimly to the Mole. "It's five or six miles to the nearest town, and we shall just have to walk it. The sooner we make a start the better."

"But what about Toad?" asked the Mole anxiously, as they set off together. "We can't leave him here, sitting in the middle of the road by himself, in the distracted state he's in! It's not safe. Suppose another Thing were to come along?"

"O, *forget* Toad," said the Rat savagely, "I've done with him!"

They had not proceeded very far on their way, however, when there was a pattering of feet behind them, and Toad caught up with them and thrust a paw inside the elbow of each of them, still breathing short and staring vacantly.

"Now, look here, Toad!" said the Rat sharply, "as soon as we get to the town, you'll have to go straight to the police station, and see if they know anything about that motorcar and who it belongs to, and lodge a complaint against it. And then you'll have to go to a blacksmith's or a wheelwright's and arrange for the cart to be fetched and mended and put right again. It'll take time, but it's not quite a hopeless smash. Meanwhile, the Mole and I will go to an inn and find comfortable rooms where we can stay till the cart's ready, and till your nerves have recovered from their shock."

"Police station! Complaint!" murmured Toad dreamily. "Me *complain* of that beautiful, that heavenly vision that has been bestowed up me! *Mend* the *cart!* I've done with carts forever. I never want to see the cart, or hear of it, again. O, Ratty! You can't think how obliged I am to you for consenting to come on this trip! I wouldn't have gone without you and then I might never have seen that—that swan, that sunbeam, that thunder-bolt! I might never have heard that entrancing sound, or smelled that bewitching smell! I owe it all to you, my best of friends!"

The Rat turned from him in despair. "You see what it is?" he said to the Mole, addressing him across Toad's head: "He's quite hopeless. I give it up—when we get to the town we'll go to the railway station, and with luck we may pick up a train there that'll get us back to River Bank tonight. And if ever you catch me going a-pleasuring with this provoking animal again—" He snorted, and during the rest of that weary trudge addressed his remarks exclusively to Mole.

On reaching the town they went straight to the station and deposited Toad in the waiting room, giving a porter twopence [TUP-ens] to keep a strict eye on him. They then left the horse at an inn stable, and gave what directions they could about the cart and its contents. Eventually, a slow train having landed them at a station not very far from Toad Hall, they escorted the spellbound, sleepwalking Toad to his door, put him inside it, and instructed his housekeeper to feed him, undress him, and put him to bed. Then they got out their boat from the boat-house, sculled down the river home, and at a very late hour sat down to supper in their own cozy riverside parlor, to the Rat's great joy and contentment.

The following evening the Mole, who had risen late and taken things very easy all day, was sitting on the bank fishing, when the Rat, who had been looking up his friends and gossip-ing, came strolling along to find him. "Heard the news?" he said. "There's nothing else being talked about, all along the river bank. Toad went up to Town by an early train this morn-ing. And he has ordered a large and very expensive motorcar."

# Wynken, Blynken, and Nod

### by
### EUGENE FIELD


Wynken, Blynken, and Nod one night
  Sailed off in a wooden shoe—
Sailed on a river of crystal light,
  Into a sea of dew.
"Where are you going, and what do you wish?"
  The old moon asked the three.
"We have come to fish for the herring fish
  That live in this beautiful sea;
  Nets of silver and gold have we,"
    Said Wynken,
    Blynken,
    And Nod.

The old moon laughed and sang a song,
  As they rocked in the wooden shoe,
And the wind that sped them all night long
  Ruffled the waves of dew.
The little stars were the herring fish
  That lived in that beautiful sea—
"Now cast your nets wherever you wish,
  Never afeared are we!"
  So cried the stars to the fishermen three:
    Wynken,
    Blynken,
    And Nod.

All night long their nets they threw
  To the stars in the twinkling foam—
Then down from the sky came the wooden shoe,
  Bringing the fishermen home;
'Twas all so pretty a sail, it seemed
  As if it could not be;

And some folk thought 'twas a dream they'd dreamed
  Of sailing that beautiful sea;
But I shall name you the fishermen three:
    Wynken,
    Blynken,
    And Nod.

Wynken and Blynken are two little eyes,
  And Nod is a little head,
And the wooden shoe that sailed the skies
  Is a wee one's trundle bed;
So shut your eyes while Mother sings
  Of wonderful sights that be,
And you shall see the beautiful things
  As you rock in the misty sea
  Where the old shoe rocked the fishermen three:
    Wynken,
    Blynken,
    And Nod.

# My Bed Is a Boat

## by
## ROBERT LOUIS STEVENSON

**Vocabulary and pronunciation guide:**
    **nurse:** nursemaid; governess; nanny
        (If you choose, substitute "Mom" or "Dad"
        for "nurse" in line 2; if "Dad," also use "He" in line 3.)
    **fast:** firmly attached; secured in place

> My bed is like a little boat;
>     Nurse helps me in when I embark;
> She girds me in my sailor's coat
>     And starts me in the dark.
>
> At night, I go on board and say
>     Good night to all my friends on shore;
> I shut my eyes and sail away
>     And see and hear no more.
>
> And sometimes things to bed I take,
>     As prudent sailors have to do;
> Perhaps a slice of wedding cake,
>     Perhaps a toy or two.
>
> All night across the dark we steer;
>     But when the day returns at last,
> Safe in my room, beside the pier,
>     I find my vessel fast.

# Dick Whittington and His Cat

**About the story:**

*History tells us that there was, indeed, a Richard Whittington—a wealthy man of commerce who (about six hundred years ago) served as sheriff of London and three times as mayor of London and who contributed vast sums for charitable and public purposes. What history does not say is that Richard Whittington ever owned a cat—much less a cat that was responsible for his success and fortune. The cat legend first appeared two centuries after Whittington's death, although similar stories can be found in the folklore of Persia, Denmark, and Italy as far back as the thirteenth century.*

*Still, it is the Dick Whittington legend that has been retold by English-speaking families for many generations, thereby securing for him and his wonderful cat a permanent place in our hearts, if not in our history.*

**Approximate reading time:** 20 minutes

**Vocabulary and pronunciation guide:**

  **guinea** [GINN-ee]: an old English coin worth one pound and five pence

  **halfpenny** [HAY-pen-ee]: an old English coin worth one half of a penny

  **rogue** [ROWG]: a scoundrel

  **Barbary Coast:** the coast of northern Africa

  **plague** [PLAYG]: a calamity, affliction, or nuisance

  **farthing:** an old English coin worth one quarter of a penny

  **genteel** [jen-TEEL]: refined; elegant

*L*ong ago, in the reign of King Edward the Third of England, there lived a little boy called Dick Whittington. His father and mother had died while he was very young, and so, with no one to care for him and being too young to work, Dick became a ragged little fellow who begged for whatever he could all around his little village. His begging usually got him very little in the way of dinner and sometimes nothing at all for breakfast, for the people who lived in the village were very poor themselves and could not spare him much more than the parings of potatoes and now and then a hard crust of bread.

Now, while Dick Whittington was a very poor boy, he was also a very sharp boy, and would listen at every chance to whatever was talked about in the village. On Sunday he was sure to get near the farmers who discussed all matter of things in the churchyard before the preacher arrived; and at least once a week you could see him leaning against the signpost of the village, taking in the varied conversations of the people who met and chatted on their way to or from the next market town along the road; and when the barbershop door was open, there he was, listening to everything the gossipy customers were telling. In this way, Dick heard many strange things about the great city of London, for the simple country people of that day thought that Londoners were all rich gentlemen and ladies and that the London streets were paved with gold.

One day a large wagon, drawn by eight fine horses with bells on their bridles, passed through the village while Dick was standing by the signpost. He thought that such an elegant wagon and team must be on its way to London, and so, summoning up all his courage, he asked the wagoner to let him walk by the side of the wagon for the rest of the journey. When the wagoner saw Dick's ragged clothes and when he learned that Dick had neither father nor mother, he granted the boy's simple request, and the two set off down the road together.

Nobody knows how little Dick obtained food or drink along the road, nor how he could walk so far—for it was a long, long journey—nor what he did at night for a place to sleep. Perhaps some good-natured people in the towns that he passed through felt sorry for him and gave him something to eat; perhaps the wagoner allowed him to sleep in the wagon at night. However it was, Dick arrived safely in London, where he was in such a hurry to see the golden pavements that he did not even stay to thank the kind wagoner, but ran off as fast as his legs could carry him through the many streets, thinking all the while that he would soon come upon those that were paved with gold. Dick had seen a guinea [GINN-ee] only three times in his own little village, but he remembered what a great deal of money it brought in change, and he thought that now he had only to take up some little bits of the pavement to have as much money as he could wish for.

Poor Dick ran till he was tired, and had quite forgotten his friend, the wagoner. But now it had grown dark, and every street he had come upon had been nothing but dirt and no speck of gold anywhere. He lay down in a dark corner and cried himself to sleep. On the next day and the next, he wandered about, asking everybody he met to give him a halfpenny [HAY-pen-ee] to keep him from starving. Only two or three persons gave him halfpennies, and so the boy was soon quite weak and faint for want of food.

Half-starved, he laid himself down on the doorstep of a grand house that was owned by a rich merchant named Mr. Fitzwarren. Here he was soon seen by the cook, a most ill-tempered creature, who called out to him:

"What business have you here, you lazy rogue [ROWG]? You beggars are everywhere these days. Away with you this minute or I'll douse you with some hot dishwater, and we'll see how fast you can jump!"

Just at this time Mr. Fitzwarren himself came home to dinner, and when he saw this dirty, ragged boy lying at the door, he said to him, "Why do you lie there, my lad? You seem old enough to work; are you just too lazy?"

"No, indeed, sir," said Dick to him. "That is not the case at all, for I would gladly work if I knew anyone who would hire me, but I do not, and now I believe I am very sick for want of food."

"Poor fellow," answered Mr. Fitzwarren. "Get up, and let us see what ails you."

Dick now tried to rise, but he was too weak to stand; after all, he had not eaten anything for three days and was no longer able to run about and beg for halfpennies from people in the streets. So the kind merchant ordered him to be taken into the house, and a good dinner given to him, and that he should do whatever dirty work he was able to for the cook.

Little Dick could have lived very happily in this good family, if it had not been for the ill-natured cook who scolded him from morning till night and took a switch to him at the slightest provocation.

At last her treatment of him came to the attention of Miss Alice, Mr. Fitzwarren's daughter, who warned the cook that if she mistreated Dick again, she would no longer be allowed to cook in the Fitzwarren house.

Now, although the cook was ill-tempered, the butler was quite different. He had lived in the family many years, and was an elderly, kindhearted man. Long ago he had had a son of his own who died at about Dick's age, and so he could not help feeling pity for the poor boy, and he sometimes gave Dick a halfpenny to buy gingerbread or a toy, for toys were far cheaper at that time than they are now.

The butler was very fond of reading, and often he would entertain the other servants, after they had completed their day's work, by reading amusing stories to them. Little Dick took great pleasure in hearing these tales, which made him wish very much to learn to read, too. So the next time the butler gave him a halfpenny, he bought a little book with it and, with the butler's help, Dick soon learned his letters and, before very long, he learned to read.

About this time, Miss Alice was going out for a morning walk and, because all the servants were busy and because little Dick had a suit of good clothes that Mr. Fitzwarren had given him to go to church on Sundays, he was told to put on his suit and walk behind her on her stroll. As they went along, Miss Alice saw a poor woman with two children, all three being quite badly off indeed. She pulled out her pocketbook to give the poor woman some money, but as she was putting it into her purse again, she unknowingly dropped it on the ground and walked on. It was lucky that Dick was behind and saw what she had done. He picked up the purse and gave it back to Miss Alice again.

A few days later, Miss Alice was sitting with the window open, amusing herself with her favorite parrot, when the parrot suddenly flew away to the branch of a high tree, and all the servants were afraid to chase after it. As soon as Dick heard of this, he ran out and climbed up the tree as nimbly as a squirrel, and after a great deal of trouble—for the parrot hopped about from branch to branch—he caught the bird and brought it back down safely to Miss Alice, who thanked him and was even more fond of him ever after.

The ill-tempered cook (who was somewhat kinder now) was not the only hardship that Dick had to overcome. His bed was in the attic, where there were so many holes in the floor and the walls that every night he was awakened in his sleep by the rats and mice, which often ran over his face and made such a noise that he sometimes thought the walls were tumbling down about him. One day a gentleman, who came to see Mr. Fitzwarren, required his shoes to be cleaned. Dick took great pains to make them shine, and the gentleman gave him a penny for his work. With this Dick thought he would buy a cat, and so the next day, seeing a little girl with a cat under her arm, he went up to her and asked if she would let him have it for a penny. The girl said she would, and gladly, for her family had more cats than they could keep; she also told Dick that this cat was an especially good mouser.

Dick hid the cat in the attic, and always took care to save part of his own dinner for her. In a short time he had no more trouble from the rats and mice, and he slept as soundly as he could wish.

Soon after this, Mr. Fitzwarren—whose living was made by selling goods of every kind in ports around the world—had a ship that was ready to sail, and, because he thought it right that all his servants should have the opportunity to make some money on his ventures, he called them into the parlor and asked them what they would send out to be sold to the natives in the land where this ship was sailing. They all had something that they were willing to sell, except poor Dick who had neither money nor goods and so could send nothing at all. For this reason he did not join the others in the parlor, but Miss Alice guessed what was wrong and called for him to come in. "I'll give you this ring, and you can sell it as your own," she said, but Mr. Fitzwarren wouldn't hear of it: Dick could risk only what was his outright. Well, the only thing he owned outright was his cat, which he had bought for the penny he had earned.

"Fetch your cat then, my good boy," said Mr. Fitzwarren, "and let her go."

Dick went upstairs and brought down his cat, and with tears in his eyes gave her to the ship's captain, for he said he would now be kept awake all night by the rats and mice. The entire group laughed at the strange parcel that Dick was shipping, but Miss Alice felt pity for the poor boy and gave him a penny with which to buy another cat.

Weeks passed, and the ill-tempered cook returned to her cruel treatment of Dick, and always made fun of him for sending his cat to sea. At last poor little Dick couldn't bear this abuse any longer, and he decided to pack up his very few things and run away early the next morning, which is exactly what he did.

He had traveled only a few miles when, resting on a large stone at the side of a crossroad, he pondered which of the roads he should take. He heard the church bells ringing in the distance, but instead of their usual sound, they seemed to him to be saying:

> "Turn again Whittington,
> Lord Mayor of London."

"Lord Mayor of London!" said Dick to himself. "Why, I would gladly put up with almost any discomfort now to be Lord Mayor of London when I grow to be a man! Well, I will go back to live at the Fitzwarrens', and I won't mind the cuffing and scolding of the cook, for I am to be Lord Mayor of London one day."

And he did go back, and was lucky enough to get into the house and set about his work before the old cook awoke that morning.

Meanwhile, the ship—with the cat on board—was a long time at sea, and was driven at last by the winds to the Barbary

Coast, a land unknown to the English at that time. The natives came down to the shore in great numbers to see the sailors, who looked very unlike themselves. These natives were quite friendly and were very eager to buy the fine things that the ship's captain had on board to sell. He wrapped up some of the finest merchandise and had it taken to the king of this new land, who was so pleased that he sent for the captain and the first mate to be brought to his palace.

When the two Englishmen arrived at the palace, they were seated on rich carpets patterned with gold and silver flowers. The king and queen greeted them and ordered huge dishes of rare foods to be brought to their guests for dinner. But just as soon as the dishes were uncovered, scores of rats and mice rushed in and helped themselves to every delicacy, splashing the gravy and spilling platters of meat all about the room. The captain was quite surprised at this, as you might expect, being in a palace and all, and he asked the king's servants whether they found these vermin to be rather unpleasant.

"Oh! yes," they said, "and the king would give half his riches to get rid of them, for they not only waste his dinner, as you can see, but they disturb him even in his bedroom, and we must stand guard over him so that he might be able to sleep."

The captain was ready to jump for joy when he heard this. He thought of poor Dick's cat, and he told the king he had a creature on board his ship that would rid him of all the rats and mice.

Well, the king was even more glad than the captain, and he said, "Bring this creature to me, and if it can do what you say, I will give you your ship full of gold in payment for her."

"Run, run," said the queen, "for I long to see the dear creature that will do this great service for us."

Away ran the captain to the ship while another dinner was prepared at the palace. He took Puss (for that was what Dick had named her) under his arm and came back in time to see the dishes almost covered with rats and mice again, and the second dinner likely to be lost in the same way as the first. When the cat saw these creatures, she did not wait for instructions, but jumped out of the captain's arms, and in a few minutes laid almost all the rats and mice dead at her feet. The rest of them, in a fright, scampered away to their holes.

The king and queen were delighted to be rid of such a plague [PLAYG] so easily, for ever since they could remember they had not had a comfortable meal by day or a quiet sleep by night. The captain held Puss out for the queen to hold, but she was afraid to touch a creature that was able to kill so many rats and mice. However, when she saw how gentle the cat seemed, and how glad she was at being stroked by the captain, she ventured to stroke her too, and took Puss up on her lap and petted her until Puss purred herself to sleep.

In gratitude for Puss's actions, the king bought the captain's entire cargo, and gave him a great deal of gold besides, which was worth far more, in payment for this wondrous cat. The captain then took leave of the king and queen, and with all his ship's crew set sail with a fair wind for England, and after a happy voyage, arrived safe at London.

On the next morning, when Mr. Fitzwarren had just come into his business office and had just seated himself at his large, handsome desk, there was a knock at his door.

"Who is there?" he asked.

"A friend," answered someone, opening the door, when who should it be but the captain and the first mate of the ship, who had just arrived from the Barbary Coast. They were followed by several of the crew carrying a portion of the vast golden treasure that the king had paid for the ship's cargo and for Dick's wonderful cat. When the merchant was told about how the king had come to be so generous and how most of the treasure was owing to Dick Whittington, in payment for his cat, he called out to his servants:

> "Go fetch him, we will tell him of the same,
> Pray call him Mister Whittington by name."

Mr. Fitzwarren now showed himself to be a truly good man, for when some of the clerks and accountants in the office suggested that so great a treasure was too much for such a boy as Dick, he answered, "God forbid that I should keep the value of a single penny from him! It is all his own, and he shall have every farthing's worth of it to himself."

He then sent for Dick, who happened to be scouring the cook's kettles, and was quite dirty; so dirty that he tried to excuse himself from going, but Mr. Fitzwarren wouldn't hear of it. As you might expect, poor Dick thought that he was about to be punished for some wrongdoing, or at the very least that he was to be made fun of, as the servants often did in the kitchen. But Mr. Fitzwarren assured him that they meant him no harm. "Indeed, *Mister* Whittington," he said, "the captain has sold your cat to the King of Barbary and has brought you in return for her more riches than I possess in the whole world; and I wish you may long enjoy them!"

Poor Dick hardly knew how to behave himself for joy. He begged his master to take as much of the treasure as he wanted, since it was all due to his kindness, after all.

"No, no," answered Mr. Fitzwarren, "this is all your own, and I have no doubt that you will use it well."

But the poor fellow was too kindhearted to keep it all to himself, so he made a handsome gift to the captain, the mate, and every one of the sailors, and afterwards to his friend the butler and to the rest of Mr. Fitzwarren's servants—even to the cook who had been so mean to him. After this, Mr. Fitzwarren advised him to send for barbers, tailors, and cobblers to outfit him like a true gentleman, which he did, and soon he looked as genteel [jen-TEEL] and handsome as any young man in all the fair city of London.

Such a dashing figure was he, in fact, that kind Miss Alice, who used to think of him with pity, now looked upon him as her sweetheart; the more so, no doubt, because Dick was now always thinking what he could do to please her, and giving her the prettiest presents that could possibly be. Mr. Fitzwarren soon saw their love for each other, and proposed to join them in marriage, and to this they both readily agreed.

History tells us that Mr. Whittington and his lady lived in great splendor and were very happy. He became sheriff of London in the year 1360 and was Lord Mayor for several terms after that. They entertained King Henry the Fifth in their home many times, and on one such occasion, the king praised Dick Whittington for his gallantry by saying, "Never had a prince such a subject," to which Dick responded, "Never had a subject such a king."

Mr. Whittington soon received the honor of knighthood, and so became *Sir* Richard Whittington. With his great wealth he helped many poor people avoid the suffering he endured as a boy; he built a church, a hospital, a college, and established scholarships for needy students. Such was his fame that, until the year 1780, the figure of Sir Richard Whittington, with his cat in his arms, could be seen carved in stone over the archway of the old prison at Newgate.

# Hiawatha's Childhood

from *The Song of Hiawatha*
by
HENRY WADSWORTH LONGFELLOW

Vocabulary and pronunciation guide:
sinews [SIN-youz]: tendons
ere [AIR]: before

By the shores of Gitche Gumee,
By the shining Big-Sea-Water,
Stood the wigwam of Nokomis,
Daughter of the Moon, Nokomis.
Dark behind it rose the forest,
Rose the black and gloomy pine trees,
Rose the firs with cones upon them;
Bright before it beat the water,
Beat the clear and sunny water,
Beat the shining Big-Sea-Water.

There the wrinkled old Nokomis
Nursed the little Hiawatha,
Rocked him in his linden cradle,
Bedded soft in moss and rushes,
Safely bound with reindeer sinews [SIN-youz];
Stilled his fretful wail by saying,
"Hush! the Naked Bear will hear thee!"
Lulled him into slumber, singing,
"Ewa-yea! my little owlet!
Who is this that lights the wigwam?
With his great eyes lights the wigwam?
Ewa-yea! my little owlet!"

Many things Nokomis taught him
Of the stars that shine in heaven;
Showed him Ishkoodah, the comet,
Ishkoodah, with fiery tresses;

Showed the Death Dance of the spirits,
Warriors with their plumes and war clubs,
Flaring far away to northward
In the frosty nights of Winter;
Showed the broad, white road in heaven,
Pathway of the ghosts, the shadows,
Running straight across the heavens,
Crowded with the ghosts, the shadows.

At the door on summer evenings
Sat the little Hiawatha,
Heard the whispering of the pine trees,
Heard the lapping of the waters,
Sounds of music, words of wonder;
"Minnie-wawa!" said the pine trees.
"Mudway-aushka!" said the water.

Saw the firefly, Wah-wah-taysee,
Flitting through the dusk of evening,
With the twinkle of its candle
Lighting up the brakes and bushes,
And he sang the song of children,
Sang the song Nokomis taught him:
"Wah-wah-taysee, little firefly,
Little, flitting, white-fire insect,
Little, dancing, white-fire creature,
Light me with your little candle,
Ere [AIR] upon my bed I lay me,
Ere in sleep I close my eyelids!"

Saw the moon rise from the water,
Rippling, rounding from the water,
Saw the flecks and shadows on it,
Whispered, "What is that, Nokomis?"
And the good Nokomis answered,
"Once a warrior, very angry,
Seized his grandmother, and threw her
Up into the sky at midnight;
Right against the moon he threw her;
'Tis her body that you see there."

Saw the rainbow in the heaven,
In the eastern sky, the rainbow,
Whispered, "What is that, Nokomis?"
And the good Nokomis answered:
"'Tis the heaven of flowers you see there;
All the wild-flowers of the forest,
All the lilies of the prairie,
When on earth they fade and perish,
Blossom in that heaven above us."

When he heard the owls at midnight,
Hooting, laughing in the forest,
"What is that?" he cried in terror;
"What is that?" he said, "Nokomis?"
And the good Nokomis answered:
"That is but the owl and owlet,
Talking in their native language,
Talking, scolding at each other."

Then the little Hiawatha
Learned of every bird its language,
Learned their names and all their secrets,
How they built their nests in Summer,
Where they hid themselves in Winter,
Talked with them whene'er he met them,
Called them "Hiawatha's Chickens."

Of all beasts he learned the language,
Learned their names and all their secrets,
How the beavers built their lodges,
Where the squirrels hid their acorns,
How the reindeer ran so swiftly,
Why the rabbit was so timid,
Talked with them whene'er he met them,
Called them "Hiawatha's Brothers."

# Pandora's Box

from *A Wonder-Book*
by
NATHANIEL HAWTHORNE

**About the story:**

*Nathaniel Hawthorne is, perhaps, best known for his dark, highly symbolic tales of romance and guilt in colonial New England (*The Scarlet Letter *and* The House of the Seven Gables, *for example). Yet his notebooks are filled with character sketches and ideas that he intended to use in stories for children. He respected the natural awareness and understanding of children, and thought it unnecessary to write down to their level of comprehension: "It is," he said, "only the artificial and complex that bewilder them."*

*In* A Wonder-Book *and* Tanglewood Tales, *he retells the ancient myths about King Midas's golden touch (which can be found in the previous collection of read-aloud classics), the feats of Hercules, Jason and the Argonauts, and many others. Hawthorne altered the stories slightly to take away "the classic coldness, which is as repellent as the touch of marble," and the modernizing effect of these changes, as well as Hawthorne's skill as a children's writer, can be seen in the following tale of uncontainable curiosity.*

# Part One

**Approximate reading time for Part One:** 14 minutes
**Vocabulary and pronunciation guide:**
**Epimetheus** [epp-ih-MEETH-ee-us]
**Pandora** [pan-DOOR-ah]

**eventide:** evening
**whence:** from where
**vexation:** an irritation, affliction
**peevishly:** in an ill-tempered, complaining manner
**staff:** a long stick or pole used for support when walking
**mischievous:** [MISS-chih-vuss]
**roguishly** [ROE-gish-lee]

*L*ong, long ago, when this old world was in its tender infancy, there was a child, named Epimetheus [epp-ih-MEETH-ee-us], who never had either father or mother. And, that he might not be lonely, another child, fatherless and motherless like himself, was sent from a far country, to live with him and be his playmate and helpmate. Her name was Pandora [pan-DOOR-ah].

The first thing that Pandora saw, when she entered the cottage where Epimetheus dwelt, was a great box. And almost the first question that she put to him, after crossing the threshold, was this—"Epimetheus, what have you in that box?"

"My dear little Pandora," answered Epimetheus, "that is a secret, and you must be kind enough not to ask any questions about it. The box was left here to be kept safely, and I do not myself know what it contains."

"But who gave it to you?" asked Pandora. "And where did it come from?"

"That is a secret too," replied Epimetheus.

"How provoking!" exclaimed Pandora, pouting her lip. "I wish the great ugly box were out of the way!"

"Oh come, don't think of it anymore," cried Epimetheus. "Let us run out of doors and have some nice play with the other children."

It is thousands of years since Epimetheus and Pandora were alive; and the world, nowadays, is a very different sort of thing from what it was in their time. Then, everybody was a child. There needed no fathers and mothers to take care of the children, because there was no danger, nor trouble of any kind, and no clothes to be mended, and there was always plenty to eat and drink. Whenever a child wanted his dinner, he found it growing on a tree; and, if he looked at the tree in the morning, he could see the expanding blossom of that night's supper; or, at eventide, he saw the tender bud of tomorrow's breakfast. It was a very pleasant life indeed. No labor to be done, no schoolbooks to be studied; nothing but sports and dances, and sweet voices of children talking, or caroling like birds, or gushing out in merry laughter, throughout the livelong day.

What was most wonderful of all, the children never quarreled among themselves; neither had they any crying fits; nor, since time first began, had a single one of these little mortals ever gone off into a corner, and sulked. Oh, what a good time was that to be alive in! The truth is, those ugly little winged monsters, called Troubles, which are now almost as numerous as mosquitoes, had never yet been seen on the earth. It is probable that the very greatest agitation that a child had ever experienced was Pandora's vexation at not being able to discover the secret of the mysterious box.

This was at first only the faint shadow of a Trouble; but, every day, it grew more and more substantial, until, before a great while, the cottage of Epimetheus and Pandora was less sunshiny than those of the other children.

"Whence can the box have come?" Pandora continually kept saying to herself and to Epimetheus. "And what in the world can be inside of it?"

"Always talking about this box!" said Epimetheus, at last, for he had grown extremely tired of the subject. "I wish, dear Pandora, you would try to talk of something else. Come, let us go and gather some ripe figs, and eat them under the trees, for our supper. And I know a vine that has the sweetest and juiciest grapes you ever tasted."

"Always talking about grapes and figs!" cried Pandora peevishly.

"Well, then," said Epimetheus, who was a very good-tempered child, like a multitude of children in those days, "let us run out and have a merry time with our playmates."

"I am tired of merry times, and don't care if I never have any more!" answered our peevish little Pandora. "And, besides, I never do have any. This ugly box! I am so taken up with thinking about it all the time. I insist upon your telling me what is inside of it."

"As I have already said fifty times over, I do not know!" replied Epimetheus, getting a little vexed. "How, then, can I tell you what is inside?"

"You might open it," said Pandora, looking sideways at Epimetheus, "and then we could see for ourselves."

"Pandora, what are you thinking of?" exclaimed Epimetheus.

And his face expressed so much horror at the idea of looking into the box, which had been confided to him on the condition of his never opening it, that Pandora thought it best not to suggest it anymore. Still, however, she could not help thinking and talking about the box.

"At least," said she, "you can tell me how it came here."

"It was left at the door," replied Epimetheus, "just before you came, by a person who looked very smiling and intelligent, and who could hardly help laughing as he put it down. He was dressed in an odd kind of a cloak, and had on a cap that seemed to be made partly of feathers, so that it looked almost as if it had wings."

"What sort of a staff had he?" asked Pandora.

"Oh, the most curious staff you ever saw!" cried Epimetheus. "It was like two serpents twisting around a stick, and was carved so naturally that I, at first, thought the serpents were alive."

"I know him," said Pandora thoughtfully. "Nobody else has such a staff. It was Quicksilver, and he brought me here, as well as the box. No doubt he intended it for me; and, most probably, it contains pretty dresses for me to wear, or toys for you and me to play with, or something very nice for us both to eat!"

"Perhaps so," answered Epimetheus, turning away. "But until Quicksilver comes back and tells us so, we have neither of us any right to lift the lid of the the box."

"What a dull boy he is!" muttered Pandora, as Epimetheus left the cottage. "I do wish he had a little more enterprise!"

For the first time since her arrival, Epimetheus had gone out without asking Pandora to accompany him. He went to gather figs and grapes by himself, or to seek whatever amusement he could find, in other society than his little playmate's. He was tired to death of hearing about the box, and heartily wished that Quicksilver, or whatever was the messenger's name, had left it at some other child's door, where Pandora would never have set eyes on it. So perseveringly she did babble about this one thing! The box, the box, and nothing but the box! It seemed as if the box were bewitched, and as if the cottage were not big enough to hold it, without Pandora's continually stumbling over it, and making Epimetheus stumble over it likewise, and bruising all four of their shins.

Well, it was really hard that poor Epimetheus should have a box in his ears from morning till night; especially as the little people of the earth were so unaccustomed to vexations, in those happy days, that they knew not how to deal with them. Thus, a small vexation made as much disturbance then, as a far bigger one would in our own times.

After Epimetheus was gone, Pandora stood gazing at the box. She had called it ugly more than a hundred times; but, in spite of all that she had said against it, it was positively a very handsome article of furniture, and would have been quite an ornament to any room in which it should be placed. It was made of a beautiful kind of wood, with dark and rich veins spreading over its surface, which was so highly polished that little Pandora could see her face in it. As the child had no other looking-glass, it is odd that she did not value the box, merely on this account.

The edges and corners of the box were carved with most wonderful skill. Around the margin there were figures of graceful men and women, and the prettiest children ever seen, reclining or sporting amid a profusion of flowers and foliage; and these various objects were so exquisitely represented, and were wrought together in such harmony, that flowers, foliage, and human beings seemed to combine into a wreath of mingled beauty. But here and there, peeping forth from behind the carved foliage, Pandora once or twice fancied that she saw a face not so lovely, or something or other that was disagreeable, and which stole the beauty out of all the rest. Nevertheless, on looking more closely, and touching the spot with her finger, she could discover nothing of the kind. Some face, that was really beautiful, had been made to look ugly by her catching a sideways glimpse at it.

The most beautiful face of all was done in what is called high relief, in the center of the lid. There was nothing else, save the dark, smooth richness of the polished wood, and this one face in the center, with a garland of flowers about its brow. Pandora had looked at this face a great many times, and imagined that the mouth could smile if it liked, or be grave when it chose, the same as any living mouth. The features, indeed, all wore a very lively and rather mischievous [MISS-chih-vuss] expression, which looked almost as if it might burst out of the carved lips, and utter itself in words.

Had the mouth spoken, it would probably have said something like this:

"Do not be afraid, Pandora! What harm can there be in opening the box? Never mind that poor, simple Epimetheus! You are wiser than he, and have ten times as much spirit. Open the box, and see if you do not find something very pretty!"

The box, I had almost forgotten to say, was fastened; not by a lock, nor by any other such contrivance, but by a very intricate knot of gold cord. There appeared to be no end to this knot, and no beginning. Never was a knot so cunningly twisted, nor with so many ins and outs, which roguishly [ROE-gish-lee] defied the most skillful fingers to disentangle them. And yet, by the very difficulty that there was in it, Pandora was the more tempted to examine the knot, and just see how it was made. Two or three times, already, she had stooped over the box, and taken the knot between her thumb and forefinger, but without positively trying to undo it.

"I really believe," said she to herself, "that I begin to see how it was done. Perhaps I could tie it up again, after undoing it. There would be no harm in that, surely. Even Epimetheus would not blame me for that. I need not open the box, and should not, of course, without the foolish boy's consent, even if the knot were untied."

It might have been better for Pandora if she had had a little work to do, or anything to employ her mind upon, so as not to be so constantly thinking of this one subject. But children led so easy a life, before any Troubles came into the world, that they had really a great deal too much leisure. They could not be forever playing at hide-and-seek among the flower shrubs, or at blindman's buff with garlands over their eyes, or at whatever other games had been invented while Mother Earth was in her babyhood. When life is all sport, toil is the real play. There was absolutely nothing to do. A little sweeping and dusting about the cottage, I suppose, and the gathering of fresh flowers (which were only too abundant everywhere), and arranging them in vases—and poor little Pandora's day's work was over. And then, for the rest of the day, there was the box!

After all, I am not quite sure that the box was not a blessing to her in its way. It supplied her with such a variety of ideas to think of, and to talk about, whenever she had anybody to listen! When she was in good spirits, she could admire the bright polish of its sides, and the rich border of beautiful faces and foliage that ran all around it. Or, if she chanced to be ill-tempered, she could give it a push, or kick it with her naughty little foot. And many a kick did the box—but it was a mischievous box, as we shall see, and deserved all it got—many a kick did it receive. But certain it is, if it had not been for the box, our active-minded little Pandora would not have known half so well how to spend her time as she now did.

For it was really an endless employment to guess what was inside. What could it be, indeed? Just imagine, my little listeners, how busy your wits would be, if there were a great box in the house, which, as you might have reason to suppose, contained something new and pretty for your Christmas or birthday gifts. Do you think that you would be less curious than Pandora? If you were left alone with the box, might you not feel a little tempted to lift the lid? But you would not do it. Of course not! No, surely not! Only—if you thought there were toys in it, it would be so very hard to let slip an opportunity of taking just one peek! I know not whether Pandora expected any toys, for none had yet begun to be made, probably, in those days, when the world itself was one great plaything for the children that dwelt upon it. But Pandora was convinced that there was something very beautiful and valuable in the box, and therefore she felt just as anxious to take a peek as any of you children would have felt. And, possibly, a little more so; but of that I am not quite so certain.

On this particular day, however, which we have so long been talking about, her curiosity grew so much greater than it usually was, that, at last, she approached the box. She was more than half determined to open it, if she could. Ah, naughty Pandora!

# Part Two

**Approximate reading time for Part Two:** 18 minutes
**Vocabulary and pronunciation guide:**
    **intricacies** [IN-trick-uh-sees]: complexities, puzzlements
    **abominably** [uh-BAHM-in-uh-blee]: disgustingly; detestably
    **odious** [OWE-dee-us]: disgusting; offensive; repugnant

*B*efore trying to open it, however, she tried to lift it. It was heavy, quite too heavy for the slender strength of a child, like Pandora. She raised one end of the box a few inches from the floor, and let it fall again, with a pretty loud thump. A moment afterwards, she almost fancied that she heard something stir inside the box. She applied her ear as closely as possible and listened. Positively, there did seem to be a kind of stifled murmur, within! Or was it merely the ringing in Pandora's ears? Or could it be the beating of her heart? The child could not quite satisfy herself whether she had heard anything or not. But, whatever the case, her curiosity was stronger than ever.

As she drew back her head, her eyes fell upon the knot of gold cord.

"It must have been a very ingenious person who tied this

knot," said Pandora to herself. "But I think I could untie it nevertheless. I am resolved, at least, to find the two ends of the cord."

So she took the golden knot in her fingers, and pried into its intricacies [IN-trick-uh-sees] as sharply as she could. Almost without intending it, or quite knowing what she was about, she was soon busily engaged in attempting to undo it. Meanwhile, the bright sunshine came through the open window, as did likewise the merry voices of the children, playing at a distance, and perhaps the voice of Epimetheus among them. Pandora stopped to listen. What a beautiful day it was! Would it not be wiser if she were to let the troublesome knot alone, and think no more about the box, but run and join her little playmates, and be happy?

All this time, however, her fingers were half unconsciously busy with the knot; and, happening to glance at the flower-wreathed face on the lid of the enchanted box, she seemed to perceive it slyly grinning at her.

"That face looks very mischievous," thought Pandora. "I wonder whether it smiles because I am doing wrong! I have more than half a mind to run away!"

But just then, by the merest accident, she gave the knot a kind of twist, which produced a wonderful result. The gold cord untwined itself, as if by magic, and left the box without a fastening.

"This is the strangest thing I ever knew!" said Pandora. "What will Epimetheus say? And how can I possibly tie it up again?"

She made one or two attempts to restore the knot, but soon found it quite beyond her skill. It had disentangled itself so suddenly that she could not in the least remember how the strings had been doubled into one another; and when she tried to recollect the shape and appearance of the knot, it seemed to have gone entirely out of her mind. Nothing was to be done, therefore, but to let the box remain as it was until Epimetheus should come in.

"But," said Pandora, "when he finds the knot untied, he will know that I have done it. How shall I make him believe that I have not looked into the box?"

And then the thought came into her naughty little heart, that, since she would be suspected of having looked into the box, she might just as well do so at once. Oh, very naughty and very foolish Pandora! You should have thought only of doing what was right, and of leaving undone what was wrong, and not of what your playmate Epimetheus would have said or believed. And so perhaps she might, if the enchanted face on the lid of the box had not looked so bewitchingly persuasive at her, and if she had not seemed to hear, more distinctly than before, the murmur of small voices within. She could not tell whether it was fancy or no, but there was quite a little tumult of whispers in her ears—or else it was her curiosity that whispered:

"Let us out, dear Pandora—pray let us out! We will be such nice pretty playmates for you! Only let us out!"

"What can it be?" thought Pandora. "Is there something alive in the box? Well!—yes!—I am resolved to take just one peek! Only one peek; and then the lid shall be shut down as safely as ever! There cannot possibly be any harm in just one little peek!"

But it is now time for us to see what Epimetheus was doing.

This was the first time, since his little playmate had come to dwell with him, that he had attempted to enjoy any pleasure in which she did not partake. But nothing went right; nor was he nearly so happy as on other days. He could not find a sweet grape or a ripe fig (if Epimetheus had a fault, it was a little too much fondness for figs); or, if ripe at all, they were overripe, and so sweet as to be cloying. There was no mirth in his heart, such as usually made his voice gush out, of its own accord, and swell the merriment of his companions. In short, he grew so uneasy and discontented that the other children could not imagine what was the matter with Epimetheus. Neither did he himself know what ailed him, any better than they did. For you must recollect that, at the time we are speaking of, it was everybody's nature and constant habit to be happy. The world had not yet learned to be otherwise. Not a single soul or body, since these children were first sent to enjoy themselves on the beautiful earth, had ever been sick or out of sorts.

At length, discovering that, somehow or other, he put a stop to all play, Epimetheus judged it best to go back to Pandora, who was in a mood better suited to his own. But, with a hope of giving her pleasure, he gathered some flowers, and made them into a wreath, which he meant to put upon her head. The flowers were very lovely—roses, and lilies, and orange blossoms, and a great many more, which left a train of fragrance behind, as Epimetheus carried them along; and the wreath was put together with as much skill as could reasonably be expected of a child, and a boy at that.

And here I must mention that a great black cloud had been gathering in the sky for some time past, although it had not yet overspread the sun. But, just as Epimetheus reached the cottage door, this cloud began to intercept the sunshine, and thus to make the sun suddenly and sadly obscure.

He entered softly, for he meant, if possible, to steal up behind Pandora and fling the wreath of flowers over her head, before she could be aware of his approach. But, as it happened, there was no need of his treading so very lightly. He might have trod as heavily as he pleased—as heavily as a grown man —as heavily, I was going to say, as an elephant—without much probability of Pandora's hearing his footsteps. She was too intent upon her purpose. At the moment of his entering the cottage, the naughty child had put her hand to the lid, and was on the point of opening the mysterious box. Epimetheus beheld her. If he had cried out, Pandora would probably have withdrawn her hand, and the fatal mystery of the box might never have been known.

But Epimetheus himself, although he said very little about it, had his own share of curiosity to know what was inside. Perceiving that Pandora was resolved to find out the secret, he determined that his playmate should not be the only wise person in the cottage. And if there were anything pretty or valuable in the box, he meant to take half of it for himself. Thus, after all his sage speeches to Pandora about restraining her curiosity, Epimetheus turned out to be quite as foolish, and nearly as much at fault, as she. So whenever we blame Pandora for what happened, we must not forget to shake our heads at Epimetheus likewise.

As Pandora raised the lid, the cottage grew very dark and dismal, for the black cloud had now swept quite over the sun, and seemed to have buried it alive. There had, for a little while past, been a low growling and muttering, which all at once broke into a heavy peal of thunder. But Pandora, heeding nothing of all this, lifted the lid nearly upright, and looked inside. It seemed as if a sudden swarm of winged creatures brushed past her, taking flight out of the box, while, at the same instant, she heard the voice of Epimetheus, with a mournful tone, as if he were in pain.

"Oh, I am stung!" cried he. "I am stung! Naughty Pandora! Why have you opened this wicked box?"

Pandora let fall the lid, and, starting up, looked about her to see what had befallen Epimetheus. The thunder cloud had so darkened the room that she could not very clearly discern what was in it. But she heard a disagreeable buzzing, as if a great many huge flies or gigantic mosquitoes or locusts were darting about. And, as her eyes grew more accustomed to the imperfect light, she saw a crowd of ugly little shapes, with bats' wings, looking abominably [uh-BAHM-in-uh-blee] spiteful, and armed with terribly long stingers in their tails. It was one of these that had stung Epimetheus. Nor was it a great while before Pandora herself began to scream in no less pain and affright than her playmate, and making a great deal of hubbub about it. An odious [OWE-dee-us] little monster had settled on her forehead, and would have stung her I know not how deeply, if Epimetheus had not run and brushed it away.

Now, if you wish to know what these ugly things might be, which had made their escape out of the box, I must tell you that they were the whole family of earthly Troubles. There were evil Passions; there were a great many species of Cares; there were more than a hundred and fifty Sorrows; there were Diseases in a vast number of miserable and painful shapes; there were more kinds of Naughtiness than it would be of any use to talk about. In short, everything that has since afflicted the souls and bodies of mankind had been shut up in the mysterious box, and given to Epimetheus and Pandora to be kept safely, in order that the happy children of the world might never be plagued by them. Had they been faithful to their trust, all would have gone well. No grown person would ever have been sad, nor any child have had cause to shed a single tear, from that hour until this moment.

But—and you may see by this how a wrong act of any one mortal is a calamity to the whole world—by Pandora's lifting the lid of that miserable box, and by the fault of Epimetheus, too, in not preventing her, these Troubles have obtained a foothold among us, and do not seem very likely to be driven away in a hurry. For it was impossible, as you will easily guess, that the two children should keep the ugly swarm in their own little cottage. On the contrary, the first thing that they did was to fling open the doors and windows, in hopes of getting rid of them; and, sure enough, away flew the winged Troubles all abroad, and so pestered and tormented the small people everywhere about, that none of them so much as smiled for many days afterwards. And, what was very singular, all the flowers and dewy blossoms on earth, not one of which had hitherto faded, now began to droop and shed their leaves after a day or two. The children, moreover, who before seemed immortal in their childhood, now grew older, day by day, and came soon to be youths and maidens, and men and women by and by, and aged people, before they dreamed of such a thing.

Meanwhile, the naughty Pandora, and the hardly less naughty Epimetheus, remained in their cottage. Both of them had been grievously stung, and were in a good deal of pain, which seemed the more intolerable to them because it was the very first pain that had ever been felt since the world began. Of course, they were entirely unaccustomed to it, and could have no idea what it meant. Besides all this, they were in exceedingly bad moods, both with themselves and with one another. Epimetheus sat down sullenly in a corner with his back toward Pandora, while Pandora flung herself upon the floor and rested her head on the fatal and abominable box. She was crying bitterly, and sobbing as if her heart would break.

Suddenly there was a gentle little tap on the inside of the lid.

"What can that be?" cried Pandora, lifting her head.

But either Epimetheus had not heard the tap, or was too much out of sorts to notice it. At any rate, he made no answer.

"You are very unkind," said Pandora, sobbing anew, "not to speak to me!"

Again the tap! It sounded like the tiny knuckles of a fairy's hand, knocking lightly and playfully on the inside of the box.

"Who are you?" asked Pandora, with a little of her former curiosity. "Who are you, inside of this naughty box?"

A sweet little voice spoke from within, "Only lift the lid, and you shall see."

"No, no," answered Pandora, again beginning to sob, "I have had enough of lifting the lid! You are inside of the box, naughty creature, and there you shall stay! There are plenty of your ugly brothers and sisters already flying about the world. You need never think that I shall be so foolish as to let you out!"

She looked toward Epimetheus as she spoke, perhaps expecting that he would commend her for her wisdom. But the sullen boy only muttered that she was wise a little too late.

"Ah," said the sweet little voice again, "you had much better let me out. I am not like those naughty creatures that have stingers in their tails. They are no brothers and sisters of mine, as you would see at once, if you were only to get a glimpse of me. Come, come, my pretty Pandora! I am sure you will let me out!"

And, indeed, there was a kind of cheerful witchery in the tone that made it almost impossible to refuse anything this little voice asked. Pandora's heart had unexplainably grown lighter at every word that came from within the box. Epimetheus, too, though still in the corner, had turned half round, and seemed to be in rather better spirits than before.

"My dear Epimetheus," cried Pandora, "have you heard this little voice?"

"Yes, to be sure I have," answered he, but in no very good humor as yet. "And what of it?"

"Shall I lift the lid again?" asked Pandora.

"Do as you please," said Epimetheus. "You have done so much mischief already that perhaps you may as well do a little more. One other Trouble, in such a swarm as you have set adrift about the world, can make no very great difference."

"You might speak a little more kindly!" murmured Pandora, wiping her eyes.

"Ah, naughty boy!" cried the little voice within the box, in a gay and laughing tone. "He knows he is longing to see me. Come, my dear Pandora, lift up the lid. I am in a great hurry to comfort you. Only let me have some fresh air, and you shall soon see that matters are not quite so dismal as you think them!"

"Epimetheus," exclaimed Pandora, "come what may, I am resolved to open the box!"

"And, as the lid seems very heavy," cried Epimetheus, running across the room, "I will help you!"

So, with one consent, the two children again lifted the lid. Out flew a sunny and smiling little character, who hovered about the room, throwing a light wherever she went. Have you never made the sunshine dance into dark corners by reflecting it from a bit of looking-glass? Well, so looked the winged cheerfulness of this fairylike stranger, amid the gloom of the cottage. She flew to Epimetheus and laid the least touch of her finger on the inflamed spot where the Trouble had stung him, and immediately the anguish of it was gone. Then she kissed Pandora on the forehead, and her hurt was cured likewise.

After performing these good deeds, the bright stranger fluttered sportively over the children's heads, and looked so sweetly at them, that they both began to think it not so very much amiss to have opened the box, since, otherwise, their cheery guest must have been kept a prisoner among those naughty imps with stingers in their tails.

"Pray, who are you, beautiful creature?" inquired Pandora.

"I am to be called Hope!" answered the sunshiny figure. "And because I am such a cheery little body, I was packed into the box, to make amends to the human race for that swarm of ugly Troubles which was destined to be let loose among them. Never fear! We shall do pretty well in spite of them all."

"Your wings are colored like the rainbow!" exclaimed Pandora. "How very beautiful!"

"Yes, they are like the rainbow," said Hope, "because, glad as my nature is, I am partly made of tears as well as smiles."

"And will you stay with us," asked Epimetheus, "for ever and ever?"

"As long as you need me," said Hope, with her pleasant smile, "—and that will be as long as you live in the world—I promise never to desert you. There may come times and seasons, now and then, when you will think that I have utterly vanished. But again, and again, and again, when perhaps you least dream of it, you shall see the glimmer of my wings on the ceiling of your cottage. Yes, my dear children, and I know something very good and beautiful that is to be given you hereafter!"

"Oh, tell us," they exclaimed, "tell us what it is!"

"Do not ask me," replied Hope, putting her finger on her rosy mouth. "But do not despair, even if it should never happen while you live on this earth. Trust in my promise, for it is true."

"We do trust you!" cried Epimetheus and Pandora, both in one breath.

And so they did; and not only they, but so has everybody trusted Hope, that has since been alive. And to tell you the truth, I cannot help being glad (though, to be sure, it was an uncommonly naughty thing for her to do) but I cannot help being glad that our foolish Pandora peeked into the box. No doubt—no doubt—the Troubles are still flying about the world, and have increased in multitude, rather than lessened, and are a very ugly set of imps, and carry most venomous stingers in their tails. I have felt them already, and expect to feel them more, as I grow older. But then that lovely and lightsome figure of Hope! What in the world could we do without her? Hope spiritualizes the earth; Hope makes it always new; and, even when the earth looks its best and brightest, Hope shows it to be only the shadow of an infinite bliss hereafter!

# I Remember, I Remember

by
**THOMAS HOOD**

**Vocabulary and pronunciation guide:**
**laburnum** [luh-BURR-num]: a tree with clusters
of yellow flowers

I remember, I remember
The house where I was born,
The little window, where the sun
Came peeping in at morn;
He never came a wink too soon
Nor brought too long a day,
But now I often wish the night
Had borne my breath away.

I remember, I remember
The roses, red and white,
The violets, and the lily-cups,
Those flowers made of light!
The lilacs, where the robin built,
And where my brother set
The laburnum [luh-BURR-num] on his birthday:
The tree is living yet!

I remember, I remember
Where I was used to swing,
And thought the air must rush as fresh,
To swallows on the wing.
My spirit flew in feathers then,
That is so heavy now;
And summer pools could hardly cool
The fever on my brow.

I remember, I remember
The fir trees, dark and high;

I used to think their slender tops
   Were close against the sky:
It was a childish ignorance,
   But now, 'tis little joy
To know I'm further off from heaven
   Than when I was a boy.

# On the Meaning of Words

from *Through the Looking-Glass*
by
## LEWIS CARROLL

**About the Story:**

*Lewis Carroll lived two lives: one as the author of such children's classics as* Alice's Adventures in Wonderland *and* Through the Looking-Glass, *and the other as the Reverend Charles Lutwidge Dodgson, a professor of mathematics at Oxford. It is as Lewis Carroll, however, that he is most remembered today, for his "nonsense" books have become not only classics for children around the world, but they are frequently discussed and quoted by philosophers, linguists, and social scientists as well.*

*Instead of writing these books for an entire audience of children, he wrote them for one particular child: Alice Liddell, the daughter of his college's dean.*

*In these adventures, both in Looking-Glass Land and in Wonderland, Alice is a seven-year-old whose curiosity leads her into a dreamworld that is filled with confrontation, politics, and inconsistencies. In the following excerpt, Alice has already entered Looking-Glass Land by walking through the mist that used to be a large mirror hanging over the fireplace. Here, everything seems to operate in reverse—just the way things appear in a looking-glass—and there are the strangest creatures, too, like talking flowers, Tweedledum, Tweedledee, and a sheep that runs a general store.*

**Approximate reading time:** 15 minutes
**Vocabulary and pronunciation guide:**
   **cravat** [kruh-VAT]: a necktie

*A*lice rubbed her eyes, and looked again. She couldn't make out what had happened at all. Was she in a shop? And was that really—was it really a *sheep* that was sitting on the other side of the counter? Rub as she would, she could make nothing more of it; she was in a little dark shop, leaning with her elbows on the counter, and opposite to her was an old Sheep, sitting in an armchair, knitting, and every now and then leaving off to look at her through a large pair of spectacles.

"What is it you want to buy?" the Sheep said at last, looking up for a moment from her knitting.

"I don't *quite* know yet," Alice said very gently. "I should like to look all round me first, if I might."

"You may look in front of you, and on both sides, if you like," said the Sheep, "but you can't look *all* round you— unless you've got eyes at the back of your head."

But these, as it happened, Alice had *not* got, so she contented herself with turning round, looking at the shelves as she came to them.

"I should like to buy an egg, please," she said timidly. "How do you sell them?"

"Fivepence for one—twopence for two," the Sheep replied.

"Then two are cheaper than one?" Alice said in a surprised tone, taking out her purse.

"Only you *must* eat them both, if you buy two," said the Sheep.

"Then I'll have *one*, please," said Alice, as she put the money down on the counter. For she thought to herself, "They might not be at all fresh, you know."

The Sheep took the money, and put it away in a box; then she said, "I never hand any item to a customer—that would never do—you must get it for yourself." And so saying, she went off to the other end of the shop, and set the egg upright on a shelf.

"I wonder *why* it wouldn't do?" thought Alice, as she groped her way among the tables and chairs, for the shop was very dark toward the back. "The egg seems to get farther away the more I walk toward it. Let me see, is this a chair? Why, it's got branches, I declare! How very odd to find trees growing here!

And actually here's a little brook! Well, this is the very strangest shop I ever saw!"

So she went on, wondering more and more at every step, as everything turned into a tree the moment she came up to it, and she quite expected the egg to do the same.

However, the egg only got larger and larger, and more and more human; when she had come within a few yards of it, she saw that it had eyes and a nose and mouth; and, when she had come close to it, she saw clearly that it was HUMPTY DUMPTY himself. "It can't be anybody else!" she said to herself. "I'm as certain of it, as if his name were written all over his face!"

It might have been written a hundred times, easily, on that enormous face. Humpty Dumpty was sitting, with his legs crossed like a Turk, on the top of a high wall—such a narrow one that Alice quite wondered how he could keep his balance —and, as his eyes were steadily fixed in the opposite direction, and he didn't take the least notice of her, she thought he must be a stuffed figure, after all.

"And how exactly like an egg he is!" she said aloud, standing with her hands ready to catch him, for she was every moment expecting him to fall.

"It's *very* provoking," Humpty Dumpty said after a long silence, looking away from Alice as he spoke, "to be called an egg—*very!*"

"I said you *looked* like an egg, Sir," Alice gently explained. "And some eggs are very pretty, you know," she added, hoping to turn her remark into a sort of compliment.

"Some people," said Humpty Dumpty, looking away from her as usual, "have no more sense than a baby!"

Alice didn't know what to say to this; it wasn't at all like conversation, she thought, as he never said anything to *her*; in fact, his last remark was evidently addressed to a tree—so she stood and softly repeated to herself—

> "Humpty Dumpty sat on a wall;
> Humpty Dumpty had a great fall.
> All the King's horses and all the King's men
> Couldn't put Humpty Dumpty together again.

"That last line is much too long for the poem," she added, almost out loud, forgetting that Humpty Dumpty would hear her.

"Don't stand chattering to yourself like that," Humpty Dumpty said, looking at her for the first time, "but tell me your name and your business."

"My *name* is Alice, but—"

"That's a stupid name!" Humpty Dumpty interrupted impatiently. "What does it mean?"

"*Must* a name mean something?" Alice asked doubtfully.

"Of course it must," Humpty Dumpty said with a short laugh; "*my* name means the shape I am—and a good handsome shape it is, too. With a name like yours, you might be any shape, almost."

"Why do you sit out here all alone?" said Alice, not wishing to begin an argument.

"Why, because there's nobody with me!" cried Humpty Dumpty. "Did you think I didn't know the answer to *that?* Ask another."

"Don't you think you'd be safer down on the ground?" Alice went on, not with any idea of making another riddle, but simply in her good-natured anxiety for the strange creature. "That wall is so *very* narrow!"

"What tremendously easy riddles you ask!" Humpty Dumpty growled out. "Of course I don't think so! Why, if ever I *did* fall off—which there's no chance of—but *if* I did—" Here he wrinkled his brow, and looked so serious and deep in thought that Alice could hardly help laughing. "If I *did* fall," he went on, "the King has promised me—yes, I'm one who has actually spoken to a King—the King has promised me—with his very own mouth—to—to—"

"To send all his horses and all his men," Alice interrupted.

"Yes, all his horses and all his men," Humpty Dumpty went on. "They'd pick me up again in a minute, *they* would! However, this conversation is going on a little too fast; let's go back to the last remark but one."

"I'm afraid I can't quite remember it," Alice said, very politely.

"In that case we start afresh," said Humpty Dumpty, "and

it's my turn to choose a subject—" ("He talks about it just as if it was a game!" thought Alice.) "So here's a question for you," he went on. "How old did you say you were?"

Alice made a short calculation, and said, "Seven years and six months."

"Wrong!" Humpty Dumpty exclaimed triumphantly. "You never said a word like it!"

"I thought you meant 'How old *are* you?' " Alice explained.

"If I'd meant that, I'd have said it," said Humpty Dumpty.

Alice didn't want to begin another argument, so she said nothing.

"Seven years and six months!" Humpty Dumpty repeated thoughtfully. "An uncomfortable sort of age. Now if you'd asked *my* advice, I'd have said 'Leave off at seven'—but it's too late now."

"I never ask advice about growing," Alice said indignantly.

"Too proud?" the other inquired.

Alice felt even more indignant at this suggestion. "I mean," she said, "that one can't help growing older."

"*One* can't, perhaps," said Humpty Dumpty; "but *two* can. With proper assistance, you might have left off at seven."

"What a beautiful belt you have on!" Alice suddenly re-marked. (They had had quite enough of the subject of age, she thought; and, if they really were to take turns in choosing subjects, it was *her* turn now.) "At least," she corrected herself on second thought, "a beautiful cravat [kruh-VAT], I should have said—no, a belt, I mean—I beg your pardon!" she added in dismay, for Humpty Dumpty looked thoroughly offended, and she began to wish she hadn't chosen that subject. "If only I knew," she thought to herself, "which was neck and which was waist!"

Evidently Humpty Dumpty was very angry, though he said nothing for a minute or two. When he *did* speak again, it was in a deep growl.

"It is a—*most*—provoking—thing," he said at last, "when a person doesn't know a cravat from a belt!"

"I know it's very ignorant of me," Alice said, in so humble a tone that Humpty Dumpty relented.

"It's a cravat, child, and a beautiful one, as you say. It's a present from the White King and Queen. There now!"

"Is it really!" said Alice, quite pleased to find that she *had* chosen a good subject after all.

"They gave it to me," Humpty Dumpty continued thoughtfully as he crossed one knee over the other and clasped his hands round it, "They gave it to me—for an un-birthday present."

"I beg your pardon?" Alice said with a puzzled air.

"I'm not offended," said Humpty Dumpty.

"I mean," said Alice, "what *is* an un-birthday present?"

"A present given when it isn't your birthday, of course," he replied.

Alice considered a little. "I like birthday presents best," she said at last.

"You don't know what you're talking about!" cried Humpty Dumpty. "How many days are there in a year?"

"Three hundred and sixty-five," said Alice.

"And how many birthdays have you?" he inquired.

"One," she replied.

"And if you take one from three hundred and sixty-five, what remains?" asked Humpty Dumpty.

"Three hundred and sixty-four, of course," she responded.

Humpty Dumpty looked doubtful. "I'd rather see that done on paper," he said.

Alice couldn't help smiling as she took out her notebook and worked the sum for him:

$$\begin{array}{r} 365 \\ -1 \\ \hline 364 \end{array}$$

Humpty Dumpty took the notebook and looked at it carefully. "That seems to be done right—" he began.

"You're holding it upside down!" Alice interrupted.

"To be sure I was!" Humpty Dumpty said gaily as she turned it round for him. "I thought it looked a little queer. As I was saying, that *seems* to be done right—though I haven't time to look it over thoroughly just now—and that shows that there are three hundred and sixty-four days when you might get un-birthday presents—"

"Certainly," said Alice.

"And only *one* for birthday presents, you know. There's glory for you!" taunted Humpty Dumpty.

"I don't know what you mean by 'glory,' " Alice said.

Humpty Dumpty smiled contemptuously. "Of course you don't—till I tell you. I meant 'there's a nice knock-down argument, for you!' "

"But 'glory' doesn't mean 'a nice knock-down argument,' " Alice objected.

"When *I* use a word," Humpty Dumpty said, in rather a scornful tone, "it means just what I choose it to mean—neither more nor less."

"The question is," said Alice, "whether you *can* make words mean so many different things."

"The question is," said Humpty Dumpty, "which is to be master—that's all."

Alice was too much puzzled to say anything; so after a minute Humpty Dumpty began again. "They've a temper, some of them—particularly verbs: they're the proudest—adjectives you can do anything with, but not verbs—however, I can manage the whole lot of them! Impenetrability! That's what I say!"

"Would you tell me please," said Alice, "what that means?"

"Now you talk like a reasonable child," said Humpty Dumpty, looking very much pleased. "I meant by 'impenetrability' that we've had enough of that subject, and it would be just as well if you'd mention what you mean to do next, as I suppose you don't mean to stop here all the rest of your life."

"That's a great deal to make one word mean," Alice said in a thoughtful tone.

"When I make a word do a lot of work like that," said Humpty Dumpty, "I always pay it extra."

"Oh!" said Alice. She was too much puzzled to make any other remark.

"Ah, you should see 'em come round me on a Saturday night," Humpty Dumpty went on, wagging his head gravely from side to side, "for to get their wages, you know."

(Alice didn't venture to ask what he paid them with; and so, you see, I can't tell *you*.) . . .

"That's all," said Humpty Dumpty. "Good-bye."

This was rather sudden, Alice thought; but, after such a *very* strong hint that she ought to be going, she felt that it would hardly be civil to stay. So she got up, and held out her hand. "Good-bye, till we meet again!" she said as cheerfully as she could.

"I shouldn't know you again if we *did* meet," Humpty Dumpty replied in a discontented tone, giving her one of his fingers to shake, "you're so exactly like other people."

"The face is what one goes by, generally," Alice remarked in a thoughtful tone.

"That's just what I complain of," said Humpty Dumpty. "Your face is the same as everybody has—the two eyes, so—" (marking their places in the air with his thumb) "nose in the middle, mouth under. It's always the same. Now if you had the two eyes on the same side of the nose, for instance—or the mouth at the top—that would be *some* help."

"It wouldn't look nice," Alice objected. But Humpty Dumpty only shut his eyes, and said, "Wait till you've tried."

Alice waited a minute to see if he would speak again, but, as he never opened his eyes or took any further notice of her, she said "Good-bye!" once more, and, getting no answer to this, she quietly walked away. But she couldn't help saying to herself, as she went, "of all the unsatisfactory——" (she repeated this aloud, as it was a great comfort to have such a long word to say) "of all the unsatisfactory people I *ever* met——"

# *Jabberwocky*

by
**LEWIS CARROLL**

**About the poem:**

*Like the story of Alice and Humpty Dumpty that pre-
cedes this poem, "Jabberwocky" is taken from* **Through
the Looking-Glass.** *Indeed, in the original work, Alice
asks Humpty Dumpty to interpret the poem for her.*

*This is* not *a poem for interpreting, just for enjoying.
The words and verses will create different pictures in the
minds of different children; no "correct" definitions or
pictures were intended, or are possible.*

*Even the pronunciations will vary from reader to
reader, but they should not vary from reading to reading.
Therefore, please set aside some additional time for prac-
ticing this poem—even more than for other read-alouds.
Lewis Carroll's whimsical vocabulary in "Jabberwocky" has been unsettling to oral readers for more than
a century; indeed, the author himself felt obliged to offer
a pronunciation guide for at least some of these unusual
words in his "Preface to the 1896 Edition":*

**Pronounce "slithy" as if it were the two words "sly,
thee"; make the "g" hard in "gyre" and "gimble"; and
pronounce "rath" to rhyme with "bath."**

'Twas brillig, and the slithy toves
   Did gyre and gimble in the wabe;
All mimsy were the borogoves,
   And the mome raths outgrabe.

"Beware the Jabberwock, my son!
   The jaws that bite, the claws that catch!
Beware the Jubjub bird, and shun
   The frumious Bandersnatch!"

——— 99 ———

He took his vorpal sword in hand:
    Long time the manxome foe he sought—
So rested he by the Tumtum tree,
    And stood awhile in thought.

And, as in uffish thought he stood,
    The Jabberwock, with eyes of flame,
Came whiffling through the tulgey wood,
    And burbled as it came!

One, two! One, two! And through and through
    The vorpal blade went snicker-snack!
He left it dead, and with its head
    He went galumphing back.

"And hast thou slain the Jabberwock?
    Come to my arms, my beamish boy!
O frabjous day! Callooh! Callay!"
    He chortled in his joy.

'Twas brillig, and the slithy toves
    Did gyre and gimble in the wabe;
All mimsy were the borogoves,
    And the mome raths outgrabe.

# Listening Level II

## (Ages 8 and up)

*I have come to believe that children's elementary-school years represent the most important period in their read-aloud lives. Not only do children attain fully 90 percent of their adult vocabulary during this period, but they also develop their tastes in literature: They become interested in reading certain books, or certain types of books.*

*Among the most precious benefits of reading aloud—both at home and in school—is that the books children have read to them are likely to be the books they want to read for themselves. So here, with both their current and future pleasure in mind, I have included a chapter from* Little Women *and several from* Treasure Island *along with shorter pieces from such giants as Mark Twain, O. Henry, and Helen Keller.*

*Perhaps a warning is in order here: You may find your children pestering you for readings of the remaining chapters of these novels or for readings of other works by these authors. If so, take heart in knowing that you may later find them choosing these works for their own reading, and then give yourself a firm pat on the back for a job well done.*

# A Miserable, Merry Christmas

## from *The Autobiography of Lincoln Steffens*

**About the story:**

*Today, the name of Lincoln Steffens is almost always associated with his "muckraking" days in the East, when he worked as a writer and editor for New York newspapers and magazines that woke up the social consciousness of the nation with exposés of corruption in politics and business. The excerpt presented here, however, shows a far different Lincoln Steffens—a boy growing up in the frontier days of Sacramento, where getting a pony of his own could be the fulfillment of a dream, and not getting that pony could be the most memorable heartbreak of a lifetime.*

**Approximate reading time:** 10 minutes
**Vocabulary and pronunciation guide:**
  **disheveled** [dih-SHEV-eld]: mussed up; rumpled
  **bade** [BAD]: past tense of *bid*; asked

What interested me in our new neighborhood was not the school, nor the room I was to have in the house all to myself, but the stable which was built back of the house. My father let me direct the making of a stall, a little smaller than the other stalls, for my pony, and I prayed and hoped and my sister Lou believed that that meant that I would get the pony, perhaps for Christmas. I pointed out to her that there were three other stalls and no horses at all. This I said in order that she should answer it. She could not. My father, when I asked about the building of the stalls, said that some day we might have horses and a cow; meanwhile a stable added to the value of the house. "Some day" is a pain to a boy who lives in and knows only "now." My good little sisters, to comfort me, remarked that Christmas was coming, but Christmas was *always* coming, and grownups were always talking about it, asking you what you wanted and then giving you what they wanted you to have. Though everybody knew what I wanted, I told them all again. My mother knew that I told God, too, every night. I wanted a pony, and to make sure that they understood, I declared that I wanted nothing else.

"Nothing but a pony?" my father asked.

"Nothing," I said.

"Not even a pair of high boots?" he persisted.

That was hard. I did want boots, but I stuck to the pony. "No, not even boots," I returned, somewhat reluctantly.

"Nor candy?" he went on. "There ought to be something to fill your stocking with, and Santa Claus can't put a pony into a stocking."

That was true, and he couldn't lead a pony down the chimney either. But no. "All I want is a pony," I said. "If I can't have a pony, give me nothing."

Now I had been looking myself for the pony I wanted, going to sales stables, inquiring of horsemen, and I had seen several that would do. My father let me "try" them. I tried so many ponies that I was learning fast to sit a horse. I chose several, but my father always found some fault with them. I was in despair. When Christmas was at hand I had given up all hope of a pony, and on Christmas Eve I hung up my stocking along with my sisters', of whom, by the way, I now had three. I haven't mentioned them or their coming because, you understand, they were girls, and girls, young girls, counted for nothing in my manly life. They did not mind me either; they were so happy that Christmas Eve that I caught some of their merriment. I speculated on what I'd get; I hung up the biggest stocking I had, and we all went reluctantly to bed to wait till morning. Not to sleep; not right away. We were told that we must not only sleep promptly, we must not wake up till seven-thirty the next morning—or if we did, we must not go to the fireplace for our Christmas. Impossible.

We did sleep that night, but we woke up at six A.M. We lay in our beds and debated through the open doors whether to obey till, say, half-past six. Then we bolted. I don't know who started it, but there was a rush. We all disobeyed; we raced to disobey and get first to the fireplace in the front room downstairs. And there they were, the gifts, all sorts of wonderful things, mixed-up piles of presents; only, as I disentangled the mess, I saw that my stocking was empty; it hung limp; not a thing in it; and under and around it—nothing. My sisters had knelt down, each by her pile of gifts; they were squealing with delight, till they looked up and saw me standing there in my nightgown with nothing. They left their piles to come to me and look with me at my empty place. Nothing. They felt my stocking: nothing.

I don't remember whether I cried at that moment, but my sisters did. They ran with me back to my bed, and there we all cried till I became indignant. That helped some. I got up, dressed, and driving my sisters away, I went alone out into the yard, down to the stable, and there, all by myself, I wept. My mother came out to me by and by; she found me in my pony stall, sobbing on the floor, and she tried to comfort me. But I heard my father outside; he had come part way with her, and she was having some sort of angry quarrel with him. She tried to comfort me; urged me to come to breakfast. I could not; I wanted no comfort and no breakfast. She left me and went on into the house with sharp words for my father.

I don't know what kind of a breakfast the family had. My sisters said it was "awful." They were ashamed to enjoy their own toys. They came to me, and I was rude. I ran away from them. I went around to the front of the house, sat down on the steps, and, as the crying was over, I ached. I was wronged, I was hurt—I can feel now what I felt then, and I am sure that if one could see the wounds upon our hearts, there would be found still upon mine a scar from that terrible Christmas morning. And my father, the practical joker, he must have been hurt, too, a little. I saw him looking out of the window. He was watching me or something for an hour or two, drawing back the curtain ever so little lest I catch him, but I saw his face, and I think I can see now the anxiety upon it, the worried impatience.

After—I don't know how long—surely an hour or two— I was brought to the climax of my agony by the sight of a man riding a pony down the street, a pony and a brand-new saddle; the most beautiful saddle I ever saw, and it was a boy's saddle; the man's feet were not in the stirrups; his legs were too long. The outfit was perfect; it was the realization of all my dreams, the answer to all my prayers. A fine new bridle, with a light curb bit. And the pony! As he drew near, I saw that the pony was really a small horse, what we called an Indian pony, a bay, with black mane and tail, and one white foot and a white star on his forehead. For such a horse as that I would have given, I could have forgiven, anything.

But the man, a disheveled [dih-SHEV-eld] fellow with a blackened eye and a fresh-cut face, came along, reading the numbers on the houses, and, as my hopes—my impossible hopes—rose, he looked at our door and passed by, he and the pony, and the saddle and the bridle. Too much. I fell upon the steps, and having wept before, I broke now into such a flood of tears that I was a floating wreck when I heard a voice.

"Say, kid," it said, "do you know a boy named Lennie Steffens?"

I looked up. It was the man on the pony, back again, at our hitching rail.

"Yes," I spluttered through my tears. "That's me."

"Well," he said, "then this is your horse. I've been looking all over for you and your house. Why don't you put your number where it can be seen?"

"Get down," I said, running out to him.

He went on saying something about "ought to have got here at seven o'clock; told me to bring the nag here and tie him to your post and leave him for you. But, hell, I got into a drunk —and a fight—and a hospital, and—"

"Get down," I said.

He got down, and he boosted me up to the saddle. He offered to fit the stirrups to me, but I didn't want him to. I wanted to ride.

"What's the matter with you?" he said, angrily. "What you crying for? Don't you like the horse? He's a dandy, this horse. I know him of old. He's fine at cattle; he'll drive 'em alone."

I hardly heard, I could scarcely wait, but he persisted. He adjusted the stirrups, and then, finally, off I rode, slowly, at a walk, so happy, so thrilled, that I did not know what I was doing. I did not look back at the house or the man, I rode off up the street, taking note of everything—of the reins, of the pony's long mane, of the carved leather saddle. I had never seen anything so beautiful. And mine! I was going to ride up past Miss Kay's house. But I noticed on the horn of the saddle some stains like raindrops, so I turned and trotted home, not to the house but to the stable. There was the family, father, mother, sisters, all working for me, all happy. They had been putting in place the tools of my new business: blankets, curry-comb, brush, pitchfork—everything, and there was hay in the loft.

"What did you come back so soon for?" somebody asked. "Why didn't you go on riding?"

I pointed to the stains. "I wasn't going to get my new saddle rained on," I said. And my father laughed. "It isn't raining," he said. "Those are not raindrops."

"They are tears," my mother gasped, and she gave my father a look which sent him off to the house. Worse still, my mother offered to wipe away the tears still running out of my eyes. I gave her such a look as she had given him, and she went off after my father, drying her own tears. My sisters remained and we all unsaddled the pony, put on his halter, led him to his stall; tied and fed him. It began really to rain; so that the rest of that memorable day we curried and combed that pony. The girls braided his mane, forelock, and tail, while I pitchforked hay to him and curried and brushed, curried and brushed. For a change we brought him out to drink; we led him up and down, blanketed like a racehorse; we took turns at that. But the best, the most inexhaustible fun, was to clean him. When we went reluctantly to our midday Christmas dinner, we all smelled of horse, and my sisters had to wash their faces and hands. I was asked to, but I wouldn't, till my mother bade [BAD] me look in the mirror. Then I washed up—quick. My face was caked with the muddy lines of tears that had coursed over my cheeks to my mouth. Having washed away that shame, I ate my dinner, and as I ate I grew hungrier and hungrier. It was my first meal that day, and as I filled up on the turkey and the stuffing, the cranberries and the pies, the fruit and the nuts—as I swelled, I could laugh. My mother said I still choked and sobbed now and then, but I laughed, too. I saw and enjoyed my sisters' presents till—I had to go out and attend to my pony, who was there, really and truly there—the promise, the beginning, of a happy double life. And—I went and looked to make sure—there was the saddle, too, and the bridle.

But that Christmas, which my father had planned so carefully, was it the best or the worst I ever knew? He often asked me that; I never could answer as a boy. I think now that it was both. It covered the whole distance from brokenhearted misery to bursting happiness—too fast. A grownup could hardly have stood it.

# The Village Blacksmith

by
**HENRY WADSWORTH LONGFELLOW**

**Vocabulary and pronunciation guide:**
> **sexton:** a person responsible for the maintenance of a
> church

Under the spreading chestnut-tree
The village smithy stands;
The smith, a mighty man is he,
With large and sinewy hands;
And the muscles of his brawny arms
Are strong as iron bands.

His hair is crisp, and black, and long.
His face is like the tan;
His brow is wet with honest sweat,
He earns whate'er he can,
And looks the whole world in the face,
For he owes not any man.

Week in, week out, from morn till night,
You can hear his bellows blow;
You can hear him swing his heavy sledge,
With measured beat and slow,
Like a sexton ringing the village bell,
When the evening sun is low.

And children coming home from school
Look in at the open door;
They love to see the flaming forge,
And hear the bellows roar,
And catch the burning sparks that fly
Like chaff from a threshing-floor.

He goes on Sunday to the church,
And sits among his boys;
He hears the parson pray and preach,
He hears his daughter's voice,
Singing in the village choir,
And it makes his heart rejoice.

It sounds to him like her mother's voice,
Singing in Paradise!
He needs must think of her once more,
How in the grave she lies;
And with his hard, rough hand he wipes
A tear out of his eyes.

Toiling—rejoicing—sorrowing,
Onward through life he goes;
Each morning sees some task begun,
Each evening sees it close;
Something attempted, something done,
Has earned a night's repose.

Thanks, thanks to thee, my worthy friend,
For the lesson thou hast taught!
Thus at the flaming forge of life
Our fortunes must be wrought;
Thus on its sounding anvil shaped
Each burning deed and thought!

# Jo's Literary Efforts

from *Little Women*
by
LOUISA MAY ALCOTT

**About the story:**

*Although Louisa May Alcott published dozens of novels as well as many poems and short stories during her lifetime, she is principally remembered as the author of one book:* **Little Women.** *This classic tale of family life in nineteenth-century New England is largely autobiographical and recalls many of the episodes that the author and her three sisters actually experienced. The poverty of her family was more severe and painful than that of the March family in* **Little Women,** *but, just as in the chapter presented here, it was the family's desperate need for money that led the young Louisa (Jo in the story) to write stories, poems, fairy tales—anything that would sell.*

*In achieving this goal, she learned something about the price of success and about the feeling of accomplishment; it remains an appropriate lesson today, for children and adults alike.*

**Approximate reading time:** 17 minutes
**Vocabulary and pronunciation guide:**
> **vortex:** a whirlwind or whirlpool
> **askew** [uh-SKYOO]: to one side; awry
> **forsook:** abandoned; deserted
> **Sphinx:** This monster plagued the Greek city of Thebes until Oedipus solved her riddle: "What walks on four feet in the morning, two at noon, and three at night?" (Answer: Human beings walk on all fours as infants, upright as adults, and with a cane when they are old.)
> **somber** [SOHM-burr]: gloom; melancholy

**hieroglyphics** [high-row-GLIFF-icks]: ancient Egyptian writings using pictures or symbols

**covertly** [KUHV-ert-lee]: secretly

**amiable** [AA-me-uh-bull]: friendly; good-natured

**lurid** [LURE-id]: shockingly vivid; sensational

**digress** [dye-GRESS]: to ramble or wander from the main idea

**metaphysical:** dealing with the nature of being and reality; therefore, highly abstract or theoretical

**ogre** [OH-gurr]: a man-eating giant

*F*ortune suddenly smiled upon Jo, and dropped a good-luck penny in her path. Not a golden penny, exactly, but I doubt if half a million would have given more real happiness than did the little sum that came to her in this way.

Every few weeks she would shut herself up in her room, put on her scribbling suit, and "fall into a vortex," as she expressed it, writing away at her novel with all her heart and soul, for till that was finished she could find no peace. Her "scribbling suit" consisted of a black woolen pinafore on which she could wipe her pen at will, and a cap of the same material, adorned with a cheerful red bow, into which she bundled her hair when the decks were cleared for action. This cap was a beacon to the inquiring eyes of her family, who during these periods kept their distance, merely popping in their heads semi-occasionally, to ask, with interest, "Does genius burn, Jo?" They did not always venture even to ask this question, but took an observation of the cap, and judged accordingly. If this expressive article of dress was drawn low upon the forehead, it was a sign that hard work was going on; in exciting moments it was pushed rakishly askew [uh-SKYOO], and when despair seized the author it was plucked wholly off, and cast upon the floor. At such times the intruder silently withdrew; and not until the red bow was seen gayly erect upon the gifted brow, did anyone dare address Jo.

She did not think herself a genius by any means; but when the writing fit came on, she gave herself up to it with entire abandon, and led a blissful life, unconscious of want, care, or bad weather, while she sat safe and happy in an imaginary world, full of friends almost as real and dear to her as any in the flesh. Sleep forsook her eyes, meals stood untasted, day and night were all too short to enjoy the happiness which blessed her only at such times, and made these hours worth loving, even if they bore no other fruit. The divine inspiration usually lasted a week or two, and then she emerged from her "vortex," hungry, sleepy, cross, or despondent.

She was just recovering from one of these attacks when she was prevailed upon to escort Miss Crocker to a lecture, and in return for her virtue was rewarded with a new idea. It was a lecture on the Pyramids, and Jo rather wondered at the choice of such a subject for such an audience—being, as it was, composed of common folk, not of scholars—but she took it for granted that some great social evil would be remedied or some great want supplied by unfolding the glories of the Pharaohs to an audience whose thoughts were busy with the price of coal and flour, and whose lives were spent in trying to solve harder riddles than that of the Sphinx.

They were early; and while Miss Crocker fixed the heel of her stocking, Jo amused herself by examining the faces of the people who occupied the seats near them. On her left were two matrons, with massive foreheads, and bonnets to match, discussing Woman's Rights and knitting. Beyond sat a pair of humble lovers, artlessly holding each other by the hand, a somber [SOHM-burr] spinster eating peppermints out of a paper bag, and an old gentleman taking his preparatory nap behind a yellow bandanna. On her right, her only neighbor was a studious-looking lad absorbed in a newspaper, or rather, a pictorial sheet, which carried illustrated short stories just brimming with action and adventure, however exaggerated or unlikely. Pausing to turn a page, the lad saw her looking, and, with boyish good nature, offered half his paper, saying bluntly, "Want to read it? That's a first-rate story."

Jo accepted with a smile, for she had never outgrown her liking for lads, and soon found herself involved in the maze of love, mystery, and murder that was usual in such publications, for the story belonged to that class of light literature in which the passions have a holiday, and when the author's inventiveness fails, a grand catastrophe clears the stage of one-half the story's characters, leaving the other half to exult over their downfall.

"Prime, isn't it?" asked the boy, as her eye went down the last paragraph of her portion.

"I think you and I could do as well as that if we tried," returned Jo, amused at his admiration of such trash.

"I should think I was a pretty lucky chap if I could," he responded. "She makes a good living out of such stories, they say," and he pointed to the name of Mrs. S. L. A. N. G. Northbury, under the title of the tale.

"Do you know her?" asked Jo, with sudden interest.

"No," the lad answered, "but I read all her pieces, and I know a fellow who works in the office where this paper is printed."

Jo's interest in the "art" form began to warm. "Do you think the author makes a good living out of stories like this?" she inquired, looking more respectfully at the agitated group in the illustration and the thickly sprinkled exclamation points that adorned the page.

"I'll say she does!" the boy replied knowingly. "She understands what folks like, and gets paid well for writing it."

Here the lecture began, but Jo heard very little of it, for while Professor Sands was droning on about hieroglyphics [highrow-GLIFF-icks], she was covertly [KUHV-ert-lee] taking down the address of the paper, and boldly resolving to try for the hundred-dollar prize offered in its columns for a sensational story. By the time the lecture ended and the audience awoke, she had built up a splendid fortune for herself (not the first founded upon paper), and was already deep in the concoction of her story, being unable to decide whether the duel should come before the elopement or after the murder.

She said nothing of her plan at home, but fell to work the next day, much to the disquiet of her mother, who always looked a little anxious when "genius took to burning." Jo had never tried this style before, contenting herself with very mild romances for the local literary journal. Her theatrical experience and miscellaneous reading were of service now, for they gave her some idea of dramatic effect, and supplied plot, language, and costumes. Her story was as full of desperation and despair as her limited acquaintance with those uncomfortable emotions enabled her to make it, and, having located it in Lisbon, she wound up with an earthquake as a striking and appropriate conclusion. The manuscript was mailed without anyone's notice, accompanied by a note, modestly saying that if the tale didn't get the prize, which the writer hardly dared expect, she would be very glad to receive any sum it might be considered worth.

Six weeks is a long time to wait, and a still longer time for a girl to keep a secret; but Jo did both, and was just beginning to give up all hope of ever seeing her manuscript again, when a letter arrived which almost took her breath away; for on opening it, a check for a hundred dollars fell into her lap. For a minute she stared at it as if it had been a snake, then she read her letter and began to cry. If the amiable [AA-me-uh-bull] gentleman who wrote that kindly note could have known what intense happiness he was giving a fellow-creature, I think he would devote his leisure hours, if he has any, to that amusement; for Jo valued the letter more than the money, because it was encouraging; and after years of effort it was *so* pleasant to find that she had learned to do something, though it was only to write a lurid [LURE-id] story.

A prouder young woman was seldom seen than she, when, having composed herself, she electrified the family by appearing before them with the letter in one hand, the check in the other, announcing that she had won the prize. Of course there was a great jubilee, and when she showed them her copy of the story, everyone read and praised it; though after her father had told her that the language was good, the romance fresh and hearty, and the tragedy quite thrilling, he shook his head, and said in his unworldly way:

"You can do better than this, Jo. Aim at the highest, and never mind the money."

"I think the money is the best part of it," said Amy. "What *will* you do with such a fortune?" she asked, looking at the check with a reverential eye.

"Send Beth and mother to the seaside for a month or two," answered Jo promptly.

"Oh, how splendid!" cried Beth, who had clapped her thin hands, and taken a long breath, as if pining for fresh ocean breezes. "But no, I can't do it, dear; it would be so selfish," she continued, motioning away the check, which her sister waved before her.

"Ah, but you *shall* go," Jo insisted. "I've set my heart on it; that's what I tried for, and that's why I succeeded. I never do well when I think of myself alone, so it will help me to work for you, don't you see? Besides, Marmee needs the change, and she won't leave you, so you *must* go. Won't it be fun to see you come home plump and rosy again? Hurrah for Dr. Jo, who always cures her patients!"

To the seaside they went, after much discussion; and though Beth didn't come home as plump and rosy as could be desired, she was much better, while Mrs. March declared she felt ten years younger; so Jo was satisfied with the investment of her prize money, and fell to work with a cheery spirit, bent on earning more of those delightful checks. She did earn several that year, and began to feel herself a power in the house; for by the magic of a pen, her "rubbish" turned into comforts for them all. Her story titled "The Duke's Daughter" paid the butcher's bill. "A Phantom Hand" put down a new carpet, and the "Curse of the Coventry's" proved the blessing of the Marches in the way of groceries and gowns.

Wealth is certainly a most desirable thing, but poverty has its sunny side, and one of the sweet uses of adversity is the genuine satisfaction that comes from hearty work of head or hand; and to the inspiration of necessity, we owe half the wise, beautiful, and useful blessings of the world. Jo enjoyed a taste of this satisfaction, and ceased to envy richer girls, taking great comfort in the knowledge that she could supply her own wants, and need ask no one for a penny.

Little notice was taken of her stories, but they found a market; and, encouraged by this fact, she resolved to make a bold stroke for fame and fortune. Having copied her novel for the fourth time, read it to all her confidential friends, and submitted it with fear and trembling to three publishers, she at last received an offer for it, on condition that she would cut it down one-third, and omit all the parts that she particularly admired.

She called a family council, and put it to them this way: "Now my options are to put the book away and let it mold, pay for printing myself, or chop it up to suit the public and get what I can for it. Fame is a very good thing to have in the house, but cash is more convenient; so I wish to take the sense of the meeting on this important subject."

"Don't spoil your book, my girl," was her father's advice. "There is more in it than you know, and the idea is well worked out. Let it wait and ripen." He had, indeed, practiced what he preached, having waited patiently thirty years for fruit of his own to ripen, and being in no haste to gather it, even now, when it was sweet and mellow.

"It seems to me that Jo will profit more by making the trial than by waiting," said Mrs. March. "Criticism is the best test of such work, for it will show her both unsuspected merits and faults, and help her to do better next time. We are too partial; but the praise and blame of outsiders will prove useful, even if she gets but little money."

"Yes," said Jo, knitting her brows, "that's just it; I've been fussing over the thing so long, I really don't know whether it's good, bad, or indifferent. It will be a great help to have cool, impartial persons take a look at it, and tell me what they think of it."

"I wouldn't take out a word of it," said Meg, who firmly believed that this book was the most remarkable novel ever written. "You'll spoil it if you do, for the interest of the story is more in the minds than in the actions of the people, and it will be all a muddle if you don't explain as you go on."

"But," Jo interrupted, turning to the publisher's note, "Mr. Allen says, 'Leave out the explanations, make it brief and dramatic, and let the characters tell the story.' "

"Then do as he tells you," said Amy, who took a strictly practical view of the subject. "He knows what will sell, and we don't. Make a good, popular book, and get as much money as you can. By and by, when you've got a name, you can afford to digress [dye-GRESS], and have philosophical and metaphysical people in your novels."

"Well," said Jo, laughing, "if my people *are* 'philosophical and metaphysical,' it isn't my fault, for I know nothing about such things, except what I hear father say, sometimes. If I've got some of his wise ideas jumbled up with my romance, so much the better for me. Now, Beth, what do you say?"

"I should so like to see it printed *soon*," was all Beth said, and smiled in saying it; but there was an unconscious emphasis on the last word, and a wistful look in the eyes that never lost their childlike candor, which chilled Jo's heart, for a minute, with a foreboding fear, and she decided to make her little venture "soon."

So, with Spartan firmness, the young author laid her first-born on her table, and chopped it up as ruthlessly as any ogre [OH-gurr]. In the hope of pleasing everyone, she took everyone's advice; and, like the old man and his donkey in the fable, suited nobody.

Her father liked the metaphysical streak which had unconsciously gotten into it; so that was allowed to remain, though she had her doubts about it. Her mother thought that there *was* a trifle too much description; out, therefore, it nearly all came, and with it many necessary links in the story. Meg admired the tragedy; so Jo piled up the agony to suit her, while Amy objected to the fun, and, with the best intentions in life, Jo quenched the sprightly scenes that relieved the somber character of the story. Then, to complete the ruin, she cut it down one-third, and confidingly sent the poor little romance, like a plucked robin, out into the big, busy world, to try its fate.

Well, it was printed, and she got three hundred dollars for it; likewise plenty of praise and blame, both so much greater than she expected that she was thrown into a state of bewilderment, from which it took her some time to recover.

"You said, mother, that the critiques would help me; but how can they, when they're so contradictory that I don't know whether I've written a promising book or broken all the Ten Commandments?" cried poor Jo, turning over a heap of notices, the perusal of which filled her with pride and joy one minute, wrath and dire dismay the next. "This man says, 'An exquisite book, full of truth, beauty, and earnestness; all is sweet, pure, and healthy,'" she continued, perplexed. "The next says, 'The theory of the book is bad, full of morbid fancies, spiritualistic ideas, and unnatural characters.' Now, as I had no theory of any kind, I don't believe in Spiritualism, and I copied my characters from life, I don't see how this critic *can* be right. Another says, 'It's one of the best American novels that has appeared for years'; and the next asserts that 'though it is original, and written with great force and feeling, it is a dangerous book.' 'Tisn't! Some make fun of it, some over-praise, and nearly all insist that I had a deep theory to expound, when I only wrote it for the pleasure and the money. I wish I'd printed it whole or not at all, for I do hate to be so misjudged."

Her family and friends administered comfort and commendation liberally; yet it was a hard time for sensitive, high-spirited Jo, who meant so well, and had apparently done so ill. But it did her good, for those whose opinions had real value gave her the criticism that is an author's best education; and when the first soreness was over, she could laugh at her poor little book, yet believe in it still, and feel herself the wiser and stronger for the buffeting she had received.

"Not being a genius, like Keats, it won't kill me," she said stoutly; "and I've got the joke on my side, after all; for the parts that were taken straight out of real life are denounced as impossible and absurd, and the scenes that I made up out of my own silly head are pronounced 'charmingly natural, tender, and true.' So I'll comfort myself with that; and when I'm ready, I'll up again and try another."

# Arithmetic

## by
## CARL SANDBURG

Arithmetic is where numbers fly like pigeons in and out of your
head.

Arithmetic tells you how many you lose or win if you know
how many you had before you lost or won.

Arithmetic is seven eleven all good children go to heaven—or
five six bundle of sticks.

Arithmetic is numbers you squeeze from your head to your
hand to your pencil to your paper till you get the answer.

Arithmetic is where the answer is right and everything is nice
and you can look out of the window and see the blue sky—
or the answer is wrong and you have to start all over and try
again and see how it comes out this time.

If you take a number and double it and double it again and
then double it a few more times, the number gets bigger and
bigger and goes higher and higher and only arithmetic can
tell you what the number is when you decide to quit dou-
bling.

Arithmetic is where you have to multiply—and you carry the
multiplication table in your head and hope you won't lose it.

If you have two animal crackers, one good and one bad, and
you eat one and a striped zebra with streaks all over him eats
the other, how many animal crackers will you have if somebody offers you five six seven and you say No no no and you
say Nay nay nay and you say Nix nix nix?

If you ask your mother for one fried egg for breakfast and she
gives you two fried eggs and you eat both of them, who is
better in arithmetic, you or your mother?

# The Cop and the Anthem

by
## O. HENRY

**About the story:**

*William Sydney Porter, who later adopted the pen name O. Henry, was raised and taught by an aunt, who ran a private elementary school. Among her teaching techniques she included reading aloud to her students every day from literary masterpieces. She also would invent an opening to a story, and then have each student contribute, orally and in turn, a part that would advance that story in a creative way. Surely young William's passion for reading and his desire to write owe a great debt to this teacher's progressive practices.*

*Almost half of O. Henry's several hundred stories are set in New York City and focus on the common people there—shopkeepers, office workers, vagrants—at the turn of the century. He found in the lives of these people all the struggles that humans everywhere face—at least humans who can't protect themselves from the cruel vagaries of fate and chance. And he added to these vignettes a device that became his trademark: the surprise ending.*

*The story that follows is a famous example of O. Henry's pitting of characters against their circumstances. A version of this story, starring Charles Laughton as the vagrant, Soapy, appeared as part of the film* O. Henry's Full House *in 1952.*

**Approximate reading time:** 16 minutes

**Vocabulary and pronunciation guide:**

**hibernatorial** [high-burr-nuh-TOR-ee-al]: like a wintering animal

**Vesuvian Bay** [veh-SUE-vee-an]: at the foot of Mt. Vesuvius, near Naples, Italy

**benign** [bee-NINE]: kind; gentle

**philanthropy** [fill-AN-throw-pee]: charity

**encumbered:** hindered; burdened
**Chablis** [sha-BLEE]: a dry, white wine
**ignoble** [ig-NO-bull]: without nobility; low
**coveted** [KUH-vet-ed]: desired; wished for
**callous** [KAL-us]: hardened; unfeeling
**fatuously** [FAT-chew-us-lee]: stupidly; foolishly
**cant:** angle; slant
**litany** [LIT-an-ee]: a lengthy or repetitive series
**insular** [IN-suh-ler]: located on an island
**marquee** [mar-KEY]: a roof with a signboard overhanging the entrance to a theater
**disconsolate** [dis-CON-suh-lut]: gloomy; dismal
**solemn** [SOL-um]: somber; serious

O n his bench in Madison Square, Soapy moved uneasily. When wild geese honk high of nights, and when women without sealskin coats grow kind to their husbands, and when Soapy moves uneasily on his bench in the park, you may know that winter is near at hand.

A dead leaf fell in Soapy's lap. That was Jack Frost's card. Jack is kind to the regular denizens of Madison Square, and gives fair warning of his annual call. At the corners of four streets he hands his calling card to the North Wind, footman of the mansion of All Outdoors, so that the inhabitants thereof may make ready.

Soapy became conscious of the fact that the time had come for him to resolve himself into a singular Committee of Ways and Means to provide against the coming rigor. And therefore he moved uneasily on his bench.

The hibernatorial [high-burr-nuh-TOR-ee-al] ambitions of Soapy were not of the highest. In them were no considerations of Mediterranean cruises, of sleepy Southern skies, or of drifting in the Vesuvian [veh-SUE-vee-an] Bay. Three months at Blackwell's Prison on the Island was what his soul craved. Three months of assured board and bed and congenial company, safe from the North Wind and the bluecoats, seemed to Soapy the essence of things desirable.

For years the hospitable Blackwell's had been his winter quarters. Just as his more fortunate fellow New Yorkers had bought their tickets to Palm Beach and the Riviera each winter, so Soapy had made his humble arrangements for his annual pilgrimage to the Island. And now the time was come. On the previous night, three Sunday newspapers—distributed beneath his coat, about his ankles, and over his lap—had failed to repulse the cold as he slept on his bench near the spurting fountain in the ancient square. So the Island loomed big and timely in Soapy's mind. He scorned the provisions made in the name of charity for the city's dependents. In Soapy's opinion the Law was more benign [bee-NINE] than philanthropy [fill-AN-throw-pee]. There was an endless round of institutions, municipal and private, on which he might set out and receive lodging and food accordant with the simple life. But to one of Soapy's proud spirit, the gifts of charity are encumbered. If not in coin, you must pay in humiliation of spirit for every benefit received at the hands of philanthropy. As Caesar had his Brutus, every bed of charity must have its toll of a bath, every loaf of bread its compensation of a private and personal inquisition. Therefore, it is better to be a guest of the law, which, though conducted by rules, does not meddle unduly with a gentleman's private affairs.

Soapy, having decided to go to the Island, at once set about accomplishing his desire. There were many easy ways of doing this. The pleasantest was to dine luxuriously at some expensive restaurant; and then, when found to be unable to pay the bill, be handed over quietly and without uproar to a policeman. An accommodating judge would do the rest.

Soapy left his bench and strolled out of the square and across the level sea of asphalt, where Broadway and Fifth Avenue flow together. Up Broadway he turned, and halted at a glittering café, which served the finest wines and the choicest meats, all in a setting of unimaginable elegance.

Soapy had confidence in himself from the lowest button on his vest upward. He was shaven, and his coat was decent, and his black clip-on tie, which had been presented to him by a lady missionary on Thanksgiving Day, made at least an opening argument for his respectability. If he could reach a table in the restaurant unsuspected, success would be his. The portion of him that would show above the table would raise no doubt in the waiter's mind. A roasted mallard duck, thought Soapy, would be about the thing—with a bottle of Chablis [sha-BLEE], some fine cheese, a cordial, and a cigar. One dollar for the cigar would be enough. The total would not be so high as to call forth any supreme manifestation of revenge from the café management; and yet the meat would leave him filled and happy for the journey to his winter refuge.

But as Soapy set foot inside the restaurant door, the head-waiter's eye fell upon his frayed trousers and worn-out shoes. Strong and ready hands turned him about and conveyed him in silence and haste to the sidewalk and averted the ignoble [ig-NO-bull] fate of the menaced mallard.

Soapy turned off Broadway. It seemed that his route to the coveted [KUH-vet-ed] Island would not be as luxurious as he had imagined. Some other way of achieving his three-month vacation must be thought of.

At the corner of Sixth Avenue, electric lights and cunningly displayed wares behind plate glass made a certain shop window stand out from the rest. Soapy took a cobblestone and dashed it through the glass. People came running around the corner, a policeman in the lead. Soapy stood still, with his hands in his pockets, and smiled at the sight of brass buttons.

"Where's the man that done that?" inquired the officer, excitedly.

"Don't you think that I might have had something to do with it?" said Soapy, not without sarcasm, but friendly, as one greets good fortune.

The policeman's mind refused to accept Soapy as even a possible culprit. Men who smash windows do not remain to discuss the event with servants of the law. They take to their heels. The policeman saw a man halfway down the block running to catch a car. With drawn club he joined in the pursuit. Soapy, with disgust in his heart, loafed along, twice unsuccessful.

On the opposite side of the street was a restaurant of no great pretensions. It catered to large appetites and modest purses. Its crockery and atmosphere were thick; its soup and table linens thin. Into this place Soapy took his worn-out shoes and telltale trousers without challenge. At a table he sat and consumed beefsteak, flapjacks, doughnuts, and pie. And then to the waiter he admitted the fact that the minutest coin and himself were strangers.

"Now, get busy and call a cop," said Soapy. "And don't keep a gentleman waiting."

"No cop for youse!" said the waiter, with a voice like butter cakes and an eye like the cherry in a Manhattan cocktail. "Hey, Con!" he bellowed to a huge friend waiting tables across the room.

Neatly upon his left ear on the callous [KAL-us] pavement the two waiters pitched Soapy. He arose joint by joint, as a carpenter's rule opens, and beat the dust from his clothes. Arrest seemed but a rosy dream. The Island seemed very far away. A policeman who stood in front of a drugstore two doors away laughed and walked down the street.

Five blocks Soapy traveled before his courage permitted him to woo capture again. This time the opportunity presented what he fatuously [FAT-chew-us-lee] termed to himself a "cinch." A young woman of a modest and pleasing appearance was standing before a show window gazing with sprightly interest at its display of shaving mugs and inkstands, and two yards from the window a large policeman of severe demeanor leaned against a fireplug.

It was Soapy's design to assume the role of the despicable and detestable "masher." The refined and elegant appearance of his victim and the proximity to the conscientious cop encouraged him to believe that he would soon feel the pleasant official clutch upon his arm that would ensure his winter quarters at the prison on the island.

Soapy straightened the lady missionary's ready-made tie, dragged his shrinking cuffs into the open, set his hat at a killing cant, and sidled toward the young woman. He made eyes at her, lurid glances punctuated with suggestive winks; he smiled and smirked and went brazenly through the impudent and contemptible litany [LIT-an-ee] of the "masher." With half an eye, Soapy saw that the policeman was watching him with a fixed stare. The young woman moved away a few steps, and again bestowed her absorbed attention upon the shaving mugs in the window. Soapy followed, boldly stepping to her side, raised his hat and said:

"Ah, there, Bedelia! Don't you want to come and play in my yard?"

The policeman was still looking. The persecuted young woman had but to beckon a finger and Soapy would be practically en route to his insular [IN-suh-ler] haven. Already he imagined he could feel the cozy warmth of the police station. The young woman faced him and, stretching out a hand, caught Soapy's sleeve.

"Sure, Mack," she said, joyfully, "if you'll buy me a pail of suds, I'll do anything you want. I'd have spoke to you sooner, but the cop was watching."

With the young woman playing the clinging ivy to his oak, Soapy walked past the policeman, overcome with gloom. He seemed doomed to liberty.

At the next corner he shook off his companion and ran. He came to a stop in the theater district, where women in furs and men in handsome coats moved gaily in the wintry air. A sudden fear seized Soapy that some dreadful enchantment had rendered him immune to arrest. The thought brought a little of panic upon him, and when he came upon another policeman lounging grandly under a gleaming marquee [mar-KEY], the idea of "disorderly conduct" flashed into his mind.

On the sidewalk Soapy began to yell drunken gibberish at the top of his harsh voice. He danced, howled, raved, and, to his credit, gave a performance worthy of any actor in the district.

The policeman twirled his club, turned his back to Soapy, and remarked to a citizen:

" 'Tis one of them Yale lads celebratin' the goose egg they give to the Hartford College. Noisy, but no harm. We've instructions to lave them be."

Disconsolate [dis-CON-suh-lut], Soapy ceased his unavailing racket. Would never a policeman lay hands on him? The Island seemed but a dream to him now. He buttoned his thin coat against the chilling wind.

In a cigar store he saw a well-dressed man lighting a cigar

under a swinging light. His silk umbrella he had set by the door on entering. Soapy stepped inside, snatched the umbrella, and sauntered off with it slowly. The man from the cigar store followed hastily after him.

"My umbrella," he called out sternly to Soapy.

"Oh, is it?" sneered Soapy, adding insult to petty larceny. "Well, why don't you call a policeman? I took it. Your umbrella! Why don't you call a cop? There stands one on the corner."

The umbrella owner slowed his steps. Soapy did likewise, but a terrible feeling told him that luck would again run against him. The policeman looked at the two curiously.

"Of course," said the umbrella man—"that is—well, you know how these mistakes occur—I—if it's your umbrella, I hope you'll excuse me—I picked it up this morning in a restaurant—If you recognize it as yours, why—I hope you'll—"

"Of course it's mine," said Soapy, viciously.

The ex-umbrella man retreated. The policeman hurried to assist a tall blonde in an opera cloak who was chancing to cross the street in front of a streetcar that was approaching only two blocks away.

Soapy walked eastward through a street damaged by improvements. He hurled the umbrella wrathfully into an excavation and muttered oaths against all policemen. Because he wanted to fall into their clutches, they seemed to regard him as a king who could do no wrong.

After some time, Soapy reached one of the avenues to the east where the glitter and turmoil was but faint. He set his face down this path toward Madison Square, for the homing instinct survives even when the home is a park bench.

But on an unusually quiet corner, Soapy came to a standstill. Here was an old church, quaint and rambling and gabled. Through one violet-stained window, a soft light glowed, where, no doubt, the organist loitered over the keys, making sure of his mastery of the coming Sunday anthem. For there drifted out to Soapy's ears sweet music that caught and held him transfixed against the iron fence.

The moon was above, lustrous and serene; vehicles and pedestrians were few; sparrows twittered sleepily in the eaves—

for a little while the scene might have been a country church-yard. And the anthem that the organist played cemented Soapy to the iron fence, for he had known it well in the days when his life contained such things as mothers and roses and ambitions and friends and immaculate thoughts and collars.

The combination of Soapy's receptive state of mind and the influences about the old church wrought a sudden and wonderful change in his soul. He viewed with swift horror the pit into which his life had tumbled, the degraded days, unworthy desires, dead hopes, wrecked faculties, and base motives that made up his existence.

And also in a moment his heart responded thrillingly to this novel mood. An instantaneous and strong impulse moved him to battle with his desperate fate. He would pull himself out of the mire; he would make a man of himself again; he would conquer the evil that had taken possession of him. There was time; he was comparatively young yet; he would resurrect his old eager ambitions and pursue them without faltering. Those solemn [SOL-um] but sweet organ notes had set up a revolution in him. Tomorrow he would go into the roaring downtown district and find work. A fur importer had once offered him a place as a driver. He would find him tomorrow and ask for the position again. He would be somebody in the world. He would—

Soapy felt a hand laid on his arm. He looked quickly around into the broad face of a policeman.

"What are you doin' here?" asked the officer.

"Nothin," said Soapy.

"Then come along," said the policeman. "We have to keep the streets clean of vagrants like you."

And the next morning, Soapy heard the judge in the Police Court say, "Three months on the Island."

# Barbara Frietchie

by
**JOHN GREENLEAF WHITTIER**

**Vocabulary and pronunciation guide:**
**o'er** [OAR]: a one-syllable pronunciation of *over*
**bier** [rhymes with NEAR]: a coffin

Up from the meadows rich with corn,
Clear in the cool September morn,

The clustered spires of Frederick stand
Green-walled by the hills of Maryland.

Round about them orchards sweep,
Apple and peach tree fruited deep,

Fair as the garden of the Lord
To the eyes of the famished rebel horde,

On that pleasant morn of the early fall
When Lee marched over the mountain-wall;

Over the mountains winding down,
Horse and foot, into Frederick town.

Forty flags with their silver stars,
Forty flags with their crimson bars,

Flapped in the morning wind; the sun
Of noon looked down and saw not one.

Up rose old Barbara Frietchie then,
Bowed with her fourscore years and ten;

Bravest of all in Frederick town,
She took up the flag the men hauled down;

In her attic window the staff she set,
To show that one heart was loyal yet.

Up the street came the rebel tread,
Stonewall Jackson riding ahead.

Under his slouched hat left and right
He glanced; the old flag met his sight.

"Halt!"—the dust-brown ranks stood fast.
"Fire!"—out blazed the rifle-blast.

It shivered the window, pane and sash;
It rent the banner with seam and gash.

Quick, as it fell, from the broken staff
Dame Barbara snatched the silken scarf.

She leaned far out on the window-sill,
And shook it forth with a royal will.

"Shoot, if you must, this old gray head,
But spare your country's flag," she said.

A shade of sadness, a blush of shame,
Over the face of the leader came;

The nobler nature within him stirred
To life at that woman's deed and word;

"Who touches a hair of yon gray head
Dies like a dog! March on!" he said.

All day long through Frederick street
Sounded the tread of marching feet:

All day long that free flag tossed
Over the heads of the rebel host.

Ever its torn folds rose and fell
On the loyal winds that loved it well;

And through the hill-gaps sunset light
Shone over it with a warm good-night.

Barbara Frietchie's work is o'er [OAR],
And the Rebel rides on his raids no more.

Honor to her! and let a tear
Fall, for her sake, on Stonewall's bier [rhymes with NEAR].

Over Barbara Frietchie's grave,
Flag of Freedom and Union, wave!

Peace and order and beauty draw
Round thy symbol of light and law;

And ever the stars above look down
On thy stars below in Frederick town!

# Beowulf's Fight with Grendel

## from *Beowulf*

**About the story:**
> *This heroic epic was written perhaps a thousand years ago by an unknown author in an ancient dialect now called Old English. Originally, it was a long, unrhymed poem telling of the adventures of Beowulf, a noble from what is now southern Sweden, whose bravery saved the people of Denmark. Beowulf's battle with the monster Grendel is presented here; in the original epic, Beowulf also fights gory battles with other monsters, including Grendel's mother—a hideous beast who sought revenge against Beowulf for the killing of her son.*

**Approximate reading time:** 10 minutes
**Vocabulary and pronunciation guide:**
> **Beowulf** [BAY-ah-wolf]
> **fen:** low, swampy land
> **moor:** an elevated tract of wasteland covered with shrubs and thick grasses
> **ogre** [OH- gurr]: a man-eating giant; hideous monster
> **mail:** body armor made from interlinked rings of steel
> **thanes:** warrior companions of a king; knights
> **whence:** from where
> **ere** [AIR]: before
> **bade** [BAD]: past tense of *bid;* invited
> **scourge** [SKURJ]: a cause of suffering or trouble
> **sinews** [SIN-youz]: muscles and tendons

*L* ong, long ago in the land of the Danes, there lived a great king named Hrothgar. The old men of his country loved him and bowed their knee to him gladly, and the young men obeyed him and joyfully did battle for him. For he was a valiant king and mighty in war. Never could any foe stand against him, for he defeated them all and took from them much treasure.

Old King Hrothgar used these spoils to build for himself a great palace, adorned with gold and ivory. It was bigger and finer than any hall men had ever heard of, and its fame spread over all the land. It was called Hart Hall, and there Hrothgar sat on his throne to share with his men the good things God had given him, and all lived together in peace and joy.

And so Hart Hall was filled with laughter and song and merriment. Every evening when the shadows fell, and the land grew dark without, the knights and warriors gathered within to feast. And when the feast was over, and the wine cup passed around the tables, and the great fire roared upon the hearth, and the dancing flames gleamed and flickered, making strange shadows among the gold and ivory carving on the walls, the minstrel played on his harp and sang. And from the many-windowed Hall, the light glowed cheerfully. Far over the dreary fen and moor, the gleam was shed, and the sound of song and harp awoke the deep silence of the night.

Though within the Hall there was light and gladness, without there was wrath and hate. For far on the moor there lived a wicked giant named Grendel. Hating all joy and brightness, this monster haunted the fens, prowling the night to see what evil he might do.

Very terrible was this ogre [OH-gurr] Grendel to look upon. Thick black hair hung about his face, and his teeth were long and sharp, like the tusks of an animal. His huge body and great hairy arms had the strength of ten men. He wore no armor, for his skin was tougher than any coat of mail that ever protected a knight in battle. His nails were like steel and sharper than daggers, and by his side there hung a great pouch in which he carried off those he was ready to devour.

Now day by day this fearsome giant was tortured to hear the sounds of laughter and of merriment. Day by day the music of the harp and the songs of the minstrel made him more and more mad with jealous hate.

Finally, he could bear it no longer, and one night, creeping through the darkness, after the feast and merriment had ended, he made his way to Hart Hall where the warriors slept. Their weapons and armor had been thrown aside, for they feared not any foe. And so with his eyes shooting out flame, this hideous fiend speedily slew thirty of the men with his savage claws. Howling with wicked joy, he carried them off to his dark dwelling across the moors, there to devour them.

Oh, when morning came, great was the grief in the land of the Danes. The sun shone upon the desolate Hall and revealed the foul deeds wrought by Grendel. The knights raised a great cry of sorrow, and Hrothgar, the mighty king so strong in war, sat downcast and wept over the loss and the suffering of his thanes. Hrothgar longed for a champion to avenge him and his men, but there was no one who could battle *this* monster; he was too strong, too horrible for anyone to conquer.

For as long as the knights slept in the great Hall, Grendel would return in the dark and slay his fill, carrying their bodies back to his dwelling, there to devour them at his leisure.

Soon no one would sleep beneath the great roof of Hart Hall; indeed, for twelve long years it stood empty, no man daring to enter it except by light of day. During these twelve long years, Grendel terrorized Hrothgar and the Danes. He prowled through the misty moors, hiding in dark places, and slaying both young and old. Many were his grisly deeds and many his foul crimes, for even the mightiest warriors were powerless against him.

Now there lived in a far-off land a young man called Beowulf [BAY-ah-wolf], who had the strength of thirty men. He heard of the wicked deeds of Grendel and the sorrow of the good King Hrothgar, and he saw that his duty lay in helping the King to rid his land of this evil giant. Beowulf was a mighty warrior, and he was eager to test his power against that of Grendel, and so he gathered with him fourteen companions, warriors all, and set sail for the land of the Danes.

For two days they sailed with strong winds until they spied the shining white cliffs of Daneland, and they anchored their boat beneath. The guard watching from the top of the cliffs rode down to them on horseback and, brandishing his sword, said, "Who are you who come to our shores dressed for war? I must know whence you come ere [AIR] you take a single step farther."

And Beowulf answered that they came as friends, to rid Hrothgar of his wicked enemy Grendel, and at that, the guard said that he would lead them to the king's palace. After some distance, the guard pointed ahead, saying, "There lies the great Hart Hall. No longer have ye need of me, and I must return to my watch along the coast."

Beowulf and his men saw the Hall shining like gold against the sky, and they followed the road, paved with stone, that led them to its entrance. There, Hrothgar's messenger welcomed them and bade [BAD] them enter the great Hall so that they might reveal their mission to the king of the Danes.

Beowulf led the way. His armor shone like a golden network, and his look was high and noble, as he said, "Hail, O King! To fight against Grendel single-handed have I come. I know that the terrible monster's hide is as steel armor, and therefore I shall bear neither sword nor shield, but will fight hand-to-hand with this foe, and death shall come to whomever God wills. If I die in this struggle, then my body will have no need for burial, for it will be devoured and my bones spread over the moor. But this alone I do ask: that you send my armor and my coat of mail back to my king, for there is none like it among the Goths."

Hrothgar loved the youth for his noble words, and bade him and his men sit down and share a merry feast in the great hall, which they did.

When the sun sank low in the west, all the guests arose. The king bade Beowulf and his comrades guard the hall and to be ever watchful for the evildoer. "Have courage," he said, "and know that if you rid us of this scourge [SKURJ], not a wish of yours shall be unfulfilled, if it be in my power to give it to thee." Farewells were said, for no man knew who would be alive when morning came. Soon darkness covered all the land, and Beowulf lay down to rest in the Hall. But he prepared himself strangely for the battle that would ensue: he removed his armor, his coat of mail, and his helmet, lying only in his silken coat and saying, "My strength is no less than Grendel's, and he has not learned the ways of weapons; so we shall fight this night as equals."

Having so spoken, Beowulf laid his head upon his pillow, and all around him his warriors lay down to take their rest. None among them thought ever again to see his own land, for they had heard of the terrible death that had carried off so many of the Dane folk from Hart Hall, and each expected that death also to be his. Yet so reckless were they of life that soon they slept. They who were to guard the great Hall slept—all save one. Beowulf alone, watchful and waiting for the evil Grendel, impatiently longed for the coming battle.

Through the creeping mists that covered the moorland strode the Evil Thing; right to the Hall he came. The bolts and bars on the giant door gave way at his touch, and he trod quickly over the marble floor of the Hall. Loud he laughed, wild, demonlike laughter, as he gazed at the troop of kinsmen lying together asleep. Here truly was a giant feast spread out before him. He slavered as he mused about sucking the life out of each one before daybreak.

Beowulf, watchful and angry, curbed his wrath and waited to see how the monster would attack. He did not have long to wait.

Quickly stretching forth a claw, Grendel seized a sleeping warrior, and before the unlucky thane could awake, Grendel had crushed his bones, drunk his blood, and swallowed the lifeless body.

Then Grendel stretched forth his claw again, this time to seize Beowulf from his bed. But Beowulf, raising himself upon his elbow, reached out his hand and caught the monster by the arm. Never before had Grendel felt such a mighty grip, and he cried out in pain, a roar that resounded throughout the Hall. Hotter and hotter grew his anger, but deeper and deeper grew his fear. He longed to flee and return to his demon lair, but he could not free himself from this powerful grasp. Beowulf then stood upright, tightening even more his grasp upon the ogre.

Grendel roared again and up and down the Hall he raged, with Beowulf holding him fast in his grip. Louder and louder grew the din, and fiercer and wilder grew the battle, but finally the end of the fight drew near.

The sinews [SIN-youz] in Grendel's shoulder snapped, and the bones cracked. The ogre now was certain that death awaited him in that mighty Hall, and with a cry that echoed throughout Daneland, he tore himself free, and fled, wounded to the death, leaving his arm in Beowulf's mighty grip.

Sobbing forth his death song, Grendel fled over the misty moorland until he reached his home in the lake of the Water Dragons, and there plunged in. The dark waves closed over him, and he sank for the last time to his watery dwelling.

Loud were the songs of triumph and great was the rejoicing in Hart Hall, for Beowulf had made good his boast. He had cleansed the Hall of the wicked monster, and the Dane folk could sleep peacefully once again. When morning came, and the news was spread over the land, many a warrior arrived from far and near. They tracked Grendel's gory footsteps until they came to the lake of the Water Dragons. There they gazed upon the water as it boiled and seethed, colored dark with the poison blood of the ogre. Then back with light hearts they sped, praising their hero.

The great Hall was cleansed, the walls hung anew with cloth of gold, the whole place was made fair and straight, for only the roof had been left altogether unhurt after the fight. A merry feast was held, during which the King presented Beowulf many wonderful treasures, and riches were bestowed upon his brave companions as well. "From now on I will love you as if you were my own son," Hrothgar said to Beowulf; "you shall want for nothing in this world, and your fame shall live forever."

Little could they imagine then, in all their joy and revelry, that though Grendel was dead indeed, there would be other— still more terrible—monsters that Beowulf must slay before peace would come at last to the land of the Danes.

# June

## from *The Vision of Sir Launfal*
## by
## JAMES RUSSELL LOWELL

**Vocabulary and pronunciation guide:**
    **mean:** common; ordinary; lowly
    **o'errun** [oar-RUN]: two-syllable pronunciation
      of *overrun*
    **dumb:** unable to speak

And what is so rare as a day in June?
    Then, if ever, come perfect days;
Then Heaven tries earth if it be in tune,
    And over it softly her warm ear lays:
Whether we look, or whether we listen,
We hear life murmur, or see it glisten;
Every clod feels a stir of might,
    An instinct within it that reaches and towers,
And, groping blindly above it for light,
    Climbs to a soul in grass and flowers;
The flush of life may well be seen
    Thrilling back over hills and valleys;
The cowslip startles in meadows green,
    The buttercup catches the sun in its chalice,
And there's never a leaf nor a blade too mean
    To be some happy creature's palace;
The little bird sits at his door in the sun,
    Atilt like a blossom among the leaves,
And lets his illumined being o'errun
    With the deluge of summer it receives;
His mate feels the eggs beneath her wings,
And the heart in her dumb breast flutters and sings;
He sings to the wide world, and she to her nest,—
In the nice ear of Nature which song is the best?

Now is the high-tide of the year,
    And whatever of life hath ebbed away
Comes flooding back with a ripply cheer,
    Into every bare inlet and creek and bay;
Now the heart is so full that a drop overfills it,
We are happy now because God wills it;
No matter how barren the past may have been,
'Tis enough for us now that the leaves are green;
We sit in the warm shade and feel right well
How the sap creeps up and the blossoms swell;
We may shut our eyes, but we cannot help knowing
That skies are clear and grass is growing. . . .

# The Celebrated Jumping Frog of Calaveras County

by
**MARK TWAIN**

**About the story:**

*This is the story that changed Samuel Langhorne Clemens, the newspaper reporter, into Mark Twain, the most famous American writer who ever lived. Although Twain had used this pen name on some of his previous articles for the* **Virginia City Territorial Enterprise,** *it was the publication of the jumping frog story in 1865 that spread his name and fame across the country.*

*This tale is more than just a humorous sketch about how a clever stranger outsmarted a compulsive gambler; its real importance comes from the way in which the author tells this tale. Although the narrator here is a well-spoken Easterner, it is the vernacular speech of the unlearned Simon Wheeler that became discussed and quoted in the parlors of genteel society, where previously only "polite" or "dignified" writing would be accepted. The "local color" language of the West, as well as representative dialects from other regions, was, from this time on, not only popular but appropriate for both humorous and serious literature.*

*Although this story will still hold its own if read aloud without the intended dialect, I urge you to try your hand at duplicating Simon Wheeler's accent. Practice reciting some paragraphs out loud as you familiarize yourself with the story; you'll get the hang of it in no time. Ready? "Well, thish-yer Smiley had a yaller one-eyed cow that didn't have no tail, only just a short stump like a bannanner, and—"*

**Approximate reading time:** 15 minutes
**Vocabulary and pronunciation guide:**
  **Calaveras County** [Kal-uh-VAIR-us]: part of the Califor-
    nia gold country east of San Francisco
  **garrulous** [GAIR-uh-lus]: talkative; wordy
  **interminable** [in-TUR-min-uh-bull]: wearisome; pro-
    longed; endless
  **transcendent:** remarkable; surpassing others
  **flume:** a chute through which water is made to flow
  **forecastle** [FOKE-sul]: on a ship, the part of the upper
    deck nearest the bow
  **quail shot:** small metal pellets used in shotgun shells

*I*n compliance with the request of a friend of mine, who
wrote me from the East, I called on good-natured, garrulous [GAIR-uh-lus] old Simon Wheeler, and inquired
about my friend's friend, Leonidas W. Smiley, as requested to
do, and I hereunto append the result. I have a lurking suspicion that *Leonidas W.* Smiley is a myth; that my friend never
knew such a personage; and that he only conjectured that, if I
asked old Wheeler about him, it would remind him of his in-
famous *Jim* Smiley, and he would go to work and bore me
nearly to death with some infernal reminiscence of him as long
and as tedious as it would be useless to me. If that was the
design, it certainly succeeded.

I found Simon Wheeler dozing comfortably by the barroom
stove of the old dilapidated tavern in the ancient mining camp
of Angel's, and I noticed that he was fat and bald-headed, and
had an expression of winning gentleness and simplicity upon
his tranquil countenance. He roused up and gave me "Good
day." I told him a friend of mine had commissioned me to
make some inquiries about a cherished companion of his boy-
hood named *Leonidas W.* Smiley—*Reverend Leonidas W.* Smiley
—a young minister of the Gospel, who he had heard was at
one time a resident of Angel's Camp. I added that if Mr.
Wheeler could tell me anything about this Reverend Leonidas
W. Smiley, I would feel under many obligations to him.

Simon Wheeler backed me into a corner and blockaded me there with his chair, and then sat me down and reeled off the monotonous narrative which follows this paragraph. He never smiled, he never frowned, he never changed his voice from the gentle-flowing key to which he tuned the initial sentence, he never betrayed the slightest suspicion of enthusiasm; but all through the interminable [in-TUR-min-uh-bull] narrative there ran a vein of impressive earnestness and sincerity, which showed me plainly that, so far from his imagining that there was anything ridiculous or funny about his story, he regarded it as a really important matter, and admired its two heroes as men of transcendent genius in *finesse*. As I said before, I asked him to tell me what he knew of Reverend Leonidas W. Smiley, and he replied as follows. I let him go on in his own way, and never interrupted him once:

"Reverend Leonidas W. H'm, Reverend Le————well, there was a feller here once by the name of *Jim* Smiley, in the winter of '49—or maybe it was the spring of '50—I don't recollect exactly, somehow, though what makes me think it was one or the other is because I remember the big flume wasn't finished when he first come to the camp; but anyway, he was the curiousest man about always betting on anything that turned up you ever see, if he could get anybody to bet on the other side; and if he couldn't, he'd change sides. Any way that suited the other man would suit him—any way just so's he got a bet, *he* was satisfied. But still he was lucky, uncommon lucky —he most always come out winner. He was always ready and laying for a chance; there couldn't be no solit'ry thing mentioned but that feller'd offer to bet on it, and take any side you please, as I was just telling you. If there was a horserace, you'd find him flush, or you'd find him busted at the end of it; if there was a dogfight, he'd bet on it; if there was a catfight, he'd bet on it; if there was a chicken-fight, he'd bet on it; why, if there was two birds setting on a fence, he would bet you which one would fly first; or if there was a camp-meeting, he would be there reg'lar, to bet on Parson Walker, which he judged to be the best exhorter about here, and so he was, too, and a good man. If he even seen a straddle-bug start to go anywheres, he would bet you how long it would take him to get wherever he was going to, and if you took him up, he would foller that straddle-bug to Mexico but what he would find out where he was bound for and how long he was on the road. Lots of the boys here has seen that Smiley, and can tell you about him. Why, it never made no difference to *him*—he would bet on *any*thing—the dangdest feller. Parson Walker's wife laid very sick once, for a good while, and it seemed as if they warn't going to save her; but one morning he came in, and Smiley asked how she was, and he said she was considerable better— thank the Lord for his inf'nit mercy—and coming along so smart that, with the blessing of Prov'dence, she'd get well yet; and Smiley, before he thought, says, 'Well, I'll risk two-and-a-half that she don't anyway.'

"Thish-yer Smiley had a mare—the boys called her the fif-teen-minute nag, but that was only in fun, you know, because, of course, she was faster than that—and he used to win money on that horse, for all she was so slow and always had the asthma, or the distemper, or the consumption, or something of that kind. They used to give her two or three hundred yards' start, and then pass her under way; but always at the last part of the race she'd get excited and desperate-like, and come ca-vorting and straddling up, and scattering her legs around lim-ber, sometimes in the air, and sometimes out to one side amongst the fences, and kicking up m-o-r-e dust, and raising m-o-r-e racket with her coughing and sneezing and blowing her nose—and always fetch up at the stand just about a neck ahead, as near as you could measure.

"And he had a little small bull-pup, that to look at him you'd think he warn't worth a cent but to set around and look ornery and lay for a chance to steal something. But as soon as money was up on him, he was a different dog; his under-jaw'd begin to stick out like the forecastle [FOKE-sul] of a steamboat, and his teeth would uncover, and shine savage like the furnaces. And a dog might tackle him, and bully-rag him, and bite him, and throw him over his shoulder two or three times, and An-drew Jackson—which was the name of the pup—Andrew Jackson would never let on but what *he* was satisfied, and hadn't expected nothing else—and the bets being doubled and doubled on the other side all the time, till the money was all up; and then all of a sudden he would grab that other dog just by the j'int of his hind leg and freeze to it—not chaw, you understand, but only just grip and hang on till they throwed up the sponge, if it was a year. Smiley always come out winner on that pup, til! he harnessed a dog once that didn't have no hind legs, because they'd been sawed off by a circular saw, and when the thing had gone along far enough, and the money was all up, and he come to make a snatch for his pet hold, he saw in a minute how he'd been imposed on, and how the other dog had him in the door, so to speak, and he 'peared surprised, and then he looked sorter discouraged-like, and didn't try no more to win the fight, and so he got shucked out bad. He give Smiley a look, as much to say his heart was broke and it was *his* fault for putting up a dog that hadn't no hind legs for him to take hold of, which was his main dependence in a fight, and then he limped off a piece and laid down and died. It was a good pup, was that Andrew Jackson, and would have made a name for hisself if he'd lived, for the stuff was in him, and he had genius—I know it, because he hadn't no opportunities to speak of, and it don't stand to reason that a dog could make such a fight as he could under them circumstances if he hadn't no talent. It always makes me feel sorry when I think of that last fight of his'n, and the way it turned out.

"Well, thish-yer Smiley had rat-terriers, and chicken-cocks, and tomcats, and all them kind of things, till you couldn't rest, and you couldn't fetch nothing for him to bet on but he'd match you. He ketched a frog one day, and took him home, and said he calc'lated to educate him; and so he never done nothing for these three months but set in his back yard and learn that frog to jump. And you bet you he *did* learn him, too. He'd give him a little punch behind, and the next minute you'd see that frog whirling in the air like a doughnut—see him turn one summerset, or maybe a couple, if he got a good start, and come down flatfooted and all right, like a cat. He got him up so in the matter of catching flies, and kept him in practice so constant, that he'd nail a fly every time as far as he could see him. Smiley said all a frog needed was education and he could do most anything—and I believe him. Why, I've seen him set Dan'l Webster down here on this floor—Dan'l Webster was the name of the frog—and sing out, 'Flies, Dan'l, flies!' and quicker'n you could wink, he'd spring straight up, and snake a fly off'n the counter there, and flop down on the floor again as solid as a gob of mud, and fall to scratching the side of his head with his hind foot as indifferent as if he hadn't no idea he'd been doin' any more'n any frog might do. You never see a frog so modest and straightfor'ard as he was, for all he was so gifted. And when it come to fair and square jumping on the dead level, he could get over more ground at one straddle than any animal of his breed you ever see. Jumping on a dead level was his strong suit, you understand; and when it come to that, Smiley would ante up money on him as long as he had a cent. Smiley was monstrous proud of his frog, and well he might be, for fellers that had traveled and been everywheres all said he laid over any frog that ever *they* see.

"Well, Smiley kept the beast in a little lattice box, and he used to fetch him downtown sometimes and lay for a bet. One day a feller—a stranger in the camp, he was—come across him with his box, and says:

" 'What might it be that you've got in the box?'

"And Smiley says, sorter indifferent like, 'It *might* be a parrot, or it *might* be a canary, maybe, but it ain't—it's only just a frog.'

"An' the feller took it, and looked at it careful, and turned it round this way and that, and says, 'H'm—so 'tis. Well, what's *he* good for?'

" 'Well,' Smiley says, easy and careless, 'he's good enough for *one* thing, I should judge—he can outjump any frog in Calaveras County.'

"The feller took the box again, and took another long, particular look, and give it back to Smiley, and says, very deliberate, 'Well, I don't see no p'ints about that frog that's any better'n any other frog.'

" 'Maybe you don't,' Smiley says. 'Maybe you understand frogs, and maybe you don't understand 'em; maybe you've had experience, and maybe you ain't only a amature as it were. Anyways, I've got *my* opinion, and I'll risk forty dollars that he can outjump any frog in Calaveras County.'

"And the feller studied a minute, and then says, kinder sad

like, 'Well, I'm only a stranger here, and I ain't got no frog; but if I had a frog, I'd bet you.'

"And then Smiley says, 'That's all right—that's all right—if you'll hold my box a minute, I'll go and get you a frog.' And so the feller took the box, and put up his forty dollars along with Smiley's, and set down to wait.

"So he set there a good while thinking and thinking to hisself, and then he got the frog out and pried his mouth open and took a teaspoon and filled him full of quail shot—filled him pretty near up to his chin—and set him on the floor. Smiley he went to the swamp and slopped around in the mud for a long time, and finally he ketched a frog, and fetched him in, and give him to this feller, and says:

" 'Now, if you're ready, set him alongside of Dan'l, with his forepaws just even with Dan'l, and I'll give the word.' Then he says, 'One—two—three—jump!' and him and the feller touched up the frogs from behind, and the new frog hopped off, but Dan'l gave a heave, and hysted up his shoulders—so —like a Frenchman, but it wasn't no use—he couldn't budge; he was planted as solid as an anvil, and he couldn't no more stir than if he was anchored out. Smiley was a good deal surprised, and he was disgusted, too, but he didn't have no idea what the matter was, of course.

"The feller took the money and started away; and when he was going out at the door, he sorter jerked his thumb over his shoulder—this way—at Dan'l, and says again, very deliberate, 'Well,' he says, '*I* don't see no p'ints about that frog that's any better'n any other frog.'

"Smiley he stood scratching his head and looking down at Dan'l a long time, and at last he says, 'I wonder what in the nation that frog throw'd off for—I wonder if there ain't something the matter with him—he 'pears to look mighty baggy, somehow.' And he ketched Dan'l by the nape of the neck, and lifted him up and says, 'Why, blame my cats, if he don't weigh five pounds!' and turned him upside down, and he belched out a double handful of shot. And then he see how it was, and he was the maddest man—he set the frog down and took out after that feller, but he never ketched him. And—"

[Here Simon Wheeler heard his name called from the front

yard, and got up to see what was wanted.] And turning to me as he moved away, he said: "Just set where you are, stranger, and rest easy—I ain't going to be gone a second."

But, by your leave, I did not think that a continuation of the history of the enterprising vagabond *Jim* Smiley would be likely to afford me much information concerning the *Reverend Leonidas W.* Smiley, and so I started away.

At the door I met the sociable Wheeler returning, and he buttonholed me and recommenced:

"Well, thish-yer Smiley had a yaller one-eyed cow that didn't have no tail, only just a short stump like a bannanner, and—"

However, lacking both time and inclination, I did not wait to hear about the afflicted cow, but took my leave.

# Stopping by Woods on a Snowy Evening

by
**ROBERT FROST**

Whose woods these are I think I know.
His house is in the village though;
He will not see me stopping here
To watch his woods fill up with snow.

My little horse must think it queer
To stop without a farmhouse near
Between the woods and frozen lake
The darkest evening of the year.

He gives his harness bells a shake
To ask if there is some mistake.
The only other sound's the sweep
Of easy wind and downy flake.

The woods are lovely, dark and deep.
But I have promises to keep,
And miles to go before I sleep,
And miles to go before I sleep.

# from *The Story of My Life*

by
## HELEN KELLER

**About the Story:**

*When she was nineteen months old, Helen Keller lost her sight and hearing forever. Yet, through the extraordinary efforts of an ingenious and compassionate teacher— Anne Mansfield Sullivan—she learned how to learn. Her curiosity was insatiable: she wanted to know and to do everything. At ten years of age, she resolved that she would learn how to speak, which she did—in English, French, and German. She was graduated from Radcliffe College, with honors, at age twenty-four, and went on to tour the world, writing and giving lectures supporting the improvement of conditions for the handicapped.*

*Many people have become familiar with the early struggles between the determined Anne Sullivan and the undisciplined, combative Helen Keller through* **The Miracle Worker,** *a play by William Gibson, made into a motion picture in 1962, with Oscar-winning performances by Anne Bancroft and Patty Duke. The excerpt presented here is Helen Keller's own account of her miraculous transformation.*

**Approximate reading time:** 11 minutes
**Vocabulary and pronunciation guide:**

**gesticulated** [jess-TICK-you-late-ed]: made gestures
**akin** [uh-KIN]: similar
**tempest:** a violent outburst or uproar
**languor** [LANG-gurr]: fatigue; weakness; spiritlessness
**tangible** [TAN-jih-bull]: able to be touched, real
**sounding-line:** a weighted line marked in fathoms and used for determining the depth of water

The beginning of my life was simple and much like every other little life. I came, I saw, I conquered, as the first baby in the family always does.

I am told that while I was still in baby clothes I showed many signs of an eager, self-asserting disposition. Everything that I saw other people do I insisted upon imitating. At six months I could pipe out "Howdee," and one day I attracted everyone's attention by saying "Tea, tea, tea" quite plainly. They tell me I walked the day I was a year old. My mother had just taken me out of the bathtub and was holding me in her lap, when I was suddenly attracted by the flickering shadows of leaves that danced in the sunlight on the smooth floor. I slipped from my mother's lap and almost ran toward them. The impulse gone, I fell down and cried for her to take me up in her arms.

These happy days did not last long. One brief spring, musical with the song of robin and mockingbird, one summer rich in fruit and roses, one autumn of gold and crimson sped by and left their gifts at the feet of an eager, delighted child. Then, in the dreary month of February, came the illness which closed my eyes and ears and plunged me into the unconsciousness of a newborn baby. They called it "acute congestion of the stomach and brain." The doctor thought I could not live. Early one morning, however, the fever left me as suddenly and mysteriously as it had come. There was great rejoicing in the family that morning, but no one, not even the doctor, knew that I should never see or hear again.

I fancy I still have confused recollections of that illness. I especially remember the tenderness with which my mother tried to soothe me in my waking hours of fret and pain, and the agony and bewilderment with which I awoke after a tossing half-sleep, and turned my eyes, so dry and hot, to the wall, away from the once-loved light, which came to me dim and yet more dim each day. But, except for these fleeting memories, if, indeed, they be memories, it all seems very unreal, like a nightmare. Gradually I got used to the silence and darkness that surrounded me and forgot it had ever been different.

I cannot recall what happened during the first months after my illness. I only know that I sat in my mother's lap and clung to her dress as she went about her household duties. My hands felt every object and observed every motion, and in this way I learned to know many things. Soon I felt the need of some communication with others and began to make crude signs. A shake of the head meant "No" and a nod, "Yes," a pull meant "Come" and a push, "Go." Was it bread I wanted? Then I would imitate the acts of cutting the slices and buttering them. If I wanted my mother to make ice cream for dinner, I made the sign for working the freezer and shivered, indicating cold.

I do not remember when I first realized that I was different from other people. I had noticed that my mother and my friends did not use signs as I did when they wanted anything done, but talked with their mouths. Sometimes I stood between two persons who were conversing and touched their lips. I could not understand, and this annoyed me greatly. I moved my lips and gesticulated [jess-TICK-you-late-ed] frantically without result. This made me so angry at times that I kicked and screamed until I was exhausted.

I think I knew when I was naughty, for I knew that it hurt Ella, my nursemaid, to kick her, and when my fit of temper was over, I had a feeling akin [uh-KIN] to regret. But I cannot remember any instance in which this feeling prevented me from repeating the naughtiness when I failed to get what I wanted. I was strong, active, indifferent to consequences. I knew my own mind well enough and always had my own way, even if I had to fight tooth and nail for it.

About this time I found out the use of a key. One morning I locked my mother up in the pantry, where she had to remain for three hours because no one was around to help her. She kept pounding on the door, while I sat outside on the porch steps and laughed with glee as I felt the jar of the pounding. Even after my teacher, Miss Sullivan, arrived, I sought an early opportunity to lock her in her room. I went upstairs with something which my mother had made me understand I was to give to Miss Sullivan; but no sooner had I given it to her than I slammed the door shut, locked it, and hid the key under the wardrobe cabinet in the hall. I could not be forced to tell where the key was, and so my father had to get a ladder and take Miss Sullivan out through the window—much to my delight. Months later, I produced the key.

Meanwhile the desire to express myself grew. The few signs I used became less and less adequate, and my failures to make myself understood were invariably followed by outbursts of passion. I felt as if invisible hands were holding me, and I made frantic efforts to free myself. I struggled—not that struggling helped matters, but the spirit of resistance was strong within me; I generally broke down in tears and physical exhaustion. If my mother happened to be near, I crept into her arms, too miserable even to remember the cause of the tempest. After a while the need of some means of communication became so urgent that these outbursts occurred daily, sometimes hourly.

My parents were deeply grieved and perplexed. We lived a long way from any school for the blind or the deaf, and it seemed unlikely that anyone would come to such an out-of-the-way place as Tuscumbia, Alabama, to teach a child who was both deaf and blind. Indeed, friends and relatives sometimes doubted whether I *could* be taught. But my father was persistent and was eventually advised, by Dr. Alexander Graham Bell, to write to the Perkins Institution in Boston, which he did, and in a few weeks there came a kind letter of reply notifying us that a teacher had been found.

The most important day I remember in all my life is the one on which my teacher, Anne Mansfield Sullivan, came to me. I am filled with wonder when I consider the immeasurable contrast between the two lives which it connects. It was the third of March, 1887, three months before I was seven years old.

On the afternoon of that eventful day, I stood on the porch, dumb, expectant. I guessed vaguely from my mother's signs and from the hurrying to and fro in the house that something unusual was about to happen, so I went to the door and waited on the steps. The afternoon sun penetrated the mass of honeysuckle that covered the porch, and fell on my upturned face. My fingers lingered almost unconsciously on the familiar leaves and blossoms which had just come forth to greet the sweet southern spring. I did not know what the future held of marvel or surprise for me. Anger and bitterness had preyed upon me continually for weeks and a deep languor [LANG-gurr] had succeeded this passionate struggle.

Have you ever been at sea in a dense fog, when it seemed as

if a tangible [TAN-jih-bull] white darkness shut you in, and the great ship, tense and anxious, groped her way toward the shore, and you waited with beating heart for something to happen? I was like that ship before my education began, only I was without compass or sounding-line, and had no way of knowing how near the harbor was. "Light! Give me light!" was the wordless cry of my soul, and the light of love shone on me in that very hour.

I felt approaching footsteps. I stretched out my hand as I supposed to my mother. Someone took it, and I was caught up and held close in the arms of her who had come to reveal all things to me, and, more than all things else, to love me.

The morning after my teacher came, she led me into her room and gave me a doll. The little blind children at the Perkins Institution had sent it, but I did not know this until afterward. When I had played with it a little while, Miss Sullivan slowly spelled into my hand the word "d-o-l-l." I was at once interested in this finger play and tried to imitate it. When I finally succeeded in making the letters correctly, I was flushed with childish pleasure and pride. Running downstairs to my mother I held up my hand and made the letters for doll. I did not know that I was spelling a word or even that words existed; I was simply making my finger go in monkey-like imitation. In the days that followed, I learned to spell in this uncomprehending way a great many words, among them *pin, hat, cup,* and a few verbs like *sit, stand,* and *walk.* But my teacher had been with me several weeks before I understood that everything has a name.

One day, while I was playing with my new doll, Miss Sullivan put my big rag doll into my lap also, spelled "d-o-l-l" into my hand, and tried to make me understand that "d-o-l-l" applied to both. Earlier in the day we had had a tussle over the words "m-u-g" and "w-a-t-e-r." Miss Sullivan had tried to impress it upon me that "m-u-g" is *mug* and that "w-a-t-e-r" is *water,* but I persisted in confusing the two. In despair she had dropped the subject for the time, only to renew it at the first opportunity. I became impatient at her repeated attempts and, seizing the new doll, I dashed it upon the floor. I was keenly delighted when I felt the fragments of the broken doll at my

feet. Neither sorrow nor regret followed my passionate outburst. I had not loved the doll. In the still, dark world in which
I lived there was no strong sentiment or tenderness. I felt my
teacher sweep the fragments to one side of the hearth, and I
had a sense of satisfaction that the cause of my discomfort was
removed. She brought me my hat, and I knew I was going out
into the warm sunshine. This thought, if a wordless sensation
may be called a thought, made me hop and skip with pleasure.

We walked down the path to the well-house, attracted by
the fragrance of the honeysuckle with which it was covered.
Someone was drawing water and my teacher placed my hand
under the spout. As the cool stream gushed over one hand,
she spelled into the other the word *water*, first slowly, then
rapidly. I stood still, my whole attention fixed upon the mo-
tions of her fingers. Suddenly I felt a misty consciousness as of
something forgotten—a mystery of language was revealed to
me. I knew then that "w-a-t-e-r" meant the wonderful cool
something that was flowing over my hand. That living word
awakened my soul, gave it light, hope, joy, set it free! There
were barriers still, it is true, but barriers that could in time be
swept away.

I left the well-house eager to learn. Everything had a name,
and each name gave birth to a new thought. As we returned to
the house, every object that I touched seemed to quiver with
life. That was because I saw everything with the strange, new
sight that had come to me. On entering the door I remembered
the doll I had broken. I felt my way to the hearth and picked
up the pieces. I tried vainly to put them together. Then my
eyes filled with tears; for I realized what I had done, and for
the first time I felt repentance and sorrow.

I learned a great many new words that day. I do not remember what they all were, but I do know that *mother, father, sister,*
and *teacher* were among them—words that were to make the
world blossom for me. It would have been difficult to find a
happier child than I was as I lay in my crib at the close of that
eventful day and lived over the joys it had brought me, and for
the first time longed for a new day to come.

# The Deacon's Masterpiece, or The Wonderful One-Hoss Shay

by
**OLIVER WENDELL HOLMES**

**Vocabulary and pronunciation guide:**
> **one-hoss shay:** a chaise; a two-wheeled, one-horse carriage with a folding top
> **Georgius Secundus:** England's German-born King George the Second
> **Braddock's army:** General Edward Braddock was killed in action during the French and Indian Wars
> **felloe:** the outside rim of a wheel
> **thill:** a horse is harnessed between slender poles called *thills*
> **whipple-tree:** a wooden bar to which the traces are attached

Have you heard of the wonderful one-hoss shay,
That was built in such a logical way
It ran a hundred years to a day,
And then, of a sudden, it—ah, but stay,
I'll tell you what happened without delay,
Scaring the parson into fits,
Frightening people out of their wits—
Have you ever heard of that, I say?

Seventeen hundred and fifty-five.
*Georgius Secundus* was then alive—
Snuffy old drone from the German hive.
That was the year when Lisbon-town
Saw the earth open and gulp her down,
And Braddock's army was done so brown,
Left without a scalp to its crown.
It was on the terrible Earthquake day
That the Deacon finished the one-hoss shay.

Now in building of chaises, I tell you what,
There is always *somewhere* a weakest spot—
In hub, tire, felloe, in spring or thill,
In panel, or crossbar, or floor, or sill,
In screw, bolt, thoroughbrace—lurking still,
Find it somewhere you must and will—
Above or below, or within or without—
And that's the reason, beyond a doubt,
A chaise *breaks down*, but doesn't *wear out*.

But the Deacon swore (as Deacons do,
With an "I dew vum," or an "I tell *yeou*")
He would build one shay to beat the taown
'N' the keounty 'n' all the kentry raoun';
It should be so built that it *couldn't* break daown.
"Fur," said the Deacon, "'t's mighty plain
Thut the weakes' place mus' stan' the strain;
'N' the way t' fix it, uz I maintain,
    Is only jest
T' make that place uz strong uz the rest."

So the Deacon inquired of the village folk
Where he could find the strongest oak,
That couldn't be split nor bent nor broke—
That was for spokes and floor and sills;
He sent for lancewood to make the thills;
The crossbars were ash, from the straightest
    trees;
The panels of white-wood, that cuts like cheese,
But last like iron for things like these;
The hubs of logs from the "Settler's ellum"—
Last of its timber—they couldn't sell 'em,
Never an ax had seen their chips,
And the wedges flew from between their lips,
Their blunt ends frizzled like celery tips;
Step and prop-iron bolt and screw,
Spring, tire, axle, and linchpin too,
Steel of the finest, bright and blue;
Thoroughbrace bison-skin, thick and wide;

Boot, top, dasher, from tough old hide
Found in the pit when the tanner died.
That was the way he "put her through."
"There!" said the Deacon, "naow she'll dew!"

Do! I tell you, I rather guess
She was a wonder, and nothing less!
Colts grew horses, beards turned gray,
Deacon and deaconess dropped away,
Children and grandchildren—where were they?
But there stood the stout old one-hoss shay
As fresh as on Lisbon-earthquake-day!

EIGHTEEN HUNDRED;—it came and found
The Deacon's masterpiece strong and sound.
Eighteen hundred increased by ten;—
"Hahnsum kerridge" they called it then.
Eighteen hundred and twenty came;—
Running as usual; much the same.
Thirty and forty at last arrive,
And then come fifty, and FIFTY-FIVE.

Little of all we value here
Wakes on the morn of its hundredth year
Without both feeling and looking queer.
In fact, there's nothing that keeps its youth,
So far as I know, but a tree and truth.
(This is a moral that runs at large;
Take it.—You're welcome.—No extra charge.)

FIRST OF NOVEMBER—the Earthquake day,—
There are traces of age in the one-hoss shay,
A general flavor of mild decay,
But nothing local, as one may say.
There couldn't be—for the Deacon's art
Had made it so like in every part
That there wasn't a chance for one to start.
For the wheels were just as strong as the thills,
And the floor was just as strong as the sills,

And the panels just as strong as the floor,
And the whipple-tree neither less nor more,
And the back crossbar as strong as the fore,
And spring and axle and hub *encore*.
And yet, *as a whole*, it is past a doubt
In another hour it will be *worn out!*

First of November, 'Fifty-five!
This morning the parson takes a drive.
Now, small boys, get out of the way!
Here comes the wonderful one-hoss shay, .
Drawn by a rat-tailed, ewe-necked bay.
"Huddup!" said the parson. —Off went they.
The parson was working his Sunday's text—
Had got to *fifthly*, and stopped perplexed
At what the—Moses—was coming next.
All at once the horse stood still,
Close by the meet'n'-house on the hill.
First a shiver, and then a thrill,
Then something decidedly like a spill,—
And the parson was sitting upon a rock,
At half past nine by the meet'n'-house clock,—
Just the hour of the earthquake shock!
What do you think the parson found,
When he got up and stared around?
The poor old chaise in a heap or mound,
As if it had been to the mill and ground!
You see, of course, if you're not a dunce,
How it went to pieces all at once—
All at once, and nothing first,—
Just as bubbles do when they burst.

End of the wonderful one-hoss shay.
Logic is logic. That's all I say.

# from *Treasure Island*

by
ROBERT LOUIS STEVENSON

About the story:

*Robert Louis Stevenson lived to be only forty-four years old, but his works became enshrined as masterpieces of the Victorian age, not only in his native Scotland, but throughout the world. Although he was an accomplished essayist and travel writer, he is remembered today chiefly for his poetry and his adventure novels. Two of these poems, "My Bed Is a Boat" (page 59) and "Requiem" (page 184, the last lines of which became his epitaph) are presented in this volume. His novels—including such classics as* Kidnapped, The Black Arrow, Dr. Jekyll and Mr. Hyde, *and* The Master of Ballantrae *—have brought to life some of the most memorable characters in all of literature.*

*In* Treasure Island *(its first four chapters are presented here), we follow the dangerous adventures of Jim Hawkins as he passes from childhood into manhood, under the "guidance" of Long John Silver. Seeing the movie versions of this tale (especially the Wallace Beery/Jackie Cooper adaptation from 1934 and the 1950 Disney version with Robert Newton as Long John Silver) does not diminish at all the excitement or the wonder this story can create as a read-aloud.*

# Part One

**Approximate reading time for Part One:** 23 minutes
**Vocabulary and pronunciation guide:**
>    **saber** [SAY-burr]: a heavy sword, often curved
>    **connoisseur** [con-uh-SURR]: an expert in matters
>        of taste
>    **grog shop:** a tavern
>    **a man who sailed before the mast:** a seaman on a ship;
>        a common sailor
>    **fourpenny:** an old English coin (with a value of approx-
>        imately eight cents)
>    **diabolic:** like the devil; fiendish
>    **the Spanish Main:** the seas and land around the north
>        coast of South America and the Caribbean
>    **Dr. Livesey** [LIV-zee]
>    **suffice** [suff-ICE]: be sufficient or satisfactory
>    **hoarfrost:** a silvery-white frost that forms during still,
>        clear nights
>    **talons** [TAL-unz]: the claws of a bird or animal
>    **bade** [BAD]: past tense of *bid*
>    **prophetic** [pro-FET-ick]: like a prophet or a prophecy;
>        predicting something that is about to happen

*I*n order to tell the entire story of Treasure Island, I must go back to the time when my father kept the Admiral Benbow Inn, and the brown old seaman, with the saber [SAY-burr] cut, first took up his lodging under our roof.

I remember him as if it were yesterday, as he came plodding to the inn door, his sea-chest following behind him in a hand cart. He was a tall, strong, heavy, nut-brown man, and his hair was tied in a pigtail that fell over the shoulders of his soiled blue coat. His hands were ragged and scarred, with black, broken nails, and across one cheek was a white saber scar. I remember him looking round the cove and whistling to himself as he did so, and then breaking out in that old sea-song that he sang so often afterwards in a high, old, tottering voice:

> "Fifteen men on the dead man's chest—
> Yo-ho-ho, and a bottle of rum!"

Then he rapped on the door with a bit of stick like a handspike that he carried, and when my father appeared, called roughly for a glass of rum. This, when it was brought to him, he drank slowly, like a connoisseur [con-uh-SURR], lingering on the taste, and still looking about him at the cliffs and up at our signboard.

"This is a handy cove," says he, at length, "and a pleasant place for a grog shop. Do you get much company, mate?"

My father told him no, very little company, he was sorry to say.

"Well, then," said he, "this is the berth for me. Here you, matey," he cried to the man who pushed the hand-cart, "bring up alongside and unload my chest. I'll stay here a bit," he continued. "I'm a plain man; rum and bacon and eggs is what I want, and that point up the coast to watch ships from. What might you call me? You might call me captain. Oh, I see what you're at—there," and he threw down three or four gold pieces on the floor. "You can tell me when I've worked through that," says he, looking as fierce as a commander.

And, indeed, bad as his clothes were, and coarsely as he spoke, he had none of the appearances of a man who sailed before the mast, but seemed like a mate or a skipper, accustomed to be obeyed or to strike. The man who came with the hand-cart told us that the stagecoach had set him down yesterday morning at the Royal George Inn, and that there he had inquired about what inns were along the coast. Hearing ours well spoken of, I suppose, and described as lonely, he apparently had chosen it from the others for his place of residence. And that was all we could learn of our guest.

He was a very silent man by custom. All day he hung round the cove, or upon the cliffs, with a brass telescope; all evening he sat in a corner of the parlor next to the fire, and drank rum and water very strong. Mostly he would not speak when spoken to; only look up sudden and fierce, and blow through his nose like a foghorn; and we and the people who came about our house soon learned to let him be. Every day, when he came back from his stroll, he would ask if any seafaring men had gone by along the road. At first we thought it was the wish for company of his own kind that made him ask this question, but at last we began to see that he only wished to avoid them. When a seaman put up at the Admiral Benbow (as now and then some did, those who came by the coast road on their way to Bristol), he would look in at him through the curtained door before he entered the parlor, and he was always sure to be as silent as a mouse.

For me, at least, there was no secret about the matter, for I was, in a way, his lookout in these matters. He had taken me aside one day, and promised me a silver fourpenny on the first of every month if I would only keep my "weather-eye open for a seafaring man with one leg," and let him know the moment he appeared. Often enough, when the first of the month came round, and I applied to him for my wage, he would only blow through his nose at me, and stare me down. But before the week was out, he was sure to think better of it, bring me my fourpenny piece, and repeat his orders to look out for "the seafaring man with one leg."

How that one-legged man haunted my dreams, I need scarcely tell you. On stormy nights, when the wind shook the four corners of the house, and the surf roared along the cove and up the cliffs, I would see him in a thousand forms, and with a thousand diabolic expressions. Now the leg would be cut off at the knee, now at the hip; now he was a monstrous kind of creature who had never had but one leg, and that in the middle of his body. To see him leap and run and pursue me over hedge and ditch was the worst of nightmares. And altogether I paid pretty dear for my monthly fourpenny piece, in the shape of these abominable phantoms.

But though I was so terrified by the idea of the seafaring man with one leg, I was far less afraid of the captain himself than anybody else who knew him. There were nights when he drank a bit more rum than his head would carry, and then, sometimes, he would sit and sing his wicked, old, wild sea-songs, paying mind to no one in the room. But other times, he would order drinks for the house, and then force all the trembling company to listen to his stories or to join in the chorus of his songs. Often I have heard the house shake with "Yo-ho-ho, and a bottle of rum," all the patrons joining in for dear life, with the fear of death upon them, and each singing louder than the other, to avoid being noticed by the captain. For in these fits he was a most domineering and intimidating creature; he would slap his hand on the table with a command for silence; he would fly up in a passion of anger at a question, or sometimes because no question was asked, and so the audience must not be following his story. Nor would he allow anyone to leave the inn till he had drunk himself sleepy and reeled off to bed.

His stories were what frightened people worst of all. Dreadful stories they were; about hanging, and walking the plank, and storms at sea, and wild deeds and places along the Spanish Main. By his own account he must have lived his life among some of the wickedest men that God ever allowed upon the sea, and the language in which he told these stories shocked our plain country people almost as much as the crimes that he described. My father was always saying the inn would be ruined, for people would soon cease coming there to be bullied and humiliated and sent home frightened beyond sleep, but I really believe the captain's presence actually did our business good. People were frightened at the time, but on looking back they rather liked it; it was a fine excitement in a quiet country life, and there was even a party of the younger men who pretended to admire him, calling him a "true sea-dog" and a "real old salt" and the like, and saying that he was the sort of man that made England so feared on the sea.

In one way, indeed, he brought near ruin to us, for he kept on staying week after week, and then month after month, so that all the money he'd put up on his arrival had been long exhausted, and still my father never had the heart to demand more from him. Whenever he as much as mentioned it, the captain blew through his nose so loudly, you might say he roared, and stared my poor father right out of the room. I have seen my father wringing his hands after such a rebuff, and I am sure the annoyance and the terror he lived in must have greatly hastened his early and unhappy death.

All the time he lived with us the captain made no change whatever in his clothes. When one of the turned-up corners in his cocked hat fell down, he let it hang from that day forth, though it was often a great annoyance to him. I remember the appearance of his coat, which he patched himself upstairs in his room, and which, before the end, was nothing but patches. He never wrote or received a letter, and he never spoke with anyone but the neighbors, and with these only when he was drunk on rum. The great sea-chest none of us had ever seen open.

He was only once crossed, and that was toward the end, when my poor father was far gone in a decline that eventually killed him. Dr. Livesey [LIV-zee] came late one afternoon to see the patient, took a bit of dinner from my mother, and went into the parlor to smoke a pipe until his horse could be brought back from the stable in the nearby village. I remember the contrast between the neat, bright doctor—with his white powdered wig and his pleasant manners—and that filthy, heavy, bleary-eyed pirate of ours, sitting far gone in rum with his arms on the table. Suddenly he—the captain, that is—began to pipe up his eternal song:

> "Fifteen men on the dead man's chest—
>    Yo-ho-ho, and a bottle of rum!
> Drink and the devil had done for the rest—
>    Yo-ho-ho, and a bottle of rum!"

At first I had supposed the "dead man's chest" to be that sea-chest of his upstairs in the front room, and the thought had been mingled in my nightmares along with that of the one-legged seafaring man. But by this time we had all long ceased to pay any particular notice to the song; it was however, new to Dr. Livesey, and on him I observed it did not produce an agreeable effect, for he looked up for a moment quite angrily before continuing his own conversation, which the captain's song had interrupted. At last the captain flapped his hand upon the table before him in a way we all knew to mean— "Silence!" The voices stopped at once, all but Dr. Livesey's; he went on as before, speaking clear and kind, and drawing briskly at his pipe between every word or two. The captain glared at him for a while, flapped his hand again, glared still harder, and at last broke out with a villainous, low oath: "Silence, there, between decks!"

"Were you addressing me, sir?" says the doctor; and when the ruffian had told him, with another oath, that this was so, "I have only one thing to say to you, sir," replies the doctor, "that if you keep on drinking rum, the world will soon be rid of a very dirty scoundrel!"

The old captain's fury was awful. He sprang to his feet, drew and opened a sailor's jackknife, and, balancing it open on the palm of his hand, threatened to pin the doctor to the wall.

The doctor never so much as moved. He spoke to him, as before, over his shoulder, and in the same tone of voice; rather high, so that all the room might hear, but perfectly calm and steady:

"If you do not put that knife this instant in your pocket, I promise, upon my honor, I'll see that you hang for threatening my life."

Then followed a battle of looks between them, but the captain soon knuckled under, put up his weapon, and resumed his seat, grumbling like a beaten dog.

"And now, sir," continued the doctor, "since I now know there's such a fellow as you in my district, I'll have an eye upon you day and night. I'm not only a doctor, you see; I'm also an officer of the law, and if I catch a breath of complaint against you, if it's only for a piece of incivility like tonight's, I'll have you hunted down and routed out of this territory. Let that suffice [suff-ICE]."

Soon after, Dr. Livesey's horse was brought to the door, and he rode away; but the captain held his peace that evening, and for many evenings to come.

It was not very long after this that there occurred the first of the mysterious events that rid us at last of the captain, though not, as you will see, of his affairs. It was a bitter cold winter, with long, hard frosts and heavy gales, and it was plain from the first that my poor father was little likely to see the spring. He sank daily, and my mother and I had to manage the entire inn alone; this kept us busy enough without paying much regard to our unpleasant guest.

It was one January morning, very early—a pinching, frosty morning—the cove all gray with hoarfrost, the ripple of the waves lapping softly on the stones, the sun still low and only touching the hilltops and shining far to seaward. The captain had risen earlier than usual, and set out down the beach, his cutlass swinging under his old blue coat, his brass telescope under his arm, his hat tilted back upon his head. I remember his breath hanging like smoke in his wake as he strode off, and the last sound I heard of him, as he rounded the big rock, was a loud snort of indignation, as though his mind was still on Dr. Livesey.

Well, mother was upstairs with father, and I was setting the breakfast table awaiting the captain's return, when the parlor door opened and a man stepped in on whom I had never set my eyes before. He was a pale, greasy creature, with two fingers missing from his left hand; and, though he wore a cutlass, he did not look much like a fighter. I had always my eye open for seafaring men, with one leg or two, and I remember this one puzzled me. He was not sailorly, and yet he had a smack of the sea about him too.

I asked him what his pleasure was, and he said he would take rum; but as I was going out of the room to fetch it, he sat down upon a table and motioned me to draw near. I stayed right where I was.

"Come here, sonny," says he. "Come nearer here."

I took a step nearer.

"Is this here table for my mate Bill?" he asked, with a kind of leer.

I told him I did not know his mate Bill, and that this was for a person who stayed in our house whom we called the captain.

"Well," said he, "my mate Bill would be called the captain,

as like as not. He has a cut on one cheek, and a mighty pleasant way with him, particularly in drink, has my mate Bill. We'll put it, for argument like, that your captain has a cut on one cheek—and we'll put it, if you like, that that cheek's the right one. Ah, well! I told you. Now, is my mate Bill in this here house?"

I told him he was out walking.

"Which way, sonny?" he asked. "Which way is he gone?"

And when I had pointed out the rock, and told him how the captain was likely to return, and how soon, and answered a few other questions, "Ah," said he, "this'll be as good as drink to my mate Bill."

The expression on his face as he said these words was not at all pleasant, and I had my own reasons for thinking that the stranger was mistaken, even supposing he meant what he said. But it was no affair of mine, I thought; and, besides, it was difficult to know what to do. The stranger kept hanging about just inside the door, peering round the corner like a cat waiting for a mouse. Once I stepped out myself into the road, but he immediately called me back, and, as I did not obey quick enough for his fancy, he snarled and ordered me in with a curse that made me jump. As soon as I was back in again, he returned to his former manner, half fawning, half sneering, patted me on the shoulder and told me that I was a good boy, and that he had taken quite a fancy to me. "I have a son of my own," said he, "as like you as brothers, and he's my pride and joy. But the great thing for boys is discipline, sonny—discipline. Now, if you had sailed alongside of Bill, you wouldn't have stood there to be spoke to twice—not you. That was never Bill's way, nor the way of such as sailed with him. And here, sure enough, is my mate Bill, with a spyglass under his arm, bless his old 'art, to be sure. You and me'll just go back into the parlor, sonny, and get behind the door, and we'll give Bill a little surprise—bless his 'art, I say again."

So saying, the stranger backed along with me into the parlor and put me behind him in the corner, so that we were both hidden by the opened door. I was very uneasy and alarmed, as you might imagine, and it rather added to my fears to observe that the stranger was certainly frightened himself. He cleared the hilt of his cutlass and loosened the blade in the sheath; and all the time we were waiting there, he kept swallowing as if he felt what we used to call a lump in his throat.

At last in strode the captain, slammed the door behind him, without looking to the right or left, and marched straight across the room to where his breakfast awaited him.

"Bill," said the stranger, in a voice that I thought he had tried to make bold and big.

The captain spun round on his heel and fronted us; all the brown had gone out of his face, and even his nose was blue; he had the look of a man who sees a ghost, or the devil, or something worse, if anything can be; and, upon my word, I felt sorry to see him turn so suddenly old and sick.

"Come on, Bill, you know me; you know an old shipmate, Bill, surely," said the stranger.

The captain made a sort of gasp.

"Black Dog!" said he.

"And who else?" returned the other, getting more at his ease. "Black Dog as ever was, come to see his old shipmate Billy, at the Admiral Benbow Inn. Ah, Bill, Bill, we have seen a sight of times, us two, since I lost them two talons [TAL-unz]," holding up his mutilated hand.

"Now, look here," said the captain, "you've run me down; here I am; well, then, speak up: what is it?"

"That's you, Bill," returned Black Dog, "you always come right to the point of it, Billy. Well, I'll have a glass of rum from this dear child here, as I've took such a liking to, and we'll sit down, if you please, and talk square, like old shipmates."

When I returned with the rum, they were already seated on either side of the captain's breakfast table—Black Dog next to the door, and sitting sideways, so as to have one eye on his old shipmate, and one, as I thought, on his retreat.

He bade [BAD] me go and leave the door wide open. "None of your keyholes for me, sonny," he said, and I left them together, and retired into the bar.

For a long time, though I certainly did my best to listen, I could hear nothing but a low rumble of discourse; but at last the voices began to grow louder, and I could pick up a word or two, mostly curses, from the captain.

"No, no, no, no, and an end of it!" he cried once. And again, "If it comes to hanging, everyone hangs, say I."

Then all of sudden there was a tremendous explosion of oaths and other noises—the chair and table went over in a lump, a clash of steel followed, and then a cry of pain, and the next instant, I saw Black Dog in full flight and the captain hotly pursuing, both with drawn cutlasses, and blood streaming from Black Dog's left shoulder. Just at the door, the captain aimed at the fugitive one last tremendous slash, which would certainly have split him to the bone had it not been intercepted by our big signboard with its picture of Admiral Benbow painted on it. You can still see the notch on the lower edge of the signboard to this day.

That blow was the last of the battle. Once out upon the road, Black Dog, in spite of his wound, fled at a goodly pace and disappeared over the edge of the hill in half a minute. The captain, for his part, stood staring at the signboard like a bewildered man. Then he passed his hand over his eyes several times, and at last turned back into the house.

"Jim," says he, "rum"; and as he spoke, he reeled a little and caught himself with one hand against the wall.

"Are you hurt?" cried I.

"Rum," he repeated. "I must get away from here. Rum! Rum!"

I ran to fetch it, but I was quite shaken by all that had just happened, and I broke one glass and spilled the rum from another; and while I was still getting in my own way, I heard a loud fall in the parlor, and, running in, beheld the captain lying full length on the floor. At the same instant, my mother, alarmed by the cries and fighting, came running downstairs to help me. Between us we raised his head. He was breathing very loud and hard, but his eyes were closed, and his face a horrible color.

"Dear, deary me," cried my mother, "what a disgrace upon the house! And your poor father sick!"

We had no idea what to do to help the captain, nor any other thought but that he had got his death-wound in the scuffle with the stranger. I got the rum, to be sure, and tried to put it down his throat; but his teeth were tightly shut, and his jaws as strong as iron. It was a happy relief for us when the door opened and Dr. Livesey came in, on his visit to my father.

"Oh, doctor," we cried, "what shall we do? Where is he wounded?"

"Wounded? Nonsense!" said the doctor. "He's no more wounded than you or I. The man has had a stroke, as I warned him. Now, Mrs. Hawkins, just you run upstairs to your husband, and tell him, if possible, nothing about it. For my part, I must do my best to save this fellow's worthless life; and Jim here will get me a basin."

When I got back with the basin, the doctor had already ripped up the captain's sleeve, and exposed his great brawny arm. It was tattooed in several places. "Here's luck," "A fair wind," and "Billy Bones his fancy" were very neatly and clearly drawn on the forearm, and up near the shoulder there was a sketch of a gallows and a man hanging from it—done, as I thought, with considerable artistry.

"Prophetic [pro-FET-ick]," said the doctor, touching this picture with his finger. "And now, Master Billy Bones, if that be your name, we'll have a look at the color of your blood. "Jim," he said, "are you afraid of blood?"

"No, sir," said I.

"Well, then," said he, "you hold the basin"; and with that he took his knife and opened a vein.

A great deal of blood was taken before the captain opened his eyes and looked mistily about him. First he recognized the doctor with an unmistakable frown; then his glance fell upon me, and he looked relieved. But suddenly his color changed, and he tried to raise himself, crying, "Where's Black Dog?"

"There is no Black Dog here," said the doctor, "except what you have on your own back. You have been drinking rum; you have had a stroke, precisely as I told you; and I have just, very much against my own will, dragged you headfirst out of the grave. Now, Mr. Bones—"

"That's not my name," he interrupted.

"No matter," returned the doctor, "It's a name that's written on your forearm, and I call you by it for the sake of shortness, and what I have to say to you is this: one glass of rum won't kill you, but if you take one, you'll take another and another, and I'll bet my wig that if you don't break off short, you'll die —do you understand that?—die, and you'll go to your own place, just as the Bible says. So do make an effort, will you? Here, I'll help you to your bed for once."

Between us, with much trouble, we managed to hoist him upstairs, and laid him on his bed, where his head fell back on the pillow, as if he were almost fainting.

"Now, mind you," said the doctor, "I clear my conscience— the name of rum for you is death."

And with that he went off to see my father, taking me with him by the arm.

"This is nothing," he said, as soon as he had closed the door. "I have drawn blood enough to keep him quiet for a while; he should lie for a week where he is—that is the best thing for him and you; but another stroke would finish him."

# Part Two

**Approximate reading time for Part Two:** 26 minutes
**Vocabulary and pronunciation guide:**

> **guinea** [GINN-ee]: an English gold coin worth about five dollars
> **booty:** items taken in war or robbery; plunder
> **oilcloth:** cloth treated with oil to make it waterproof
> **farthing:** a British coin worth one fourth of a penny

*A*bout noon I stopped at the captain's door with some cooling drinks and some medicine. He was lying very much as we had left him, only a little higher, and he seemed both weak and excited.

"Jim," he said, "you're the only one here that's worth anything, and you know I've been always good to you. Never a month but I've given you a silver fourpenny for yourself. And now you see, mate, I'm pretty low, and deserted by all; and, Jim, you'll bring me one noggin of rum, now won't you, matey?"

"The doctor—" I began.

But he broke in cursing the doctor, in a feeble voice, but heartily. "Doctors is all swabs," he said, "and that doctor there, why, what do he know about seafaring men? I been in places hot as pitch, and mates dropping round with yellow fever, and the blessed land a-heaving like the sea with earthquakes—what do the doctor know of lands like that?—and I lived on rum, I tell you. It's been meat and drink and man and wife to me; and if I'm not to have my rum now, well, I'm as good as done, and that's all; and my blood'll be on you, Jim and that doctor swab"; and he ran on again for a while with curses. "Look, Jim, how my fingers fidget," he continued, in the pleading tone. "I can't keep 'em still, not I. I haven't had a drop this blessed day. That doctor's a fool, I tell you. If I don't have a swallow of rum, Jim, I'll go mad; and if I start ravin'—a man who's lived as rough as I have—why I'll raise Cain. Your doctor hisself said one glass wouldn't hurt me. I'll give you a golden guinea [GINN-ee] for a glassful, Jim."

He was growing more and more excited, and this alarmed me because my father was very weak that day and needed quiet. Besides, I was reassured by the doctor's words, now quoted to me, and rather offended by the offer of a bribe.

"I want none of your money," said, I, "but what you owe my father. I'll get you one glass, and no more."

When I brought it to him, he seized it greedily, and drank it dry.

"Ay, ay," said he, "that's some better, sure enough. And now, matey, did that doctor say how long I was to lie here in this old berth?"

"A week at least," said I.

"Thunder!" he cried. "A week! I can't do that; they'd have the black spot on me by then. The lubbers is about to get wind of me this blessed moment; lubbers that couldn't keep what was theirs, and now want to snatch what is mine. Is that sea-manly behavior, now, I ask you? But I'm a saving soul. I never wasted good money of mine, nor lost it neither; and I'll trick 'em again. I'm not afraid of 'em."

As he was thus speaking, he had risen from bed with great difficulty, holding to my shoulder with a grip that almost made me cry out, and moving his legs like so much dead weight. His spirited words were in sad contrast with the weakness in his voice. He paused when he had got into a sitting position on the edge.

"That doctor's done me," he murmured. "My ears is singing. Lay me back."

But before I could do much to help him, he had fallen back again to his former place, where he lay for a while silent.

"Jim," he said at length, "you saw that seafaring man today?"

"Black Dog?" I asked.

"Ah! Black Dog," says he. "*He's* a bad 'un; but there's worse that put him up to it. Now, if I can't get away nohow, and they tip me the black spot, mind you, it's my old sea-chest they're after. You get on a horse—you can ride, can't you?—well, then, you get on a horse, and go to—well, yes, I will!—to that eternal doctor swab, and tell him to pipe all hands—police and such—and he'll nab 'em all at the Admiral Benbow—all old Flint's crew, man and boy, all of 'em that's left. I was first mate, I was, old Flint's first mate, and I'm the only one as knows the place. He gave it to me when he lay a-dying, like I am now, you see. But you won't spill it unless they get the black spot on me, or unless you see that Black Dog again, or a seafaring man with one leg, Jim—him above all."

"But what is the black spot, captain?" I asked.

"That's a summons, mate. I'll tell you if it comes to that. But you keep your weather-eye open, Jim, and I'll share with you equals, upon my honor."

He wandered on a little longer, his voice growing weaker; but soon after I had given him his medicine, he fell at last into a heavy, swoon-like sleep, in which I left him. What I should have done had all gone well I do not know. Probably I should have told the whole story to the doctor, for I was in mortal fear lest the captain should repent of his confessions and make an end of me. But my poor father died quite suddenly that evening, which put all other matters aside. Our natural distress, the visits of the neighbors, the arranging of the funeral, and all the work of the inn to be carried on in the meanwhile, kept me so busy that I scarcely had time to think of the captain, let alone to be afraid of him.

He got downstairs next morning, to be sure, and had his meals as usual, though he ate little, and had more, I am afraid, than his usual supply of rum, for he served himself from the bar, scowling and blowing through his nose, and no one dared to cross him. On the night before the funeral he was as drunk as ever, and it was shocking, in that house of mourning, to hear him singing away at his ugly old sea-song. But, because he was so weak, we all feared that he would soon die, and the doctor was suddenly taken up with a case many miles away, and was never near the house after my father's death.

I have said that the captain was weak, and, indeed, he seemed rather to grow weaker than regain his strength. He struggled up and down the stairs, and went from the parlor to the bar and back again, and sometimes put his nose out the door to smell the sea, holding on to the walls as he went for support, and breathing hard and fast like a man on a steep mountain. He never spoke to me directly, and it is my belief that he had forgotten that he had confided his secrets in me; but his temper was more violent than ever. He had an alarming way now when he was drunk of drawing his cutlass and laying it bare before him on the table. But, with all that, he paid less heed to other people now, and seemed to be shut up in his own thoughts and rather wandering. Once, for instance, to our extreme wonder, he launched into singing a completely different type of song, a kind of country love song that he must have learned in his youth before he began to follow the sea.

So things passed until, the day after the funeral, and about three o'clock on a bitter, foggy, frosty afternoon, I was standing at the door for a moment, full of sad thoughts about my father, when I saw someone drawing slowly near along the road. He was plainly blind, for he tapped before him with a stick, and wore a great green shade over his eyes and nose;

and he was hunched, as if with age or weakness, and wore a huge old tattered sea-cloak with a hood, that made him appear positively deformed. I never saw in my life a more dreadful-looking figure. He stopped a little from the inn, and, raising his voice in an odd sing-song way, addressed the air in front of him:

"Will any kind friend inform a blind man, who has lost the precious sight of his eyes in the defense of his native England —and God bless King George!—where or in what part of this country he may now be?"

"You are at the Admiral Benbow in Black Hill Cove, my good man," said I.

"I hear a voice," said he, "a young voice. Will you give me your hand, my kind young friend, and lead me in?"

I held out my hand, and the horrible, soft-spoken, eyeless creature gripped it in a moment like a vise. I was so much startled that I struggled to withdraw, but the blind man pulled me close up to him with a single tug of his arm.

"Now, boy," he said, "take me in to the captain."

"Sir," said I, "upon my word I dare not."

"Oh," he sneered, "you'll do it, all right! You'll take me in straightaway, or I'll break your arm."

And he gave it, as he spoke, a wrench that made me cry out.

"Sir," said I, "it is for yourself, I mean. The captain is not what he used to be. He sits with a drawn cutlass. Another gentleman—"

"Come, now, march!" he interrupted, and I never heard a voice so cruel and cold and ugly as that blind man's. I began to obey him at once, walking straight in at the door and toward the parlor, where our sick old buccaneer was sitting, dazed with rum. The blind man clung close to me, holding me in one iron fist, and leaning almost more of his weight on me that I could carry. "Lead me straight up to him, and when I'm in view, cry out, 'Here's a friend for you, Bill.' If you don't, I'll do this"; and with that he gave me a twist that I thought would have made me faint. Between the sound of his voice and the pain in my arm, I was so utterly terrified of the blind beggar that I forgot my terror of the captain, and as I opened the parlor door, I cried out the words he had ordered in a trembling voice.

The poor captain raised his eyes, and at one look the rum went out of him and left him staring sober. The expression of his face was not so much of terror as of mortal sickness. He made a movement to rise, but I do not believe he had enough force left in his body.

"Now, Bill, sit where you are," said the beggar. "If I can't see, I can hear a finger stirring. Business is business. Hold out your left hand. Boy, take his left hand by the wrist and bring it near to my right."

We both obeyed him to the letter, and I saw him pass something from the hollow of the hand that held his stick into the palm of the captain's, which closed upon it instantly.

"And now that's done," said the blind man; and with those words, he suddenly left hold of me and, with incredible nimbleness, skipped out of the parlor and into the road, where, as I still stood motionless, I could hear his stick go tap-tap-tapping into the distance.

It was some time before either I or the captain seemed to gather our senses, but at length, and about the same moment, I released his wrist, which I was still holding, and he drew in his hand and looked sharply into the palm.

"Ten o'clock!" he cried. "Six hours. We'll do them yet," and he sprang to his feet.

Even as he did so, he reeled, put his hand to his throat, stood swaying for a moment, and then, with a peculiar sound, fell from his whole height face down on the floor.

I ran to him at once, calling to my mother. But haste was all in vain. The captain had been struck dead by another stroke. It is a curious thing to understand, for I had certainly never liked the man, though of late I had begun to pity him, but as soon as I saw that he was dead, I burst into a flood of tears. It was the second death I had known, and the sorrow of the first was still fresh in my heart.

I lost no time, of course, in telling my mother all that I knew, and perhaps should have told her long before, and we saw ourselves at once in a difficult and dangerous position. Some of the man's money—if he had any—was certainly due to us, but it was not likely that our captain's shipmates, above all the blind beggar, would be inclined to give up their booty in payment of the dead man's debts. The captain's order to mount at once and ride for Dr. Livesey would have left my mother alone and unprotected, and so I did not consider it further. Indeed, it seemed impossible for either of us to remain much longer in the house; the slightest sound—the fall of coals in the kitchen grate, the very ticking of the clock—filled us with alarm. The neighborhood, to our ears, seemed haunted by approaching footsteps, and between the dead body on the parlor floor and the thought of that detestable blind beggar hovering near at hand, there were moments when, as the saying goes, I jumped out of my skin for fright. Something had to be done right away, and it occurred to us at last to go forth together and seek help in the neighboring village. No sooner said than done. Without waiting even to put on hats and coats, we ran out into the gathering evening and the frosty fog.

The village lay not many hundred yards away, though out of view, on the other side of the next cove; and what greatly encouraged me, it was in an opposite direction from that in which the blind man had appeared, and where he had presumably returned. We were not many minutes on the road, though we sometimes stopped to hold on to each other and listen all around. But there was no unusual sound—nothing but the low wash of the ripple and the croaking of the crows in the wood.

It was already dark when we reached the village, and I shall never forget how much I was cheered to see the yellow glow of candlelight in the doors and windows; but that, as it proved, was all the help we would get from these neighbors. For—you would have thought men would have been ashamed of themselves—no soul would consent to return with us to the Admiral Benbow. The more we told of our troubles, the more—man, woman, and child—they clung to the shelter of their houses. The name of Captain Flint, though it was strange to me, was well enough known to most of them, and it carried a great weight of terror. The short and the long of the matter was, that while we could get several who were willing enough to ride to Dr. Livesey's, which lay in another direction, not one would help us to defend the inn.

When each had had his say, my mother made them a speech.

She would not, she declared, lose money that belonged to her fatherless boy; "if none of the rest of you dare," she said, "Jim and I dare. Back we will go, the way we came, and small thanks to you big, hulking, chicken-hearted men. We'll have that chest open if we die for it. And I'll take that bag, Mrs. Crossley, if you please, to bring back our lawful money in."

Of course, I said I would go with my mother, and of course they all cried out at our foolhardiness, but even then not a man would go along with us. All they would do was to give me a loaded pistol, in case we were attacked, and to promise to have horses saddled and ready in case we were pursued on our return; one lad would also ride on to the doctor's to get help from the police.

My heart was pounding when we two set forth in the cold night upon this dangerous venture. A full moon was beginning to rise and peered redly through the upper edges of the fog, and this increased our haste, for it was plain that, before we came forth again, all would be as bright as day and our departure would be exposed to the eyes of anyone who happened to be watching. We slipped along the hedges, noiseless and swift, nor did we see or hear anything to increase our terrors, till, to our great relief, the door of the Admiral Benbow had closed behind us.

I secured the bolt at once, and we stood and panted for a moment in the dark, alone in the house with the dead captain's body. Then my mother got a candle in the bar, and, holding each other's hands, we advanced into the parlor. He lay as we had left him, on his back, with his eyes open and one arm stretched out.

"Draw down the blind, Jim," whispered my mother; "they might come and watch from outside. And now," said she, when I had done so, "we have to get the key off *that*," pointing to the lifeless figure of the captain, "and who's to touch it, I should like to know!" and she gave a kind of sob as she said the words.

I went down on my knees at once. On the floor, close to his hand, there was a little round of paper, blackened on one side. I could not doubt that this was the *black spot*, and taking it up,

I found written on the other side, in a very good, clear hand, this short message: "You have till ten tonight."

"He had till ten o'clock, mother," said I; and just as I said it, our old clock began striking. This sudden noise startled us with a shock, but the news was good, for it was only six.

"Now, Jim," she said, "that key."

I felt in his pockets, one after another. A few small coins, a thimble, and some thread and big needles, a piece of chewing tobacco bitten away at the end, his jackknife with the crooked handle, a pocket compass, and a tinderbox were all that they contained, and I began to despair.

"Perhaps it's round his neck," suggested my mother.

Summoning up all my courage, I tore open his shirt at the neck, and there, sure enough, hanging to a bit of string, which I cut with his own knife, we found the key. At this triumph we were filled with hope, and hurried upstairs without delay to the little room where he had slept so long, and where his sea-chest had stood since the day of his arrival.

It was like any other seaman's chest on the outside, the initial "B." burned on the top of it with a hot iron, and the corners somewhat smashed and broken from long, rough usage.

"Give me the key," said my mother, and though the lock was very stiff, she had turned it and thrown back the lid in a twinkling.

A strong smell of tobacco and tar rose from the interior, but nothing was to be seen on the top except a suit of very good clothes, carefully brushed and folded. They had never been worn, my mother said. Under that lay a vast assortment of odds and ends—tobacco, compasses, pistols, a watch, and trinkets of little value. But at the very bottom, underneath an old cloak stained with sea-salt, there lay a bundle of papers tied up in oilcloth, and also a canvas bag that gave forth, at a touch, the jingle of gold.

"I'll show these rogues that I'm an honest woman," said my mother. "I'll have what is due me and not a farthing over. Hold Mrs. Crossley's bag." And she began to count out money from the sailor's bag and drop it into the one that I was holding.

It was a long, difficult business, for the coins were of all countries and sizes—doubloons, and guineas, and pieces of eight, and I know not what besides, all shaken together at random. Besides this, the guineas were about the scarcest, and it was only with these that my mother could make her count.

When we were about halfway through, I suddenly put my hand upon her arm, for I had heard in the silent, frosty air a sound that brought my heart into my mouth—the tap-tapping of the blind man's stick upon the frozen road. It drew nearer and nearer, while we sat holding our breath. Then it struck sharp on the door of our inn, and then we could hear the handle being turned, and the bolt rattling as the wretched being tried to enter, and then there was a long time of silence both inside and out. At last the tapping recommenced, and, to our indescribable joy and gratitude, died slowly down the road until it ceased to be heard.

"Mother," said I, "take the whole of it and let's be going," for I was sure the bolted door must have seemed suspicious and would bring the whole lot of them next time; though how thankful I was that I had bolted it.

But my mother, frightened as she was, would not consent to take a fraction more than was due to her, and was unwilling to be content with less. It was not yet seven, she said; she knew her rights and she would have them. She was still arguing with me when a little low whistle sounded a good way off upon the hill. That was enough, and more than enough, for the both of us.

"I'll take what I have," she said, jumping to her feet.

"And I'll take this to make up for the rest," said I, picking up the oilskin packet.

Next moment we were both groping downstairs, leaving the candle by the empty chest, and next we had opened the door and were in full retreat. We had not started a moment too soon. The fog was rapidly breaking up; already the moon shone quite clear on the surrounding hills, and it was only in the exact bottom of the valley and round the tavern door that a thin veil still hung unbroken to conceal the first steps of our escape. I could see that less than halfway to the village, just beyond the bottom of the hill, we would come out into bright moonlight. Nor was this all, for the sound of several footsteps running came already to our ears, and as we looked back in their direction, a light tossing to and fro and still rapidly advancing, showed that one of the newcomers carried a lantern.

"My dear," said my mother suddenly, "take the money and run on. I am going to faint."

This was certainly the end for both of us, I thought. How I cursed the cowardice of the neighbors; how I blamed my poor mother for her honesty and her greed, for her past foolhardiness and present weakness! We were just at the little bridge, and I helped her to the edge of the bank, where, sure enough, she gave a sigh and fell on my shoulder. I do not know how I found the strength to do it at all, and I am afraid that I did not do it at all well, but I managed to drag her down the bank and a little way under the bridge. I could not move her farther, for the arch was too low to let me do more than crawl below it. So there we had to stay—my mother almost entirely exposed, and both of us within earshot of the inn.

My curiosity, in a sense, was stronger than my fear, for I could not remain where I was, but crept back to the bank again and watched the inn door from behind the shelter of a bush. Seven or eight men arrived, running hard, and among them was the blind beggar.

"Down with the door!" the beggar cried.

"Ay, ay, sir!" answered two or three, and then I could see them pause, as if they were surprised to find the door open. Four or five of the men rushed in; two remained outside with the blind man. There was a pause, then a voice shouting from the house: "Bill's dead!"

The blind man swore at them and cried out:

"Search him, some of you shirking lubbers, and the rest of you aloft and get the chest."

I could hear their feet rattling up our old stairs, so that the house must have shook with it. Promptly afterwards, fresh sounds of astonishment arose; the window of the captain's room was thrown open with a slam and a jingle of broken glass; and a man leaned out into the moonlight, head and shoulders, and addressed the blind beggar on the road below him.

"Pew," he called to him, "someone's been here before us; they've opened the chest and searched it thorough."

"Is it there?" roared Pew.

"The money's there," came the reply.

The blind man cursed the money.

"Flint's packet, I mean. Here, you below there, see if it's on Bill," he commanded.

At that, another fellow came to the door of the inn. "Bill's been overhauled a'ready," said he, "nothin' left."

"It's these people of the inn—it's that boy," fumed the blind man, Pew. "I wish I had put his eyes out! They must be close by; they can't be far. Scatter and look for them, dogs. Oh, shiver my soul," he cried, "if I only had eyes!"

"Hang it, Pew," grumbled one of the men, "we've already got the doubloons."

"You fools," snarled Pew, "you'd have your hands on thousands, you'd be as rich as kings if you could find it, and you're ready to settle for cheap. There wasn't one of you dared face Bill, and I did it—a blind man! And I'm to lose my chance for you! I'm to be a poor, crawling beggar, sponging for rum, when I might be riding in a coach!"

Just then the same whistle that had alarmed my mother and me while we were counting the dead man's money sounded through the night, but this time twice repeated. I had thought it to be the blind man's call, summoning his crew to attack, but I now found that it was a signal from the hillside toward the village, a signal to warn them of approaching danger. Then, another sound—the tramp of horses in full gallop, and I knew that Dr. Livesey's men had come to our rescue. At this the buccaneers turned at once and ran, separating in every direction, so that in half a minute not a sign of them remained but Pew. Him they had deserted, and he remained behind, tapping up and down the road in a frenzy, and groping and calling for his comrades. He ran just a few steps past me, crying:

"Johnny, Black Dog, Dirk," and other names, "you won't leave old Pew, mates—not old Pew!"

Just then the noise of the horses topped the rise, and four or five riders came in sight in the moonlight, and swept in a headlong charge down the slope. At this, Pew turned with a scream and made a dash, now utterly bewildered, right under the nearest of the coming horses. The rider tried to save him, but in vain. Down went Pew with a cry that rang high into the night; the four hoofs trampled him and went on. He fell on his side, then gently collapsed upon his face, and moved no more.

This was the end of our night of terror, but it was just the beginning of the adventures that the oilskin packet held for me. Little did I know that it contained a map of a remote island on which Captain Flint—that bloodthirsty pirate—had buried his hoard of treasure; even less did I imagine that I would soon be sailing as cabin boy on an expedition to find that treasure, along with Dr. Livesey, Squire Trelawney, and a devious "seafaring man with one leg" named Long John Silver.

# Requiem

### by
### ROBERT LOUIS STEVENSON

Under the wide and starry sky,
Dig my grave and let me lie;
Glad did I live, and gladly die,
And I lay me down with a will.

And this be the verse you grave for me:
*Here he lies where he longed to be;*
*Home is the sailor, home from sea.*
*And the hunter home from the hill.*

# Listening Level III

## (Ages 11 and up)

*When children reach junior-high or middle-school age, they assume that being read to is an enjoyment that they should have outgrown by now, one that their peers will surely think is appropriate only for "children." Consequently, even children who look forward to their daily read-aloud sessions at home with their parents are likely to join in the feigned dissent that arises when a teacher first suggests a classroom read-aloud. The dissent quickly dissipates, however, when the class chooses to enjoy itself, whether doing so is socially acceptable or not.*

*Teachers (and parents who have had an ongoing read-aloud program with their children) will find the selections here to be designed for the more mature emotional makeup and the longer attention spans of older children. Although each selection is complete in itself, each is also introductory in that it suggests a whole world ripe for future read-alouds. "The Tell-Tale Heart," for example, may excite students' interest in other Poe stories, or in similar tales of terror; knowing the story of Macbeth can make adolescents more interested in seeing this play performed, and hearing or reading other Shakespearean plays as well; Martin Luther King's "I Have a Dream" and Lincoln's "Gettysburg Address" may suggest having practiced presentations by class members of other historic speeches.*

*This is the age at which oral language comes to a crossroads; the sharing of oral readings by teachers with their students, and by parents with their children, can determine which road an adolescent will choose to follow.*

# from *The Yearling*

by
MARJORIE KINNAN RAWLINGS

**About the story:**

> *The story of twelve-year-old Jody Baxter and his pet deer, Flag, in* The Yearling *is a story about a boy's growth out of childhood into maturity. Each chapter is an episode in the life of the Baxters as they struggle to live on their farm in the Florida scrub shortly after the Civil War. It is Jody's idyllic life of innocence as a child, and his ultimate acceptance of the responsibilities and pains of adulthood, that have endeared this classic tale to generations of children and adults.*
>
> *Parents who wish to use the entire novel as a read-aloud should first be certain that their children are old enough to withstand some painful incidents in Jody's growth—not the least of which is his having to kill the deer he loves so much.*
>
> *In the following chapter, however, we see Jody the child, a Huckleberry Finn who loves to be out in nature —especially when the alternative is doing chores.*

# Part One

**Approximate reading time for Part One:** 12 minutes
**Vocabulary and pronunciation guide:**
>    **branch:** a small stream or brook
>    **deprecatory** [DEP-reck-uh-tore-ee]: apologetic; showing
>       regret
>    **scrub:** a thick growth of stunted trees or bushes

—— *187* ——

**tawny:** tan-colored
**indigo** [IN-dih-go]: a plant that yields a dark blue dye
**breeches** [BRICH-ez]: trousers
**spasmodic** [spaz-MAHD-ick]: impulsive; fleeting; as
    with a sudden, convulsive burst of energy
**flutter-mill:** a small water wheel set in a stream so that
    its paddles are pushed around an axle by the current
**frond** [FRAHND]: the whole leaf of a fern or palm, in-
    cluding the stem and leaflets
**indolently** [IN-doe-lent-lee]: lazily

*A* column of smoke rose thin and straight from the cabin chimney. The smoke was blue where it left the red of the clay. It trailed into the blue of the April sky and was no longer blue but gray. The boy Jody watched it, speculating. The fire on the kitchen hearth was dying down. His mother was hanging up pots and pans after the noon dinner. The day was Friday. She would sweep the floor with a broom and after that, if he were lucky, she would scrub it, too. If she scrubbed the floor, she would not miss him until he had reached the Glen. He stood a minute, balancing the hoe on his shoulder.

The clearing itself was pleasant if the unweeded rows of young shafts of corn were not before him. The wild bees had found the chinaberry tree by the front gate. They burrowed into the fragile clusters of lavender bloom as greedily as though there were no other flowers in the scrub; as though they had forgotten the yellow jasmine of March; the sweet bay and the magnolias ahead of them in May. It occurred to him that he might follow the swift line of flight of the black gold bodies, and so find a bee-tree, full of amber honey. The winter's cane syrup was gone and most of the jellies. Finding a bee-tree was nobler work than hoeing, and the corn could wait another day. The afternoon was alive with a soft stirring. It bored into him as the bees bored into the chinaberry blossoms, so that he must be gone across the clearing, through the pines and down the road to the running branch. The bee-tree might be near the water.

He stood his hoe against the split-rail fence. He walked down the cornfield until he was out of sight of the cabin. He swung himself over the fence on his two hands. Old Julia the hound had followed his father in the wagon to Grahamsville, but Rip the bulldog and Perk the new mongrel saw the form clear the fence and ran toward him. Rip barked deeply but the voice of the small mongrel was high and shrill. They wagged deprecatory [DEP-reck-uh-tore-ee] short tails when they recognized him. He sent them back to the yard. They watched after him indifferently. They were a sorry pair, he thought, good for nothing but the chase, the catch, and the kill. They had no interest in him except when he brought them their plates of table scraps night and morning. Old Julia was a gentle thing with humans, but her worn-toothed devotion was only for his father, Penny Baxter. Jody had tried to make up to Julia, but she would have none of him.

"You was pups together," his father told him, "ten year gone, when you was two year old and her a baby. You hurted the leetle thing, not meanin' no harm. She cain't bring herself to trust you. Hounds is often that-a-way."

He made a circle around the sheds and corncrib and cut south through the black oaks. He wished he had a dog like Grandma Hutto's. It was white and curly-haired and did tricks. When Grandma Hutto laughed and shook and could not stop, the dog jumped into her lap and licked her face, wagging its plumed tail as though it laughed with her. He would like anything that was his own; that licked his face and followed him as old Julia followed his father. He cut into the sand road and began to run east. It was two miles to the Glen, but it seemed to Jody that he could run forever. There was no ache in his legs, as when he hoed the corn. He slowed down to make the road last longer. He had passed the big pines and left them behind. Where he walked now, the scrub had closed in, walling in the road with dense sand pine, each one so thin it seemed to the boy it might make kindling by itself. The road went up an incline. At the top he stopped. The April sky was framed by the tawny sand and pines. It was as blue as his homespun shirt, dyed with Grandma Hutto's indigo [IN-dih-go]. Small clouds were stationary, like bolls of cotton. As he watched, the sunlight left the sky a moment and the clouds were gray.

"There'll come a little old drizzly rain before nightfall," he thought.

The downgrade tempted him to a lope. He reached the thick-bedded sand of the Silver Glen road. The tar-flower was in bloom, and the fetter-bush, and sparkleberry. He slowed to a walk, so that he might pass the changing vegetation tree by tree, bush by bush, each one unique and familiar. He reached the magnolia tree where he had carved the wildcat's face. The growth was a sign that there was water nearby. It seemed a strange thing to him, when earth was earth and rain was rain, that scrawny pines should grow in the scrub, while by every branch and lake and river there grew magnolias. Dogs were the same everywhere, and oxen and mules and horses. But trees were different in different places.

"Reckon it's because they can't move none," he decided. They took what food was in the soil under them.

The east bank of the road shelved suddenly. It dropped below him twenty feet to a spring. The bank was dense with magnolia and loblolly bay, sweet gum and gray-barked ash. He went down to the spring in the cool darkness of their shadows. A sharp pleasure came over him. This was a secret and lovely place.

A spring as clear as well water bubbled up from nowhere in the sand. It was as though the banks cupped green leafy hands to hold it. There was a whirlpool where the water rose from the earth. Grains of sand boiled in it. Beyond the bank, the parent spring bubbled up at a higher level, cut itself a channel through white limestone, and began to run rapidly downhill to make a creek. The creek joined Lake George, Lake George was a part of the St. John's River, the great river flowed northward and into the sea. It excited Jody to watch the beginning of the ocean. There were other beginnings, true, but this one was his own. He liked to think that no one came here but himself and the wild animals and the thirsty birds.

He was warm from his jaunt. The dusky Glen laid cool hands on him. He rolled up the hems of his blue denim breeches [BRICH-ez] and stepped with bare, dirty feet into the shallow spring. His toes sunk into the sand. It oozed softly between them and over his bony ankles. The water was so cold that for a moment it burned his skin. Then it made a rippling sound, flowing past his pipe-stem legs, and was entirely delicious. He walked up and down, digging his big toe experimentally under smooth rocks he encountered. A school of minnows flashed ahead of him down the growing branch. He chased them through the shallows. They were suddenly out of sight as though they had never existed. He crouched under a bared and overhanging live-oak root where a pool was deep, thinking they might reappear, but only a spring frog wriggled from under the mud, stared at him, and dove under the tree root in a spasmodic [spaz-MAHD-ick] terror. He laughed.

"I ain't no coon. I'd not ketch you," he called after it.

A breeze parted the canopied limbs over him. The sun dropped through and lay on his head and shoulders. It was good to be warm at his head while his hard calloused feet were cold. The breeze died away, the sun no longer reached him. He waded across to the opposite bank where the growth was more open. A low palmetto brushed him. It reminded him that his knife was snug in his pocket; that he had planned as long ago as Christmas to make himself a flutter-mill.

He had never built one alone. Grandma Hutto's son Oliver had always made one for him whenever he was home from sea. He went to work intently, frowning as he tried to recall the exact angle necessary to make the mill-wheel turn smoothly. He cut two forked twigs and trimmed them into two Y's of the same size. Oliver had been very particular to have the crossbar round and smooth, he remembered. A wild cherry grew halfway up the bank. He climbed it and cut a twig as even as a polished pencil. He selected a palm frond [FRAHND] and cut two strips of the tough fiber, an inch wide and four inches long. He cut a slit lengthwise in the center of each of them, wide enough to insert the cherry twig. The strips of palm frond must be at angles, like the arms of a windmill. He adjusted them carefully. He separated the Y-shaped twigs by nearly the length of the cherry crossbar and pushed them deep into the sand of the branch bed a few yards below the spring.

The water was only a few inches deep but it ran strongly, with a firm current. The palm-frond mill-wheel must just brush the water's surface. He experimented with depth until he was satisfied, then laid the cherry bar between the twigs. It hung motionless. He twisted it a moment, anxiously, helping it to fit itself into its forked grooves. The bar began to rotate. The current caught the flexible tip of one bit of palm frond. By the time it lifted clear, the rotation of the bar brought the angled tip of the second into contact with the stream. The small leafy paddles swung over and over, up and down. The little wheel was turning. The flutter-mill was at work. It turned with the easy rhythm of the great water-mill his father had taken him to see, where corn was ground into meal.

Jody drew a deep breath. He threw himself on the seedy sand close to the water and abandoned himself to the magic of motion. Up, over, down, up, over, down—the flutter-mill was enchanting. The bubbling spring would rise forever from the earth, the thin current was endless. The spring was the beginning of waters sliding to the sea. Unless leaves fell, or squirrels cut sweet bay twigs to drop and block the fragile wheel, the flutter-mill might turn forever. When he was an old man, as old as his father, there seemed no reason why this rippling movement might not continue as he had begun it.

He moved a stone that was matching its corners against his sharp ribs and burrowed a little, hollowing himself a nest for his hips and shoulders. He stretched out one arm and laid his head on it. A shaft of sunlight, warm and thin like a light patchwork quilt, lay across his body. He watched the flutter-mill indolently [IN-doe-lent-lee], sunk in the sand and the sunlight. The movement was hypnotic. His eyelids fluttered with the palm-leaf paddles. Drops of silver slipping from the wheel blurred together like the tail of a shooting star. The water made a sound like kittens lapping. A rain frog sang a moment and then was still. There was an instant when the boy hung at the edge of a high bank made of the soft fluff of broom-sage, and the rain frog and the starry dripping of the flutter-mill hung with him. Instead of falling over the edge, he sank into the softness. The blue, white-tufted sky closed over him. He slept.

# Part Two

**Approximate reading time for Part Two:** 16 minutes
**Vocabulary and pronunciation guide:**
    **harried** [HAIR-eed]: tormented; distressed; harassed
    **luminous** [LEW-min-us]: glowing; shining; giving off
      light
    **paling** [PAY-ling]: picket
    **sweet 'tater pone:** bread made from sweet potatoes
    **poke-greens:** the leaves and stems of the pokeweed
      plant, eaten as vegetables
    **replete** [rih-PLEET]: gorged with food; full to the utter-
      most
    **cajoled** [kuh-JOLD]: coaxed; wheedled
    **addled** [AD-uld]: confused; muddled

When he awakened, he thought he was in a place other than the branch bed. He was in another world, so that for an instant he thought he might still be dreaming. The sun was gone, and all the light and shadow. There were no black trunks of live oaks, no glossy green of magnolia leaves, no pattern of gold lace where the sun had sifted through the branches of the wild cherry. The world was all a gentle gray, and he lay in a mist as fine as spray from a waterfall. The mist tickled his skin. It was scarcely wet. It was at once warm and cool. He rolled over on his back and it was as though he looked up into the soft gray breast of a mourning dove.

He lay, absorbing the fine-dropped rain like a young plant. When his face was damp at last and his shirt was moist to the touch, he left his nest. He stopped short. A deer had come to the spring while he was sleeping. The fresh tracks came down the east bank and stopped at the water's edge. They were sharp and pointed, the tracks of a doe. They sank deeply into the sand, so that he knew the doe was an old one and large. Perhaps she was heavy with fawn. She had come down and drunk deeply from the spring, not seeing him where he slept. Then she had scented him. There was a scuffled confusion in the sand where she had wheeled in fright. The tracks up the opposite bank had long, harried [HAIR-eed] streaks behind them. Perhaps she had not drunk, after all, before she scented him, and turned and ran with that swift, sand-throwing flight. He hoped she was not now thirsty, wide-eyed in the scrub.

He looked about for other tracks. The squirrels had raced up and down the banks, but they were bold, always. A raccoon had been that way, with his feet like sharp-nailed hands, but he could not be sure how recently. Only his father could tell for certain the hour when any wild things had passed by. Only the doe had surely come and had been frightened. He turned back again to the flutter-mill. It was turning as steadily as though it had always been there. The palm-leaf paddles were frail, but they made a brave show of strength, rippling against the shallow water. They were glistening from the slow rain.

Jody looked at the sky. He could not tell the time of day in the grayness, nor how long he may have slept. He bounded up the west bank, where open gallberry flats spread without obstructions. As he stood, hesitant whether to go or stay, the rain ended as gently as it had begun. A light breeze stirred from the southwest. The sun came out. The clouds rolled together into great white billowing feather bolsters, and across the east a rainbow arched, so lovely and so various that Jody thought he would burst with looking at it. The earth was pale green, the air itself was all but visible, golden with the rain-washed sunlight, and all the trees and grass and bushes glittered, varnished with the raindrops.

A spring of delight boiled up within him as irresistibly as the spring of the branch. He lifted his arms and held them straight from his shoulders like a water-turkey's wings. He began to whirl around in his tracks. He whirled faster and faster until his ecstasy was a whirlpool, and when he thought he would explode with it, he became dizzy and closed his eyes and dropped to the ground and lay flat in the broom-sage. The earth whirled under and with him. He opened his eyes and the blue April sky and the cotton clouds whirled over him. Boy and earth and trees and sky spun together. The whirling stopped, his head cleared, and he got to his feet. He was light-headed and giddy, but something in him was relieved, and the April day could be borne again, like any ordinary day.

He turned and galloped toward home. He drew deep breaths of the pines, aromatic with wetness. The loose sand that had pulled at his feet was firmed by the rain. The return was comfortable going. The sun was not far from its setting when the long-leaf pines around the Baxter clearing came into sight. They stood tall and dark against the red-gold west. He heard the chickens clucking and quarreling and knew they had just been fed. He turned into the clearing. The weathered gray of the split-rail fence was luminous [LEW-min-us] in the rich spring light. Smoke curled thickly from the stick-and-clay chimney. Supper would be ready on the hearth and hot bread baking in the Dutch oven. He hoped his father had not returned from Grahamsville. It came to him for the first time that perhaps he should not have left the place while his father was away. If his mother had needed wood, she would be angry. Even his father would shake his head a little and say, "Son—." He heard old Caesar snort and knew his father was ahead of him.

The clearing was in a pleasant clatter. The horse whinnied at the gate, the calf bleated in its stall and the milk cow answered, the chickens scratched and cackled, and the dogs barked with the coming of food and evening. It was good to be hungry and to be fed, and the stock was eager with an expectant certainty. The end of winter had been meager; corn short, and hay, and dried cow-peas. But now in April the pastures were green and succulent and even the chickens savored the sprouts of young grass. The dogs had found a nest of young rabbits that evening, and after such tid-bits, the scraps from the Baxter supper table were a matter of some indifference. Jody saw old Julia lying under the wagon, worn out from her miles of trotting. He swung open the front paling [PAY-ling] gate and went to find his father.

Penny Baxter was at the woodpile. He still wore the coat of the broadcloth suit that he had been married in, that he now wore as badge of his gentility when he went to church, or off trading. The sleeves were too short, not because Penny had grown, but because the years of hanging through the summer dampness, and being pressed with the smoothing iron and pressed again, had somehow shrunk the fabric. Jody saw his father's hands, big for the rest of him, close around a bundle of wood. He was doing Jody's work, and in his good coat. Jody ran to him.

"I'll git it, Pa."

He hoped his willingness, now, would cover his delinquency. His father straightened his back.

"I near about give you out, son," he said.

"I went to the Glen," Jody explained.

"Hit were a mighty purty day to go," Penny said. "Or to go anywhere. How come you to take out such a fur piece?"

It was as hard to remember why he had gone as though it had been a year ago. He had to think back to the moment when he had laid down his hoe.

'Oh," he said, somewhat startled. He had it now. "I aimed to foller the honey-bees and find a bee-tree."

"You find it?" Penny asked.

Jody stared blankly.

"Dogged if I ain't forgot 'til now to look for it," he said.

He felt as foolish as a bird-dog caught chasing field mice. He looked at his father sheepishly. His father's pale blue eyes were twinkling.

"Tell the truth, Jody," he said, "and shame the devil. Wa'n't the bee-tree a fine excuse to go a-ramblin?"

Jody grinned.

"The notion takened me," he admitted, "afore I studied on the bee-tree."

"That's what I figgered," said his father. "How come me to know, was when I was drivin' along to Grahamsville, I said to myself, 'There's Jody now, and the hoein' ain't goin' to take him too long. What would I do this fine spring day, was I a boy?' And then I thought, 'I'd go a-ramblin'. Most anywhere, long as it kivered the ground.'"

A warmth filled the boy that was not the low golden sun. He nodded.

"That's the way I figgered," he said.

"But your Ma, now," Penny jerked his head toward the house, "don't hold with ramblin'. Most women-folks cain't see for their lives, how a man loves so to ramble. I never let on you wasn't here. She said, 'Where's Jody?' and I said, 'Oh, I reckon he's around some'eres.' "

He winked one eye and Jody winked back.

"Men-folks has got to stick together in the name o' peace. You carry your Ma a good bait o' wood now."

Jody filled his arms and hurried to the house. His mother was kneeling at the hearth. The spiced smells that came to his nose made him weak with hunger.

"That ain't sweet 'tater pone, is it, Ma?" he asked.

"Hit's sweet 'tater pone," she answered. "And don't you fellers be too long a time now, piddlin' and visitin'. Supper's done and ready."

He dumped the wood in the box and scurried to the lot. His father was milking Trixie.

"Ma says to git done and come on," he reported. "Must I feed old Caesar?"

"I done fed him, son, sich as I had to give the poor feller." He stood up from the three-legged milking stool. "Carry in the milk and don't trip and waste it outen the gourd like you done yestiddy. Easy, Trixie—"

He moved aside from the cow and went to the stall in the shed, where her calf was tethered.

"Here, Trixie. Soo, gal—"

The cow lowed and came to her calf.

"Easy, there. You greedy as Jody."

He stroked the pair and followed the boy to the house. They washed in turn at the water-shelf and dried their hands and faces on the roller towel hanging outside the kitchen door. Ma Baxter sat at the table waiting for them, putting helpings on their plates. Her bulky frame filled the end of the long narrow table. Jody and his father sat down on either side of her. It seemed natural to both of them that she should preside.

"You-all hongry tonight?" she asked.

"I kin hold a barrel o' meat and a bushel o' biscuit," Jody said.

"That's what you say," replied his mother. "Your eyes is bigger'n your belly."

"I'd about say the same," Penny said, "if I hadn't learned better. Goin' to Grahamsville allus do make me hongry."

"You git a snort o'moonshine there, is the reason," she said.

"A mighty small one today," he confessed. "Jim Turnbuckle treated."

"Then you shore didn't git enough to hurt you," Ma Baxter said knowingly.

Jody heard nothing; saw nothing but his plate. He had never been so hungry in his life, and after a lean winter and slow spring, with food not much more plentiful for the Baxters than for their stock, his mother had cooked a supper good enough for the preacher. There were poke-greens with bits of white bacon buried in them; sand-buggers made of potato and onion and the cooter he had found crawling yesterday; sour orange biscuits and, at his mother's elbow, the sweet potato pone. He was torn between his desire for more biscuits and another sand-bugger and the knowledge, born of painful experience, that if he ate them, he would suddenly have no room for pone. The choice was plain.

"Ma," he said, "kin I have my pone right now?"

She was at a pause in the feeding of her own large frame. She cut him, dexterously, a generous portion. He plunged into its spiced and savory goodness.

"The time it takened me," she complained, "to make that pone—and you destroyin' it before I git my breath—"

"I'm eatin' it quick," he admitted, "but I'll remember it a long time."

Supper was done with. Jody was replete [rih-PLEET]. Even his father, who usually ate like a sparrow, had taken a second helping.

"I'm full, thank the Lord," he said.

Ma Baxter sighed.

"If a feller'd light me a candle," she said, "I'd git shut o' the dishwashin' and mebbe have time to set and enjoy my-self."

Jody left his seat and lit a tallow candle. As the yellow flame wavered, he looked out of the east window. The full moon was rising.

"A pity to waste light, ain't it?" his father said, "and the full moon shinin'."

He came to the window and they watched it together.

"Son, what do it put in your head? Do you mind what we said we'd do, full moon in April?"

"I dis-remember," said Jody.

Somehow, the seasons always took him unawares. It must be necessary to be as old as his father to keep them in the mind and memory, to remember moon-time from one year's end to another.

"You ain't forgot what I told you? I'll swear, Jody. Why, boy, the bears comes outen their winter beds on the full moon in April."

"Old Slewfoot!" Jody shouted. "You said we'd lay for him when he come out!"

"That's it," acknowledged his father.

"You said we'd go where we seed his tracks comin' and goin' and criss-crossin', and likely find his bed, and him, too, comin' out in April."

"And fat. Fat and lazy," his father chimed in. "The meat so sweet, from him layin' up."

"And him mebbe easier to ketch, not woke up good," Jody offered. "When kin we go, Pa?"

"Soon as we git the hoein' done. And see bear-signs," Penny replied.

"Which-a-way will we begin huntin' him?" the boy asked.

His father thought a minute, then answered, "We'd best to go by the Glen springs and see has he come out and watered there."

"A big ol' doe watered there today," Jody said. "Whilst I was asleep. I built me a flutter-mill, Pa. It run fine."

Ma Baxter stopped the clatter of her pots and pans.

"You sly scaper," she said. "That's the first I knowed you been off. You gittin' slick as a clay road in the rain."

He shouted with laughter.

"I fooled you, Ma. Say it, Ma, I got to fool you once."

"You fooled me," she admitted. "And me standin' over the fire makin' 'tater pone—"

She was not truly angry.

"Now, Ma," he cajoled [kuh-JOLD] her, "suppose I was a varmint and didn't eat nothing' but roots and grass."

"I'd not have nothin' then to rile me," she said.

At the same time he saw her mouth twist. She tried to straighten it and could not.

"Ma's a-laughin'! Ma's a-laughin!" he cried. "You ain't riled when you laugh!"

He darted behind her and untied her apron strings. The apron slipped to the floor. She turned her bulk quickly and boxed his ears, but the blows were feather-light and playful. The same delirium came over him again that he had felt in the afternoon. He began to whirl around and around as he had done in the broom-sage.

"You knock them plates offen the table," she said, "and you'll see who's riled."

"I cain't he'p it," Jody said. "I'm dizzy."

"You're addled [AD-uld]," she said. "Jest plain addled."

It was true. He was addled with April. He was dizzy with Spring. He was as drunk as Lem Forrester on a Saturday night. His head was swimming with the strong brew made up of the sun and the air and the thin gray rain. The flutter-mill had made him drunk, and the doe's coming, and his father's hiding his absence, and his mother's making him a pone and laughing at him. He was stabbed with the candlelight inside the safe comfort of the cabin, with the moonlight around it. He pictured old Slewfoot, the great black outlaw bear with one toe missing, rearing up in his winter bed and tasting the soft air and smelling the moonlight, as he, Jody, smelled and tasted them. He went to bed in a fever and could not sleep. A mark was on him from the day's delight, so that all his life, when April was a thin green and the flavor of rain was on his tongue, an old wound would throb and a nostalgia would fill him for something he could not quite remember. A whip-poor-will called across the bright night, and suddenly he was asleep.

# Birches

## by
## ROBERT FROST

**Vocabulary and pronunciation guide:**
**bracken:** ferns

When I see birches bend to left and right
Across the lines of straighter darker trees,
I like to think some boy's been swinging them.
But swinging doesn't bend them down to stay.
Ice-storms do that. Often you must have seen them
Loaded with ice a sunny winter morning
After a rain. They click upon themselves
As the breeze rises, and turn many-colored
As the stir cracks and crazes their enamel.
Soon the sun's warmth makes them shed crystal shells
Shattering and avalanching on the snow-crust—
Such heaps of broken glass to sweep away
You'd think the inner dome of heaven had fallen.
They are dragged to the withered bracken by the load,
And they seem not to break; though once they are bowe
So low for long, they never right themselves:
You may see their trunks arching in the woods
Years afterwards, trailing their leaves on the ground
Like girls on hands and knees that throw their hair
Before them over their heads to dry in the sun.
But I was going to say when Truth broke in
With all her matter-of-fact about the ice-storm,
I should prefer to have some boy bend them
As he went out and in to fetch the cows—
Some boy too far from town to learn baseball,
Whose only play was what he found himself,
Summer or winter, and could play alone.
One by one he subdued his father's trees
By riding them down over and over again
Until he took the stiffness out of them,
And not one but hung limp, not one was left

For him to conquer. He learned all there was
To learn about not launching out too soon
And so not carrying the tree away
Clear to the ground. He always kept his poise
To the top branches, climbing carefully
With the same pains you use to fill a cup
Up to the brim, and even above the brim.
Then he flung outward, feet first, with a swish,
Kicking his way down through the air to the ground.

So was I once myself a swinger of birches.
And so I dream of going back to be.
It's when I'm weary of considerations,
And life is too much like a pathless wood
Where your face burns and tickles with the cobwebs
Broken across it, and one eye is weeping
From a twig's having lashed across it open.
I'd like to get away from earth awhile
And then come back to it and begin over.
May no fate willfully misunderstand me
And half grant what I wish and snatch me away
Not to return. Earth's the right place for love:
I don't know where it's likely to go better.
I'd like to go by climbing a birch tree,
And climb black branches up a snow-white trunk
*Toward* heaven, till the tree could bear no more,
But dipped its top and set me down again.
That would be good both going and coming back.
One could do worse than be a swinger of birches.

# Macbeth

by
## WILLIAM SHAKESPEARE
### (as retold by Charles Lamb)

**About the story:**

*Shakespeare took the basic outline for this play from historical fact: There was a brave general named Macbeth, whose murderous acts secured for him the throne of Scotland. But it is the suffering of the king and queen—ultimately doomed by the ambition that flaws their characters—and the poetry of Shakespeare's language that turns what, in a lesser hand, would have been a historical soap opera into a tragic masterpiece.*

*The poetry of this play does not, of course, show through this nineteenth-century retelling by Charles Lamb, but a few of the major speeches have been inserted here, and your children's knowledge of this rather complex plot will help them when they read the entire play for themselves or see it performed.*

**Approximate reading time:** 21 minutes

**Vocabulary and pronunciation guide:**

**heath:** an area of open land overgrown with rough grasses and shrubs

**prophesying** [PROF-eh-sigh-ing]: predicting a future event; issuing a prophecy

**condescension:** lowering oneself to equal terms with inferiors

**inordinate:** exceeding normal limits; uncontrolled

**dissuade** [dih-SWADE]: to alter someone's plans; to sway someone from a course of action

**prescient** [PREE-she-ant]: able to know events before they take place; farseeing

**cauldron:** a large pot or kettle

**Dunsinane** [Dun-sin-ain]

**impregnable** [imm-PREG-nuh-bull]: incapable of being taken by force

––––––– 203 –––––––

When Duncan the Meek reigned as King of all Scotland, there lived a great thane, or lord, called Macbeth. This Macbeth was a near kinsman to the king, and he was held in great esteem throughout the land for his valor and his conduct in the wars. Only recently, Macbeth and his fellow general, Banquo, had led the army in a decisive battle against the King of Norway and the traitorous nobleman who was known as the Thane of Cawdor.

Returning victorious from this battle, Macbeth and Banquo crossed a desolate heath, where they were stopped by the strange appearance of three figures—they looked like women, except that they had beards, and their withered skins and wild attire made them look quite unlike any earthly creatures. Macbeth called to them, when they, seemingly offended, laid each one a chapped finger upon her skinny lips, in token of silence; and the first of them saluted Macbeth, calling him by his name and title:

"All hail, Macbeth! Hail to thee, Thane of Glamis!"

The general was more than a little startled to find himself known by such creatures; but he was perplexed, indeed, when the second creature followed up that salute with:

"All hail, Macbeth! Hail to thee, Thane of Cawdor!" He was, after all, not the Thane of Cawdor, though he had captured that rebellious traitor and had dispatched him to the king for execution.

And now the third of these specters cried out, "All hail, Macbeth, that shalt be king hereafter!"

Well, this was something to conjure with. How could such a prophetic greeting ever come true when, as Macbeth well knew, the king's two sons would surely follow their father to the throne?

Then, turning to Banquo, the strange figures described him in a sort of riddle:

"Lesser than Macbeth, and greater.
Not so happy, yet much happier.
Thou shalt get kings, though thou be none,"

thus prophesying [PROF-eh-sigh-ing] that though he himself would never reign, yet his sons would become kings of Scotland. When the specters vanished into thin air, Macbeth and Banquo knew them to be witches—the three "weird sisters."

While the two generals stood pondering these strange predictions, there arrived two messengers from the king, who were empowered by him to confer upon Macbeth the title of Thane of Cawdor. This event, which so miraculously corresponded to the prediction of the witches, astonished Macbeth, and he stood rapt in amazement, unable to make any reply to the messengers. Could it be that the prediction of the third witch would likewise come true—that he would become King of Scotland, too?

Turning to Banquo, he said, "Do you not hope your children shall be kings, when what the witches promised to me has so wonderfully come to pass?" To which Banquo replied, "That hope might enkindle you to aim at the throne; but often times these ministers of darkness tell us truths in little things, just to betray us into deeds of major consequence."

Still, Macbeth could not dismiss the dream of one day being king, and the horrifying thought that he might have to kill Duncan in order to fulfill this final prophecy. But, he reasoned, there is also the possibility that fate may hold some way for him to ascend the throne without any effort on his part. He decides to leave his destiny to chance, saying:

> "If chance will have me king,
>     why, chance may crown me,
> Without my stir."

Sad it is that once the seeds of greed and power are planted, they grow of their own accord, and from that day, Macbeth bent all his thoughts toward becoming King of Scotland.

Now Macbeth had a wife, to whom he told the strange prediction of the weird sisters and its partial fulfillment. She was an evil, ambitious woman, and thought that if she and her husband could arrive at greatness, what did it matter how they got there? She spurred on the reluctant Macbeth to act on his initial thought of murdering the king, for it was, she said, the only way to ensure fulfillment of the witches' prophecy.

It so happened that the king, who out of his royal condescension would oftentimes visit the principal nobles of his court, came to the castle of Macbeth, accompanied by his two sons— Malcolm and Donalbain—and a host of lords and servants, this royal visit to honor Macbeth for his recent triumphs in the war.

The castle of Macbeth was a pleasant place; King Duncan enjoyed the sweet and delicate air he noticed all around. He was even more taken by the attentions and respect shown by his hostess, Lady Macbeth, unaware, of course, of what she had in mind for him. Oh, how she could cover her treacherous purposes with smiles, and look like the innocent flower, while, all the time, be the serpent under it.

The king, being tired from his journey, went early to bed, and two servants went with him to guard his chamber door.

Now was the middle of night, when the world seems dead, and wicked dreams enter men's minds, and none but the wolf and the murderer is about. This was the time when Lady Macbeth awoke to plot the murder of the king. She would not have undertaken a deed so abhorrent, so unladylike, except that she feared her husband's nature was "too full of the milk of human kindness" to plan and carry out a murder by himself. She knew him to be ambitious, but above all he was scrupulous, and not by nature prepared for the type of crime that accompanies inordinate ambition. Earlier, she had gotten him to consent to the murder, but now she doubted his resolution; she feared that his natural tendencies (more humane than her own) would intervene and dissuade [dih-SWADE] him in the end.

And so they had. Macbeth's resolve had weakened, and he no longer thought that Duncan's death was necessary to his success. After all, Duncan was not only his king, but his kinsman as well. Furthermore, Macbeth was the king's host, and a host is supposed to protect his guests from danger, not murder them. Then, too, he considered how merciful and good a king this Duncan had been, how lovingly he had treated his subjects —especially Macbeth himself, for it was through Duncan's generosity that Macbeth had risen so high. No, he would not murder such a man and tempt the gods who watch over and protect such kings.

But although Macbeth's better nature had risen up to argue against his proceeding any further, Lady Macbeth was a woman not easily shaken from a plan, no matter what evil was required to carry it out. She began to infuse her own spirit into his mind, giving him reason upon reason why he should not shrink from what he had undertaken to do. She pointed out how easy the deed would become if they plied the servants who guarded Duncan's door with enough wine to keep them fast asleep throughout the night. She told him to think about how soon it would all be over, and how the action of one short night would make him a king for all his days and nights to come.

This tactic having failed to bring about its desired result, she then accused him of cowardice, and she chided him for failing to stick with their original plan as he had sworn to do. He had been so bold and so courageous before, but now those qualities had left him:

> "When you durst do it, then you were a man;
> And, to be more than what you were, you would
> Be so much more the man."

Besides, she added, the blame would surely fall upon the sleeping guards.

That was enough to summon up Macbeth's courage once again for the bloody business, and, taking the dagger in his hand, he crept toward the dark room where Duncan lay. On his way, he thought he saw another dagger in the air, with the handle pointing toward him, and on the blade and at the point were drops of blood. But when he tried to take hold of it, it was nothing but air, a mere phantom of his own imagination. Casting this fear aside, he entered the king's room and dispatched him with one stroke of the dagger.

Quickly he returned to his own bedchamber, where Lady Macbeth waited anxiously. Yes, he had murdered the king, but he had seen strange visions and heard strange voices, and these now filled him with guilt and remorse, and he, despairing, cried—

> "I am afraid to think what I have done;
> Look on it again I dare not."

He told her that after the king died, a voice had wailed, "Sleep no more! Macbeth does murder sleep," which he took to mean that he would never again enjoy a peaceful night's repose.

His wife again chastised him for his frailty, and she laid out for him the steps that must now be taken. He must first wash the blood from his hands; meanwhile, she would smear the guards and their daggers with the king's blood, thereby ensuring that these unwitting servants would be blamed for the murder.

Morning came, and with it the discovery of the murder. Although Macbeth and his lady made a great show of grief, and although the evidence against the guards was compelling, still there were those—especially Banquo and the king's two sons—who suspected Macbeth of committing the treasonous act. Fearing that they too would be slain, the two princes fled —Malcolm to England and Donalbain to Ireland.

The fleeing of Malcolm and Donalbain left the throne vacant, and because Macbeth was next in line of succession, he was crowned king, and the third prophecy of the weird sisters came to pass. Macbeth and his queen, though, could not forget the last of the witches' predictions: that Macbeth should be king, yet not his children, but those of Banquo would be kings after him. The thought of this, and the thought that they had committed murder only to place Banquo's heirs upon the throne, so rankled them that they determined this prophecy must never come to be. Banquo must die, and with him his son, Fleance.

A plan was agreed upon that would accomplish these ends. They held a great banquet, to which they invited all the chief thanes, and especially Banquo and his son. Macbeth hired three professional murderers and instructed them to fall upon Banquo and Fleance as they approached the castle. This they did, that evening, but although they achieved their goal by stabbing and killing Banquo, in the scuffle Fleance escaped.

At the banquet, the queen played the hostess with regal gracefulness and attention, while Macbeth talked freely with his thanes about his friendship with, and admiration for, Banquo. Just at these words the ghost of the murdered Banquo entered the room and placed himself on the chair that Macbeth was about to occupy. Though Macbeth was a bold man, and one who could have faced the devil without trembling, at this horrible sight his cheeks turned white with fear, and he stood quite paralyzed with his eyes fixed upon the ghost. His queen and all the nobles saw nothing, except Macbeth staring at an empty chair. Lady Macbeth reproached him, whispering that it was just his imagination, as it had been when he thought he saw the dagger in the air. But Macbeth continued to see the ghost, and he addressed it with words that the queen feared would reveal their dreadful secret. Quickly she dismissed all their guests, saying that Macbeth had been ill of late and had not, it appeared, fully recovered.

Macbeth had noticed the absence of the lord Macduff from the banquet, and he surmised that Macduff was now his principal enemy. (In this judgment, he was unusually prescient [PREE-she-ant], for Macduff had already gone to England to assist Malcolm in obtaining English help in overthrowing Macbeth.) To learn what the future held for his dealings with Macduff, he decided to seek out the three weird sisters, but he was prepared to continue on his murderous path against his enemies, if that course proved necessary. He said,

> ". . . I am in blood
> Stepp'd in so far that, should I wade no more,
> Returning were as tedious as go o'er."

He sought the witches in a cave upon the heath, where they, who knew by foresight of his coming, were engaged in preparing the concoction that would conjure up the evil spirits who would reveal the future to them. They chanted:

> "Round about the cauldron go;
> In the poison'd entrails throw.
> Toad, that under cold stone
> Days and nights has thirty-one
> Swelter'd venom sleeping got,
> Boil thou first i' the charmèd pot.

Double, double toil and trouble;
Fire burn, and cauldron bubble.
Fillet of a fenny snake,
In the cauldron boil and bake;
Eye of newt and toe of frog,
Wool of bat and tongue of dog,
Adder's fork and blind-worm's sting,
Lizard's leg and howlet's wing,
For a charm of powerful trouble,
Like a hell-broth boil and bubble.
Double, double toil and trouble;
Fire burn and cauldron bubble."


And then they added to the pot dragon scales, wolves' teeth, poisonous roots, body organs, and other horrible ingredients, even the finger of a dead child! When these were boiled and then cooled with baboon's blood, they produced infernal spirits who could answer questions about future events.

The sisters demanded to know whether Macbeth would have his doubts resolved by them, or by these spirits, who were their masters. He, undaunted by the dreadful ceremonies he saw, boldly replied, "Call 'em, let me see 'em." And so they did.

With a clap of thunder, the first spirit arose in the likeness of a helmeted head, and he called Macbeth by name, and bid him beware of the Thane of Fife. Macbeth thanked him for this warning, for this confirmed that Macduff, whose title was Thane of Fife, was indeed his enemy.

And the second spirit arose in the likeness of a bloody child, and he called Macbeth by name, and bid him have no fear, "for none of woman born shall harm Macbeth." This prophecy pleased Macbeth, for if no human could harm him, then he had no need to fear Macduff. Still, just to make doubly certain of his safety, he vowed to kill Macduff anyway.

That spirit having vanished, a third arose in the form of a child wearing a crown on its head and holding a small tree in its hand. He, too, called Macbeth by name, and he, too, gave Macbeth comfort by saying,

"Macbeth shall never vanquish'd be until
Great Birnam Wood to high
   Dunsinane [DUN-sin-ain] Hill
Shall come against him."

Macbeth was overjoyed at this news, for who could uproot a forest and move it to another place? Now he was certain to live out his full life and not be killed in a rebellion. But one thing still troubled him, and he asked the spirits whether Banquo's heirs would ever reign in his kingdom. Here the cauldron sank into the ground, and a procession of eight shadows, arrayed like kings, passed by Macbeth, the last of which was Banquo's ghost, bearing a strange glass that showed the figures of many more. Macbeth knew that these were "Banquo's issue," his heirs, who would reign in Scotland after him.

Then, just when the witches vanished, in came a nobleman to report that Macduff, Thane of Fife, had been recruiting an army in England in order to help Malcolm, the eldest son of the late king, reclaim the throne that was rightfully his. Macbeth, stung with rage, ordered at once that Macduff's castle be attacked, that Macduff's wife and children be killed, and so too all who claimed the slightest relationship to Macduff.

These and many similar deeds of vengeance and brutality caused some of the chief thanes in Scotland to alienate themselves from the king. Some even fled to England to join the forces of Malcolm and Macduff, while the rest secretly wished them success. Macbeth soon became hated by nobles and common folk alike; all thought him to be a tyrant; no one loved or honored him; and he began to envy the condition of the murdered Duncan, who now slept peacefully in his grave, for no poison or treason or malice could hurt him any longer.

Meanwhile, the queen was near madness, and her doctor and servants were at a loss for a cure. She had not slept for several nights, and now was in a constant torment by what she thought was the stain of blood upon her hands. She cried,

"Out, damned spot! Out, I say! . . . Will these hands ne'er be clean? . . . Here's the smell of the blood still. All the perfumes of Arabia will not sweeten this little hand."

Persistent rubbing and washing her hands did no good at all (though, in truth, no one but she could see anything unusual in their appearance). Everyone feared that in her madness she might take her own life.

Macbeth, on the other hand, was faced with the possibility that his life would be taken by others, for the armies of Malcolm and Macduff approached nearer and nearer his own forces at the castle at Dunsinane. The prophecies of the witches had filled him with a certain confidence, for he remembered their saying that none of woman born was to hurt him, and that he would not be defeated until Birnam Wood came to Dunsinane, which, of course, could never be. So he secured himself behind the impregnable walls of his castle and sullenly waited for the invaders, despairing all the while the shambles he had made of his life, saying,

> "And that which should accompany old age,
> As honor, love, obedience, troops of friends,
> I must not look to have, but, in their stead,
> Curses, not loud but deep, mouth-honor, breath,
> Which the poor heart would fain deny, and dare not."

Not long afterward, a servant brought the news to him that his wife, the queen, was dead. Macbeth, now stricken by grief, is even more contemptuous of his wasted life. Denouncing life itself as a meaningless folly, he laments,

> "Tomorrow, and tomorrow, and tomorrow,
> Creeps in this petty pace from day to day
> To the last syllable of recorded time,
> And all our yesterdays have lighted fools
> The way to dusty death. Out, out, brief candle!
> Life's but a walking shadow, a poor player
> That struts and frets his hour upon the stage
> And then is heard no more. It is a tale
> Told by an idiot, full of sound and fury,
> Signifying nothing."

Another messenger then appeared, quite pale and shaken. He reported that from his watch on the hill, as he looked toward Birnam Wood, he saw the forest begin to move! "Liar, and slave!" fumed Macbeth. "If thou speak'st false, upon the next tree shalt thou hang alive! If thy speech be true, I care not if thou dost the same to me." Macbeth had begun to suspect the fiendish witches of deceiving him, for apparently Birnam Wood *had* come to Dunsinane.

The strange appearance that had given the messenger an idea of a moving forest was actually Malcolm's skillful use of camouflage for his troops. Malcolm had instructed each of his soldiers to cut down a bough from the trees in Birnam Wood, and hold it before him, thereby concealing their true numbers and delaying their detection from the castle walls. To the messenger, the woods appeared to move, and to Macbeth, the witches' prophecy appeared to come true.

And now a violent battle ensued, during which Macbeth avoided Macduff, remembering the counsel of the first witch. But Macduff, enraged with anger and thirsting for revenge, sought out the man who had caused the murder of his wife and children. When the two met at last, Macbeth smiled confidently, recalling another of the witches' prophecies. "I bear a charmed life," he said to his foe, "which must not yield to one of woman born."

"Despair thy charm," replied Macduff, and then he revealed that he was not born of woman, in the ordinary sense, for he was brought into the world by the hands of others (a cesarean birth).

Trembling now that he realizes how the witches have deceived him, Macbeth throws himself into a final battle, saying,

> "Lay on, Macduff,
> And damn'd be him that first cries 'Hold, enough!' "

These were his last words, for, after a desperate struggle, Macduff proved the victor, and he cut off the head of his foe as a present for Malcolm, the young and lawful king.

# Lines Written in Early Spring

### by
## WILLIAM WORDSWORTH

**Vocabulary and pronunciation guide:**
  **bower:** a leafy or wooded shelter; an arbor
  **primrose:** an early blossoming, pale yellow plant
  **periwinkle:** a trailing evergreen plant with small blue
    flowers; also called myrtle
  **lament:** to feel sorrow or regret over; to mourn


I heard a thousand blended notes,
While in a grove I sat reclined,
In that sweet mood when pleasant thoughts
Bring sad thoughts to the mind.

To her fair works did Nature link
The human soul that through me ran;
And much it grieved my heart to think
What man has made of man.

Through primrose tufts, in that green bower,
The periwinkle trailed its wreaths;
And 'tis my faith that every flower
Enjoys the air it breathes.

The birds around me hopped and played,
Their thoughts I cannot measure—
But the least motion which they made,
It seemed a thrill of pleasure.

The budding twigs spread out their fan,
To catch the breezy air;
And I must think, do all I can,
That there was pleasure there.

If this belief from heaven be sent,
If such be Nature's holy plan,
Have I not reason to lament
What man has made of man?

# The Gettysburg Address

by
**ABRAHAM LINCOLN**

**About the speech:**

*The three-day battle at Gettysburg, Pennsylvania (July 1–3, 1863), marked the turning point in the Civil War, for after Lee's forces were routed there (and Grant took Vicksburg the following day), the Confederacy would not win a major battle during the duration of the war.*

*The battle itself started quite unceremoniously, with stragglers from both armies accidentally bumping into each other on the then-peaceful streets of the city. Positions were quickly taken, and three days of heroism, military blunders, and unparalleled bloodshed ensued. When it was finally over, this single encounter had killed perhaps 28,000 of the 75,000 troops General Lee had led into the North, and Federal losses were numbered at 23,000 of their 88,000 men. More American soldiers were killed in this one battle than in the entire Vietnam War.*

*Even before these fallen wariors could be properly buried, the battlefield was declared a national cemetery. President Abraham Lincoln, as well as other dignitaries, was invited to speak at the dedication ceremony, November 19, 1863. Lincoln, it is certain, took this opportunity as a matter of great importance. He worked on his speech for some time—polishing and editing until the piece was just what he wanted. (The legend that he wrote the speech quickly on the back of an envelope during his train ride to Gettysburg is wholly without foundation.)*

*Lincoln's speech was brief—certainly by comparison with the speech that preceded it: a nearly two-hour-long, memorized oration by the statesman Edward Everett. When Lincoln finished, he himself thought the speech to have been a complete and embarrassing failure, but others, including Edward Everett, recognized its literary excellence and knew that these mere two hundred and sixty words embodied the spiritual and democratic meaning of the entire Civil War. Today the speech is considered one of the world's masterpieces, both as literature and as a statement of democracy. It is well worth whatever practice and memorization time you or your children can afford it.*

**Approximate reading time:** 2 minutes
**Vocabulary and pronunciation guide:**
    **score:** a set of twenty
    **hallow:** to make holy

*F*our score and seven years ago our fathers brought forth on this continent a new nation, conceived in liberty, and dedicated to the proposition that all men are created equal.

Now we are engaged in a great civil war, testing whether that nation, or any nation so conceived and so dedicated, can long endure. We are met on a great battlefield of that war. We have come to dedicate a portion of that field as a final resting place for those who here gave their lives that that nation might live. It is altogether fitting and proper that we should do this.

But, in a larger sense, we cannot dedicate—we cannot consecrate—we cannot hallow this ground. The brave men, living and dead, who struggled here have consecrated it far above our poor power to add or detract. The world will little note, nor long remember, what we say here, but it can never forget what they did here.

It is for us the living, rather, to be dedicated here to the unfinished work which they who fought here have thus far so nobly advanced. It is rather for us to be here dedicated to the great task remaining before us—that from these honored dead we take increased devotion to that cause for which they gave the last full measure of devotion; that we here highly resolve that these dead shall not have died in vain; that this nation, under God, shall have a new birth of freedom; and that government of the people, by the people, and for the people, shall not perish from the earth.

# I Have a Dream

by
## MARTIN LUTHER KING, Jr.

**About the speech:**

*Dr. Martin Luther King, Jr., had been the acknowledged leader of the civil rights movement since the first transit boycott in Montgomery, Alabama, in 1955. He was young, educated, respected, and, perhaps above all, he had the eloquence and oratorical power to motivate masses of people, black and white.*

*Near the end of his campaign to desegregate lunch counters and other businesses in Birmingham, Alabama, he joined a nationwide coalition of forces that sought a peaceful end to the nation's racial prejudices. These leaders organized the historic August 28, 1963, "March on Washington," in which more than 200,000 citizens gathered peaceably to hear King and other speakers call out from the steps of the Lincoln Memorial their demand for equal justice under the law.*

*Martin Luther King's I Have a Dream speech moved and uplifted the assembled crowd and the television audience as no other did that day, or has to this day. Yet many still think it was King's oratorical flair alone that made the speech so moving. Not so. As you read and recite this masterpiece, you will see that it holds up well as a piece of literature, and that its biblical phraseology and its parallels to The Gettysburg Address allow it to be commanding in any voice—even your own.*

**Approximate reading time:** 11 minutes
**Vocabulary and pronunciation guide:**

    **score:** a set of twenty

    **manacles** [MAN-uh-culz]: restraints; handcuffs

    **unalienable** [un-AA-lee-en-uh-bull] (more commonly *inalienable*): not transferable; that which cannot be rightfully taken away

**hallowed:** honored; regarded as holy

**inextricably** [in-EX-trick-uh-blee]: unable to be separated

**interposition** [in-ter-poe-ZIH-shun]: the opposition by a state to a federal action or law

**nullification:** the doctrine that a state has a legal right in refusing to obey an act of Congress

**prodigious** [pro-DIJ-us]: marvelous; amazing

**curvaceous** [kur-VAY-shus]: having beautiful curves; shapely

*F*ive score years ago, a great American, in whose symbolic shadow we stand today, signed the Emancipation Proclamation. This momentous decree came as a great beacon of light of hope to millions of Negro slaves who had been seared in the flames of withering injustice. It came as a joyous daybreak to end the long night of their captivity.

But one hundred years later, the Negro still is not free. One hundred years later, the life of the Negro is still sadly crippled by the manacles [MAN-uh-culz] of segregation and the chains of discrimination.

One hundred years later, the Negro lives on a lonely island of poverty in the midst of a vast ocean of material prosperity. One hundred years later, the Negro still languishes in the corners of American society and finds himself an exile in his own land. So we have come here today to dramatize a shameful condition.

In a sense we have come to our nation's capital to cash a check. When the architects of our republic wrote the magnificent words of the Constitution and Declaration of Independence, they were signing a promissory note to which every American was to fall heir. This note was a promise that all men, yes, black men as well as white men, would be guaranteed the unalienable [un-AA-lee-en-uh-bull] rights of life, liberty, and the pursuit of happiness.

It is obvious today that America has defaulted on this promissory note insofar as her citizens of color are concerned. Instead of honoring this sacred obligation, America has given the Negro people a bad check, which has come back marked "insufficient funds."

But we refuse to believe that the bank of justice is bankrupt. We refuse to believe that there are insufficient funds in the great vaults of opportunity of this nation. So we have come to cash this check—a check that will give us upon demand the riches of freedom and the security of justice.

We have also come to this hallowed spot to remind America of the fierce urgency of now. This is no time to engage in the luxury of cooling off or to take the tranquilizing drug of gradualism. Now is the time to make real the promises of democracy. Now is the time to rise from the dark and desolate valley of segregation to the sunlit path of racial justice. Now is the time to lift our nation from the quicksands of racial injustice to the solid rock of brotherhood. Now is the time to make justice a reality for *all* of God's children.

It would be fatal for the nation to overlook the urgency of the movement and to underestimate the determination of the Negro. This sweltering summer of the Negro's legitimate discontent will not pass until there is an invigorating autumn of freedom and equality. Nineteen sixty-three is not an end but a beginning. Those who hope that the Negro needed to blow off steam and will now be content will have a rude awakening if the nation returns to business as usual.

There will be neither rest nor tranquillity in America until the Negro is granted his citizenship rights. The whirlwinds of revolt will continue to shake the foundations of our nation until the bright day of justice emerges.

But there is something that I must say to my people who stand on the warm threshold which leads into the palace of justice. In the process of gaining our rightful place, we must not be guilty of wrongful deeds.

Let us not seek to satisfy our thirst for freedom by drinking from the cup of bitterness and hatred. We must forever conduct our struggle on the high plane of dignity and discipline. We must not allow our creative protest to degenerate into physical violence. Again and again we must rise to the majestic heights of meeting physical force with soul force.

The marvelous new militancy which has engulfed the Negro community must not lead us to a distrust of all white people, for many of our white brothers, as evidenced by their presence here today, have come to realize that their destiny is tied up with our destiny, and they have come to realize that their freedom is inextricably [in-EX-trick-uh-blee] tied to our freedom. This offense we share, mounted to storm the battlements of injustice, must be carried forth by a biracial army. We cannot walk alone.

And as we walk, we must make the pledge that we shall always march ahead. We cannot turn back. There are those who are asking the devotees of civil rights, "When will you be satisfied?" We can never be satisfied as long as the Negro is the victim of the unspeakable horrors of police brutality.

We can never be satisfied as long as our bodies, heavy with the fatigue of travel, cannot gain lodging in the motels of the highways and the hotels of the cities. We cannot be satisfied as long as the Negro's basic mobility is from a smaller ghetto to a larger one.

We can never be satisfied as long as our children are stripped of their selfhood and robbed of their dignity by signs stating "for whites only." We cannot be satisfied as long as a Negro in Mississippi cannot vote and a Negro in New York believes he has nothing for which to vote. No, we are not satisfied, and we will not be satisfied until justice rolls down like waters and righteousness like a mighty stream.

I am not unmindful that some of you have come here out of excessive trials and tribulation. Some of you have come fresh from narrow jail cells. Some of you have come from areas where your quest for freedom left you battered by the storms of persecution and staggered by the winds of police brutality. You have been the veterans of creative suffering. Continue to work with the faith that unearned suffering is redemptive.

Go back to Mississippi; go back to Alabama; go back to South Carolina; go back to Georgia; go back to Louisana; go back to the slums and ghettos of the Northern cities, knowing that somehow this situation can and will be changed. Let us not wallow in the valley of despair.

So I say to you, my friends, that even though we must face

the difficulties of today and tomorrow, I still have a dream. It is a dream deeply rooted in the American dream that one day this nation will rise up and live out the true meaning of its creed—we hold these truths to be self-evident, that *all* men are created equal.

I have a dream that one day on the red hills of Georgia, sons of former slaves and sons of former slave-owners will be able to sit down together at the table of brotherhood.

I have a dream that one day, even the state of Mississippi, a state sweltering with the heat of injustice, sweltering with the heat of oppression, will be transformed into an oasis of freedom and justice.

I have a dream that my four little children will one day live in a nation where they will not be judged by the color of their skin but by the content of their character. I have a dream today!

I have a dream that one day, down in Alabama, with its vicious racists, with its governor having his lips dripping with the words of interposition [in-ter-poe-ZIH-shun] and nullification, that one day, right there in Alabama, little black boys and black girls will be able to join hands with little white boys and white girls as sisters and brothers. I have a dream today!

I have a dream that one day every valley shall be exalted, every hill and mountain shall be made low, the rough places shall be made plain, and the crooked places shall be made straight and the glory of the Lord will be revealed and all flesh shall see it together.

This is our hope. This is the faith that I go back to the South with.

With this faith we will be able to hew out of the mountain of despair a stone of hope. With this faith we will be able to transform the jangling discords of our nation into a beautiful symphony of brotherhood.

With this faith we will be able to work together, to pray together, to struggle together, to go to jail together, to stand up for freedom together, knowing that we will be free one day. This will be the day when all of God's children will be able to sing with new meaning—"My country 'tis of thee, sweet land of liberty, of thee I sing; land where my fathers died, land of the pilgrim's pride; from every mountainside, let freedom ring"—and if America is to be a great nation, this must become true.

And so let freedom ring from the prodigious [pro-DIJ-us] hilltops of New Hampshire.

Let freedom ring from the mighty mountains of New York.

Let freedom ring from the heightening Alleghenies of Pennsylvania.

Let freedom ring from the snow-capped Rockies of Colorado.

Let freedom ring from the curvaceous [kur-VAY-shus] slopes of California.

But not only that.

Let freedom ring from Stone Mountain of Georgia.

Let freedom ring from Lookout Mountain of Tennessee.

Let freedom ring from every hill and molehill of Mississippi, from every mountainside, let freedom ring.

And when this happens, and when we allow freedom to ring, when we let it ring from every village and hamlet, from every state and city, we will be able to speed up that day when all of God's children—black men and white men, Jews and Gentiles, Catholics and Protestants—will be able to join hands and to sing in the words of the old Negro spiritual, "Free at last, free at last, thank God Almighty, we are free at last."

# Sonnet 29

## by
## WILLIAM SHAKESPEARE

**Vocabulary and pronunciation guide:**
    **bootless:** futile, useless
    **haply:** by chance or accident (by hap)

When, in disgrace with fortune and men's eyes,
I all alone beweep my outcast state,
And trouble deaf heaven with my bootless cries,
And look upon myself, and curse my fate,
Wishing me like to one more rich in hope,
Featured like him, like him with friends possessed,
Desiring this man's art and that man's scope,
With what I most enjoy contented least;
Yet in these thoughts myself almost despising,
Haply I think on thee, and then my state,
Like to the lark at break of day arising
From sullen earth, sings hymns at heaven's gate;
    For thy sweet love remembered such wealth brings
    That then I scorn to change my state with kings.

# Sonnet 116

## by
## WILLIAM SHAKESPEARE

**Vocabulary and pronunciation guide:**
> **fixèd** [FIX-ed] (pronounced as two syllables to
> fit the meter of the line): secure; immovable
> **tempest:** a violent storm; a fierce tumult
> **bark:** a sailing vessel
> **compass:** the reach or range of something (in
> this case, youthful physical appearance does
> fall within the power of Time to change)

Let me not to the marriage of true minds
Admit impediments. Love is not love
Which alters when it alteration finds,
Or bends with the remover to remove:
Oh, no! It is an ever-fixèd [FIX-ed] mark,
That looks on tempests and is never shaken;
It is the star to every wandering bark,
Whose worth's unknown, although his height be taken.
Love's not Time's fool, though rosy lips and cheeks
Within his bending sickle's compass come;
Love alters not with his brief hours and weeks,
But bears it out even to the edge of doom.
　　If this be error and upon me proved,
　　I never writ, nor no man ever loved.

# The Tell-Tale Heart

by
## EDGAR ALLAN POE

**About the story:**

*During Edgar Allan Poe's brief forty-year life—a life interspersed with long stretches of poverty, ending mysteriously in a Baltimore gutter—he developed an extraordinary creative mastery as a poet and a writer of short stories. He is best known for his gothic settings and tales—those that evoke a feeling of horror, terror, or mystery.*

*If he did not actually invent the detective story, he certainly developed and polished the form more than any other single writer. His contribution to the refinement of the mystery story in general is such that an award called an Edgar is given annually by the Mystery Writers of America to the year's best examples of mystery writing.*

**Approximate reading time:** 13 minutes
**Vocabulary and pronunciation guide:**

> **harken:** listen
> **profound:** intellectually deep or penetrating; wise
> **sagacity** [suh-GAS-ih-tee]: keen perception; shrewdness; cunning
> **crevice** [CREV-iss]: a fissure or crack
> **waned** [WAYND]: decreased; diminished
> **bade** [BAD]: (past tense of "bid"); greeted; urged
> **audacity** [awe-DASS-ih-tee]: boldness; daring
> **ere** [AIR]: before
> **vehemently** [VEE-uh-ment-lee]: passionately; energetically
> **derision** [durr-IH-zhun]: ridicule; mockery

True!—nervous—very, very dreadfully nervous I had been and am! But why *will* you say that I am mad? The disease had sharpened my senses—not destroyed—not dulled them. Above all was the sense of hearing acute. I heard all things in the heaven and in the earth. I heard many things in hell. How, then, am I mad? Harken! and observe how healthily—how calmly I can tell you the whole story.

It is impossible to say how first the idea entered my brain; but once conceived, it haunted me day and night. Object there was none. Passion there was none. I loved the old man. He had never wronged me. He had never given me insult. For his gold I had no desire. I think it was his eye! Yes, it was this! One of his eyes resembled that of a vulture—a pale blue eye, with a film over it. Whenever it fell upon me, my blood ran cold; and so by degrees—very gradually—I made up my mind to take the life of the old man, and thus rid myself of the eye forever.

Now this is the point. You fancy me mad. Madmen know nothing. But you should have seen *me*. You should have seen how wisely I proceeded—with what caution—with what fore-sight—with what deception I went to work!

I was never kinder to the old man than during the whole week before I killed him. And every night, about midnight, I turned the latch of his door and opened it—oh, so gently! And then, when I had made an opening sufficient for my head, I put in a dark lantern, all closed, closed so that no light shone out, and then I thrust in my head. Oh, you would have laughed to see how cunningly I thrust it in! I moved it slowly—very, very slowly, so that I might not disturb the old man's sleep. It took me an hour to place my whole head within the opening so far that I could see him as he lay upon his bed. Ha! —would a madman have been so wise as this? And then, when my head was well in the room, I undid the lantern cautiously —oh, so cautiously—cautiously (for the hinges creaked)—I undid it just so much that a single thin ray fell upon the vulture eye. And this I did for seven long nights—every night just at midnight—but I found the eye always closed; and so it was impossible to do the work; for it was not the old man who vexed me, but his Evil Eye. And every morning, when the day broke, I went boldly into the chamber, and spoke courageously to him, calling him by name in a hearty tone, and inquiring how he had passed the night. So, you see, he would have been a very profound old man, indeed, to suspect that every night, just at twelve, I looked in upon him while he slept.

Upon the eighth night I was more than usually cautious in opening the door. A watch's minute hand moves more quickly than did mine. Never before that night had I *felt* the extent of my own powers—of my sagacity [suh-GAS-ih-tee]. I could scarcely contain my feelings of triumph. To think that there I was, opening the door, little by little, and he not even to dream of my secret deeds or thoughts. I fairly chuckled at the idea; and perhaps he heard me; for he moved on the bed suddenly, as if startled. Now you may think that I drew back—but no. His room was as black as pitch with the thick darkness (for the shutters were tightly fastened, through fear of robbers), and so I knew that he could not see the opening of the door, and I kept pushing it on steadily, steadily.

I had my head in, and was about to open the lantern, when my thumb slipped upon the tin latch, and the old man sprang up in bed, crying out—"Who's there?"

I kept quite still and said nothing. For a whole hour I did not move a muscle, and in the meantime I did not hear him lie down. He was still sitting up in the bed, listening;—just as I have done, night after night, harkening to the death-watches in the wall.

Presently I heard a slight groan, and I knew it was the groan of mortal terror. It was not a groan of pain or grief—oh no!— it was the low stifled sound that arises from the bottom of the soul when overcharged with awe. I knew the sound well. Many a night, just at midnight, when all the world slept, it has welled up from my own bosom, deepening, with its dreadful echo, the terrors that distracted me. I say I knew it well. I knew what the old man felt, and pitied him, although I chuckled at heart. I knew that he had been lying awake ever since the first slight noise, when he had turned in the bed. His fears had been ever since growing upon him. He had been trying to fancy them causeless, but could not. He had been saying to himself—"It is nothing but the wind in the chimney—it is only a mouse crossing the floor," or "It is merely a cricket which has made a single chirp." Yes, he had been trying to comfort himself with these suppositions, but he had found all in vain. *All in vain;* because Death, in approaching him, had stalked with his black shadow before him, and enveloped the victim. And it was the mournful influence of the unperceived shadow that caused him to feel—although he neither saw nor heard—to *feel* the presence of my head within the room.

When I had waited a long time, very patiently, without hearing him lie down, I resolved to open a little—a very, very little crevice [CREV-iss] in the lantern. So I opened it—you cannot imagine how stealthily, stealthily—until, at length, a single dim ray, like the thread of the spider, shot from out the crevice and full upon the vulture eye.

It was open—wide, wide open—and I grew furious as I gazed upon it. I saw it with perfect distinctness—all a dull blue, with a hideous veil over it that chilled the very marrow in my bones; but I could see nothing else of the old man's face or person, for I had directed the ray, as if by instinct, precisely upon the damnable spot.

And now—have I not told you that what you mistake for madness is but over-acuteness of the senses?—now, I say, there came to my ears a low, dull, quick sound, such as a watch makes when enveloped in cotton. I knew *that* sound well too. It was the beating of the old man's heart. It increased my fury, as the beating of a drum stimulates the soldier into courage.

But even yet I refrained and kept still. I scarcely breathed. I held the lantern motionless. I tried to see how steadily I could maintain the ray upon the eye. Meantime, the hellish tattoo of the heart increased. It grew quicker and quicker, and louder and louder every instant. The old man's terror *must* have been extreme! It grew louder, I say, louder every moment!—do you mark me well? I have told you that I am nervous; so I am. And now at the dead hour of night, amid the dreadful silence of that old house, so strange a noise as this excited me to uncontrollable terror. Yet, for some minutes longer I refrained and stood still. But the beating grew louder, louder! I thought the heart must burst. And now a new anxiety seized me—the sound would be heard by a neighbor! The old man's hour had come! With a loud yell, I threw open the lantern and leaped into the room. He shrieked once—once only. In an instant I dragged him to the floor, and pulled the heavy bed over him. I then smiled gaily, to find the deed so far done. But, for many minutes, the heart beat on with a muffled sound. This, however, did not vex me; it would not be heard through the wall. At length it ceased. The old man was dead. I removed the bed and examined the corpse. Yes, he was stone, stone dead. I placed my hand upon the heart and held it there many minutes. There was no pulsation. He was stone dead. His eye would trouble me nor more.

If still you think me mad, you will think so no longer when I describe the wise precautions I took for the concealment of the body. The night waned [WAYND], and I worked hastily, but in silence. First of all I dismembered the corpse. I cut off the head and the arms and the legs.

I then took up three planks from the flooring of the chamber, and deposited all between the crossbeams. I then replaced the boards so cleverly, so cunningly, that no human eye—not even *his*—could have detected anything wrong. There was nothing to wash out—no stain of any kind—no blood-spot whatever. I had been too wary for that. A tub had caught all—ha! ha!

When I had made an end of these labors, it was four o'clock —still dark as midnight. As the bell sounded the hour, there came a knocking at the street door. I went down to open it with a light heart—for what had I *now* to fear? There entered three men, who introduced themselves, with perfect politeness, as officers of the police. A shriek had been heard by a neighbor during the night; suspicion of foul play had been aroused; information had been lodged at the police station, and they (the officers) had been appointed to search the premises.

I smiled—for *what* had I to fear? I bade [BAD] the gentlemen welcome. The shriek, I said, was my own in a dream. The old man, I mentioned, was vacationing in the country. I took my visitors all over the house. I bade them search—search *well*. I led them, at length, to *his* chamber. I showed them his treasures, secure, undisturbed. In the enthusiasm of my confidence, I brought chairs into the room, and desired them *here* to rest from their fatigues, while I myself, in the wild audacity [awe-DASS-ih-tee] of my perfect triumph, placed my own seat upon the very spot beneath which reposed the corpse of the victim.

The officers were satisfied. My *manner* had convinced them. I was singularly at ease. They sat, and while I answered cheerily, they chatted about familiar things. But, ere [AIR] long, I felt myself getting pale and wished them gone. My head ached, and I fancied a ringing in my ears; but still they sat and still chatted. The ringing became more distinct;—it continued and became more distinct; I talked more freely to get rid of the feeling; but it continued and gained explicitness—until, at length, I found that the noise was *not* within my ears.

No doubt I now grew *very* pale;—but I talked more fluently, and with a heightened voice. Yet the sound increased—and what could I do? It was *a low, dull, quick sound—much like a sound a watch makes when enveloped in cotton.* I gasped for breath —and yet the officers heard it not. I talked more quickly— more vehemently [VEE-uh-ment-lee]; but the noise steadily increased. Why *would* they not be gone? I paced the floor to and fro with heavy strides, as if excited to fury by the observation of the men—but the noise steadily increased. Oh God! what *could* I do? I foamed—I raved—I swore. I swung the chair upon which I had been sitting, and grated it upon the boards, but the noise arose over all and continually increased. It grew louder—louder—*louder!* —And still the men chatted pleasantly, and smiled. Was it possible they heard not? Almighty God!—no, no! They heard!—they suspected!—they *knew!*— they were making a *mockery* of my horror!—this I thought, and this I think. But anything was better than this agony! Anything was more tolerable than this derision [durr-IH-zhun]! I could bear those hypocritical smiles no longer! I felt that I must scream or die!—and now—again!—hark! louder! louder! *louder!*—

"Villains!" I shrieked, "pretend no more! I admit the deed! —tear up the planks!—here, here!—it is the beating of his hideous heart!"

# The Lottery

by
## SHIRLEY JACKSON

**About the story:**

*Like Poe, Shirley Jackson is considered a master of the gothic horror tale. This reputation is due in no small part to "The Lottery," which she wrote for* The New Yorker *magazine in 1948. More recently, she wrote a children's book about the madness of the Salem witch trials, and her novel* The Haunting of Hill House *was made into a MGM movie entitled* The Haunting. *Although she was also a talented comic writer and created many humorous sketches about everyday family life (in* Life Among the Savages, *for example), most people still identify her with the story that follows.*

*The author's view of society in this story—savage, timid, conformist, cruel—can provide a good parallel for listeners who enjoyed the lynch-mob scene from* Huckleberry Finn *in* Classics to Read Aloud to Your Children. *What happens to an individual's belief in doing right or being just, when a group, or a mob, or a whole town thinks otherwise?*

**Approximate reading time:** 20 minutes
**Vocabulary and pronunciation guide:**

> **profusely:** lavishly; abundantly
> **paraphernalia** [pair-uh-fur-NAY-lee-uh]: equipment; articles used in an activity
> **perfunctory** [purr-FUNK-tore-ee]: done mechanically and without enthusiasm, just for the sake of getting through
> **interminably** [in-TURR-min-uh-blee]: endlessly; continuing for a very long time
> **petulantly** [PETCH-you-lant-lee]: irritably; in an ill-tempered manner

The morning of June 27th was clear and sunny, with the fresh warmth of a full-summer day; the flowers were blossoming profusely and the grass was richly green. The people of the village began to gather in the square, between the post office and the bank, around ten o'clock; in some towns there were so many people that the lottery took two days and had to be started on June 26th, but in this village, where there were only about three hundred people, the whole lottery took less than two hours, so it could begin at ten o'clock in the morning and still be through in time to allow the villagers to get home for noon dinner.

The children assembled first, of course. School was recently over for the summer, and the feeling of liberty sat uneasily on most of them; they tended to gather together quietly for a while before they broke into boisterous play, and their talk was still of the classroom and the teacher, of books and reprimands. Bobby Martin had already stuffed his pockets full of stones, and the other boys soon followed his example, selecting the smoothest and roundest stones; Bobby and Harry Jones and Dickie Delacroix—the villagers pronounced this name "Dellacroy"—eventually made a great pile of stones in one corner of the square and guarded it against the raids of the other boys. The girls stood aside, talking among themselves, looking over their shoulders at the boys, and the very small children rolled in the dust or clung to the hands of their older brothers or sisters.

Soon the men began to gather, surveying their own children, speaking of planting and rain, tractors and taxes. They stood together, away from the pile of stones in the corner, and their jokes were quiet and they smiled rather than laughed. The women, wearing faded house dresses and sweaters, came shortly after their menfolk. They greeted one another and exchanged bits of gossip as they went to join their husbands. Soon the women, standing by their husbands, began to call to their children, and the children came reluctantly, having to be called four or five times. Bobby Martin ducked under his mother's grasping hand and ran, laughing, back to the pile of stones. His father spoke up sharply, and Bobby came quickly and took his place between his father and his oldest brother.

The lottery was conducted—as were the square dances, the teenage club, the Halloween program—by Mr. Summers, who had time and energy to devote to civic activities. He was a round-faced, jovial man and he ran the coal business, and people were sorry for him, because he had no children and his wife was a scold. When he arrived in the square, carrying the black wooden box, there was a murmur of conversation among the villagers, and he waved and called, "Little late today, folks." The postmaster, Mr. Graves, followed him, carrying a three-legged stool, and the stool was put in the center of the square and Mr. Summers set the black box down on it. The villagers kept their distance, leaving a space between themselves and the stool, and when Mr. Summers said, "Some of you fellows want to give me a hand?" there was a hesitation before two men, Mr. Martin and his oldest son, Baxter, came forward to hold the box steady on the stool while Mr. Summers stirred up the papers inside it.

The original paraphernalia [pair-uh-fur-NAY-lee-uh] for the lottery had been lost long ago, and the black box now resting on the stool had been put into use even before Old Man Warner, the oldest man in town, was born. Mr. Summers spoke frequently to the villagers about making a new box, but no one liked to upset even as much tradition as was represented by the black box. There was a story that the present box had been made with some pieces of the box that had preceded it, the one that had been constructed when the first people settled down to make a village here. Every year, after the lottery, Mr. Summers began talking again about a new box, but every year the subject was allowed to fade off without anything's being done. The black box grew shabbier each year; by now it was no longer completely black but splintered badly along one side to show the original wood color, and in some places faded or stained.

Mr. Martin and his oldest son, Baxter, held the black box securely on the stool until Mr. Summers had stirred the papers thoroughly with his hand. Because so much of the ritual had been forgotten or discarded, Mr. Summers had been successful in having slips of paper substituted for the chips of wood that had been used for generations. Chips of wood, Mr. Summers had argued, had been all very well when the village was tiny, but now that the population was more than three hundred and likely to keep on growing, it was necessary to use something that would fit more easily into the black box. The night before the lottery, Mr. Summers and Mr. Graves made up the slips of paper and put them in the box, and it was then taken to the safe of Mr. Summers's coal company and locked up until Mr. Summers was ready to take it to the the square next morning. The rest of the year, the box was put away, sometimes one place, sometimes another; it had spent one year in Mr. Graves's barn and another year underfoot in the post office, and sometimes it was set on a shelf in the Martin grocery and left there.

There was a great deal of fussing to be done before Mr. Summers declared the lottery open. There were the lists to make up—of heads of families, heads of households in each family, members of each household in each family. There was the proper swearing-in of Mr. Summers by the postmaster, as the official of the lottery; at one time, some people remembered, there had been a recital of some sort, performed by the official of the lottery, a perfunctory [purr- FUNK-torr-ee], tuneless chant that had been rattled off duly each year; some people believed that the official of the lottery used to stand just so when he said or sang it, others believed that he was supposed to walk among the people, but years and years ago this part of the ritual had been allowed to lapse. There had been, also, a ritual salute, which the official of the lottery had had to use in addressing each person who came up to draw from the box, but this also had changed with time, until now it was felt necessary only for the official to speak to each person approaching. Mr. Summers was very good at all this; in his clean white shirt and blue jeans, with one hand resting carelessly on the black box, he seemed very proper and important as he talked interminably [in-TURR-min-uh-blee] to Mr. Graves and the Martins.

Just as Mr. Summers finally left off talking and turned to the assembled villagers, Mrs. Hutchinson came hurriedly along the path to the square, her sweater thrown over her shoulders, and slid into place in the back of the crowd. "Clean forgot what day it was," she said to Mrs. Delacroix, who stood next to her, and they both laughed softly. "Thought my old man was out back stacking wood," Mrs. Hutchinson went on, "and then I looked out the window and the kids was gone, and then I remembered it was the twenty-seventh and came a-running." She dried her hands on her apron, and Mrs. Delacroix said, "You're in time, though. They're still talking away up there."

Mrs. Hutchinson craned her neck to see through the crowd and found her husband and children standing near the front. She tapped Mrs. Delacroix on the arm as a farewell and began to make her way through the crowd. The people separated good-humoredly to let her through; two or three people said, in voices just loud enough to be heard across the crowd, "Here comes your Missus, Hutchinson," and "Bill, she made it after all." Mrs. Hutchinson reached her husband, and Mr. Summers, who had been waiting, said cheerfully, "Thought we were going to have to get on without you, Tessie." Mrs. Hutchinson said, grinning, "Wouldn't have me leave m'dishes in the sink, now, would you, Joe?" and soft laughter ran through the crowd as the people stirred back into position after Mrs. Hutchinson's arrival.

"Well, now," Mr. Summers said soberly, "guess we better get started, get this over with, so's we can go back to work. Anybody ain't here?"

"Dunbar," several people said. "Dunbar, Dunbar."

Mr. Summers consulted his list. "Clyde Dunbar," he said. "That's right. He's broke his leg, hasn't he? Who's drawing for him?"

"Me, I guess," a woman said, and Mr. Summers turned to look at her. "Wife draws for her husband," Mr. Summers said. "Don't you have a grown boy to do it for you, Janey?" Although Mr. Summers and everyone else in the village knew the answer perfectly well, it was the business of the official of the lottery to ask such questions formally. Mr. Summers waited with an expression of polite interest while Mrs. Dunbar answered.

"Horace's not but sixteen yet," Mrs. Dunbar said regretfully. "Guess I gotta fill in for the old man this year."

"Right," Mr. Summers said. He made a note on the list he was holding. Then he asked, "Watson boy drawing this year?"

A tall boy in the crowd raised his hand. "Here," he said. "I'm drawing for m'mother and me." He blinked his eyes nervously and ducked his head as several voices in the crowd said things like "Good fellow, Jack," and "Glad to see your mother's got a man to do it."

"Well," Mr. Summers said, "guess that's everyone. Old Man Warner make it?"

"Here," a voice said, and Mr. Summers nodded.

A sudden hush fell on the crowd as Mr. Summers cleared his throat and looked at the list. "All ready?" he called. "Now, I'll read the names—heads of families first—and the men come up and take a paper out of the box. Keep the paper folded in your hand without looking at it until everyone has had a turn. Everything clear?"

The people had done it so many times that they only half listened to the directions; most of them were quiet, wetting their lips, not looking around. Then Mr. Summers raised one hand high and said, "Adams." A man disengaged himself from the crowd and came forward. "Hi, Steve," Mr. Summers said, and Mr. Adams said, "Hi, Joe." They grinned at one another humorlessly and nervously. Then Mr. Adams reached into the black box and took out a folded paper. He held it firmly by one corner as he turned and went hastily back to his place in the crowd, where he stood a little apart from his family, not looking down at his hand.

"Allen," Mr. Summers said. "Anderson . . . Bentham."

"Seems like there's no time at all between lotteries anymore," Mrs. Delacroix said to Mrs. Graves in the back row. "Seems like we got through with the last one only last week."

"Time sure goes fast," Mrs. Graves said.

"Clark . . . Delacroix," called out Mr. Summers.

"There goes my old man," Mrs. Delacroix said. She held her breath while her husband went forward.

"Dunbar," Mr. Summers said, and Mrs. Dunbar went steadily to the box while one of the women said, "Go on, Janey," and another said, "There she goes."

"We're next," Mrs. Graves said. She watched while Mr. Graves came around from the side of the box, greeted Mr. Summers gravely, and selected a slip of paper from the box. By now, all through the crowd there were men holding the small folded papers in their large hands, turning them over and over nervously. Mrs. Dunbar and her two sons stood together, Mrs. Dunbar holding the slip of paper.

"Harburt . . . Hutchinson," came the cry.

"Get up there, Bill," Mrs. Hutchinson said, and the people near her laughed.

"Jones," called Mr. Summers.

"They do say," Mr. Adams said to Old Man Warner, who stood next to him, "that over in the north village they're talking of giving up the lottery."

Old Man Warner snorted. "Pack of crazy fools," he said. "Listening to the young folks, nothing's good enough for *them.* Next thing you know, they'll be wanting to go back to living in caves, nobody work anymore, live *that* way for a while. Used to be a saying about 'Lottery in June, corn be heavy soon.' First thing you know, we'd all be eating stewed chickweed and acorns. There's *always* been a lottery," he added petulantly [PETCH-you-lant-lee]. "Bad enough to see young Joe Summers up there joking with everybody."

"Some places have already quit lotteries," Mrs. Adams said.

"Nothing but trouble in *that,*" Old Man Warner said stoutly. "Pack of young fools."

"Martin," came the call. And Bobby Martin watched his father go forward. "Overdyke . . . Percy," continued Mr. Summers.

"I wish they'd hurry." Mrs. Dunbar said to her older son. "I wish they'd hurry."

"They're almost through," her son said.

"You get ready to run tell Dad," Mrs. Dunbar said.

Mr. Summers called his own name and then stepped forward precisely and selected a slip from the box. Then he called, "Warner."

"Seventy-seventh year I been in the lottery," Old Man Warner said as he went through the crowd. "Seventy-seventh time."

"Watson." The tall boy came awkwardly through the crowd. Someone said, "Don't be nervous, Jack," and Mr. Summers said, "Take your time, son." And then "Zanini."

After that, there was a long pause, a breathless pause, until Mr. Summers, holding his slip of paper in the air, said, "All right, fellows." For a minute, no one moved, and then all the slips of paper were opened. Suddenly, all the women began to speak at once, saying, "Who is it?" "Who's got it?" "Is it the Dunbars?" "Is it the Watsons?" Then the voices began to say, "It's Hutchinson. It's Bill." "Bill Hutchinson's got it."

"Go tell your father," Mrs. Dunbar said to her older son.

People began to look around to see the Hutchinsons. Bill Hutchinson was standing quiet, staring down at the paper in his hand. Suddenly, Tessie Hutchinson shouted to Mr. Summers, "You didn't give him time enough to take any paper he wanted. I saw you. It wasn't fair."

"Be a good sport, Tessie," Mrs. Delacroix called, and Mrs. Graves said, "All of us took the same chance."

"Shut up, Tessie," Bill Hutchinson said.

"Well, everyone," Mr. Summers said, "that was done pretty fast, and now we've got to be hurrying a little more to get done in time." He consulted his next list. "Bill," he said, "you draw for the Hutchinson family. You got any other households in the Hutchinsons?"

"There's Don and Eva," Mrs. Hutchinson yelled. "Make *them* take their chance!"

"Daughters draw with their husbands' families, Tessie," Mr. Summers said gently. "You know that as well as anyone else."

"It wasn't *fair*," Tessie said.

"I guess not, Joe," Bill Hutchinson said regretfully. "My daughter draws with her husband's family, that's only fair. And I've got no other family except the kids."

"Then, as far as drawing for families is concerned, it's you," Mr. Summers said in explanation, "and as far as drawing for households is concerned, that's you, too. Right?"

"Right," Bill Hutchinson said.

"How many kids, Bill?" Mr. Summers asked formally.

"Three," Bill Hutchinson said. "There's Bill, Jr., and Nancy, and little Dave, and Tessie and me."

"All right, then," Mr. Summers said. "Harry, you got their tickets back?"

Mr. Graves nodded and held up the slips of paper. "Put them in the box, then," Mr. Summers directed. "Take Bill's and put it in."

"I think we ought to start over," Mrs. Hutchinson said, as quietly as she could. "I tell you it wasn't *fair.* You didn't give him time enough to choose. *Everybody* saw that."

Mr. Graves had selected the five slips and put them in the box, and dropped all the papers but those onto the ground, where the breeze caught them and lifted them off.

"Listen, everybody," Mrs. Hutchinson was saying to the people around her.

"Ready, Bill?" Mr. Summers asked, and Bill Hutchinson, with one quick glance around at his wife and children, nodded.

"Remember," Mr. Summers said, "take the slips and keep them folded until each person has taken one. Harry, you help little Dave." Mr. Graves took the hand of the little boy, who came willingly with him up to the box. "Take a paper out of the box, Davy," Mr. Summers said. Davy put his hand into the box and laughed. "Take just *one* paper," Mr. Summers said. "Harry, you hold it for him." Mr. Graves took the child's hand and removed the folded paper from the tight fist and held it while little Dave stood next to him and looked up at him wonderingly.

"Nancy next," Mr. Summers said. Nancy was twelve, and her school friends breathed heavily as she went forward, switching her skirt, and took a slip daintily from the box. "Bill, Jr.," Mr. Summers said, and Billy, his face red and his feet overlarge, nearly knocked the box over as he got a paper out. "Tessie," Mr. Summers said. She hesitated for a minute, looking around defiantly, and then set her lips and went up to the box. She snatched a paper out and held it behind her.

"Bill," Mr. Summers said, and Bill Hutchinson reached into the box and felt around, bringing his hand out at last with the slip of paper in it.

The crowd was quiet. A girl whispered, "I hope it's not Nancy," and the sound of the whisper reached the edges of the crowd.

"It's not the way it used to be," Old Man Warner said clearly. "People ain't the way they used to be."

"All right," Mr. Summers said. "Open the papers. Harry, you open little Dave's."

Mr. Graves opened the slip of paper and there was a general sigh through the crowd as he held it up and everyone could see that it was blank. Nancy and Bill, Jr., opened theirs at the same time, and both beamed and laughed, turning around to the crowd and holding their slips of paper above their heads.

"Tessie," Mr. Summers said. There was a pause, and then Mr. Summers looked at Bill Hutchinson, and Bill unfolded his paper and showed it. It was blank.

"It's Tessie," Mr. Summers said, and his voice was hushed. "Show us her paper, Bill."

Bill Hutchinson went over to his wife and forced the slip of paper out of her hand. It had a black spot on it, the black spot Mr. Summers had made the night before with the heavy pencil in the coal-company office. Bill Hutchinson held it up, and there was a stir in the crowd.

"All right, folks," Mr. Summers said. "Let's finish quickly."

Although the villagers had forgotten the ritual and lost the original black box, they still remembered to use stones. The pile of stones the boys had made earlier was ready; there were stones on the ground with the blowing scraps of paper that had come out of the box. Mrs. Delacroix selected a stone so large she had to pick it up with both hands and turned to Mrs. Dunbar. "Come on," she said. "Hurry up."

Mrs. Dunbar had small stones in both hands, and she said, gasping for breath, "I can't run at all. You'll have to go ahead and I'll catch up with you."

The children had stones already, and someone gave little Davy Hutchinson a few pebbles.

Tessie Hutchinson was in the center of a cleared space by now, and she held her hands out desperately as the villagers moved in on her. "It isn't fair," she said. A stone hit her on the side of the head.

Old Man Warner was saying, "Come on, come on, everyone." Steve Adams was in the front of the crowd of villagers, with Mrs. Graves beside him.

"It isn't fair, it isn't right," Mrs. Hutchinson screamed, and then they were upon her.

# How Do I Love Thee?

by
ELIZABETH BARRETT BROWNING

How do I love thee? Let me count the ways.
I love thee to the depth and breadth and height
My soul can reach, when feeling out of sight
For the ends of Being and ideal Grace.
I love thee to the level of every day's
Most quiet need, by sun and candlelight.
I love thee freely, as men strive for Right;
I love thee purely, as they turn from Praise.
I love thee with the passion put to use
In my old griefs, and with my childhood's faith.
I love thee with a love I seemed to lose
With my lost saints,—I love thee with the breath,
Smiles, tears, of all my life!—and, if God choose,
I shall but love thee better after death.

# To Build a Fire

by
## JACK LONDON

**About the story:**

*Few would have guessed from his mischievous and itinerant adolescence that Jack London would become one of the most popular and widely translated of all American authors. His fifty books and hundreds of stories, both fiction and nonfiction, would dominate the literary marketplace at the beginning of the twentieth century and would introduce a new and distinctly American style of writing.*

*At age twenty-two, when he returned to San Francisco from an unsuccessful search for fortune in the Klondike gold rush, he brought with him a whole world of experiences that would later appear in such popular and acclaimed tales of the north as* **The Call of the Wild** *and* **White Fang.**

*The story that follows is a classic in this Yukon saga, for it shows the human struggle against the powerful, harsh, and unforgiving forces of nature. Like the chapters from* **The Call of the Wild** *presented in* **Classics to Read Aloud to Your Children,** *this story is not for young children, so please don't rush them into this bleak and desolate world before they (just like the character in the story) are fully prepared for it.*

# Part One

**Approximate reading time for Part One:** 21 minutes
**Vocabulary and pronunciation guide:**
> **pall** [PAUL]: a heavy covering, such as the black cloth thrown over a coffin
> **orb:** a sphere or globe
> **Dyea** [dye-EE-ah]: a town in Alaska, now extinct
> **chechaquo** [chee-CHAH-quo]: Alaskan Indian word for an inexperienced outsider
> **unwonted:** unusual; unfamiliar
> **spirit thermometer:** an alcohol thermometer
> **reiterated** [ree-IT-er-ate-ed]: repeated
> **Klondike:** the gold region of Alaska and northwest Canada
> **conflagration** [con-flag-RAY-shun]: a great, destructive fire

Day had broken cold and gray, exceedingly cold and gray, when the man turned aside from the main Yukon trail and climbed the high earthbank where a dim and little-traveled trail led eastward through the fat spruce timberland. It was a steep bank, and he paused for breath at the top, excusing the act to himself by looking at his watch. It was nine o'clock. There was no sun nor hint of sun, though there was not a cloud in the sky. It was a clear day, and yet there seemed an intangible pall [PAUL] over the face of things, a subtle gloom that made the day dark, and that was due to the absence of sun. It had been days since he had seen the sun, and he knew that a few more days must pass before that cheerful orb, due south, would just peep above the skyline and dip immediately from view.

The man flung a look back along the way he had come. The Yukon lay a mile wide and hidden under three feet of ice. On top of this ice were as many feet of snow. It was all pure white, rolling in gentle undulations where the ice jams of the freeze-up had formed. North and south, as far as his eye could see, it was unbroken white, save for a dark hairline that curved and twisted from around the spruce-covered island to the south, and that curved and twisted away into the north, where it disappeared behind another spruce-covered island. This dark hairline was the trail—the main trail—that led south five hundred miles to the Chilcoot Pass, Dyea [dye-EE-ah], and salt water; and that led north seventy miles to Dawson, and still on to the north a thousand miles to Nulato, and finally to St. Michael on the Bering Sea, and a thousand miles and half a thousand more.

But all this—that mysterious, far-reaching hairline trail, the absence of sun from the sky, the tremendous cold, and the strangeness and weirdness of it all—made no impression on the man. It was not because he was long used to it. He was a newcomer in the land, a *chechaquo* [chee-CHAH-quo], and this was his first winter. The trouble with him was that he was without imagination. He was quick and alert in the things of life, but only in the things, and not in the significances. Fifty degrees below zero meant eighty-odd degrees of frost. Such a fact impressed him as being cold and uncomfortable, and that was all. It did not lead him to meditate upon his frailty as a creature of temperature, and upon man's frailty in general, able only to live within certain narrow limits of heat and cold; and from there on it did not lead him to the conjectural field of immortality and man's place in the universe. Fifty degrees below zero stood for a bite of frost that hurt and that must be guarded against by the use of mittens, earflaps, warm moccasins, and thick socks. Fifty degrees below zero was to him just precisely fifty degrees below zero. That there should be anything more to it than that was a thought that never entered his head.

As he turned to go on, he spat speculatively. There was a sharp, explosive crackle that startled him. He spat again. And again, in the air, before it could fall to the snow, the spittle crackled. He knew that at fifty below spittle crackled on the snow, but this spittle had crackled in the air. Undoubtedly it was colder that fifty below—how much colder he did not know. But the temperature did not matter. He was bound for the old claim on the left fork of Henderson Creek, where the boys were already. They had come over across the divide from the Indian Creek country, while he had come the roundabout way to take a look at the possibilities of getting out logs in the spring from the islands in the Yukon. He would be in to camp by six o'clock; a bit after dark, it was true, but the boys would be there, a fire would be going, and a hot supper would be ready. As for lunch, he pressed his hand against the protruding bundle under his jacket. It was also under his shirt, wrapped up in a handkerchief and lying against the naked skin. It was the only way to keep the biscuits from freezing. He smiled agreeably to himself as thought of those biscuits, each cut open and sopped in bacon grease, and each enclosing a generous slice of fried bacon.

He plunged in among the big spruce trees. The trail was faint. A foot of snow had fallen since the last sled had passed over, and he was glad he was without a sled, traveling light. In fact, he carried nothing but the lunch wrapped in the handkerchief. He was surprised, however, at the cold. It certainly was cold, he concluded, as he rubbed his numb nose and cheekbones with his mittened hand. He was a warm-whiskered man, but the hair on his face did not protect the high cheekbones and the eager nose that thrust itself aggressively into the frosty air.

At the man's heels trotted a dog, a big native husky, the proper wolf dog, gray-coated and without any visible or temperamental difference from its brother, the wild wolf. The animal was depressed by the tremendous cold. It knew that it was no time for traveling. Its instinct told it a truer tale than was told to the man by the man's judgment. In reality, it was not merely colder than fifty below zero; it was colder than sixty below, than seventy below. It was seventy-five below zero. Since the freezing point is thirty-two above zero, it meant that one hundred and seven degrees of frost obtained. The dog did not know anything about thermometers. Possibly in its brain there was no sharp consciousness of a condition of very cold such as was in the man's brain. But the brute had its instinct. It experienced a vague but menacing apprehension that subdued it and made it slink along at the man's heels, and that made it question eagerly every unwonted movement of the man as if expecting him to go into camp or to seek shelter somewhere and build a fire. The dog had learned fire, and it wanted fire, or else to burrow under the snow and cuddle its warmth away from the air.

The frozen moisture of its breathing had settled on its fur in a fine powder of frost, and especially were its jowls, muzzle, and eyelashes whitened by its crystaled breath. The man's red beard and mustache were likewise frosted, but more solidly, the deposit taking the form of ice and increasing with every warm, moist breath he exhaled. Also, the man was chewing tobacco, and the muzzle of ice held his lips so rigidly that he was unable to clear his chin when he expelled the juice. The result was that a crystal beard of the color and solidity of amber was increasing its length on his chin. If he fell down it would shatter itself, like glass, into brittle fragments. But he did not mind the appendage. It was the penalty all tobacco chewers paid in that country, and he had been out before in two cold snaps. They had not been so cold as this, he knew, but by the spirit thermometer at Sixty Mile he knew they had been registered at fifty below and at fifty-five.

He held on through the level stretch of woods for several miles and then dropped down a bank to the frozen bed of a small stream. This was Henderson Creek, and he knew he was ten miles from the forks. He looked at his watch. It was ten o'clock. He was making four miles an hour, and he calculated that he would arrive at the forks at half-past twelve. He decided to celebrate that event by eating his lunch there.

The dog dropped in again at his heels, with a tail drooping discouragement, as the man swung along the creek bed. The furrow of the old sled trail was plainly visible, but a dozen inches of snow covered the marks of the last runners. In a month no man had come up or down that silent creek. The man held steadily on. He was not much given to thinking, and just then particularly he had nothing to think about save that he would eat lunch at the forks and that at six o'clock he would be in camp with the boys. There was nobody to talk to; and, had there been, speech would have been impossible because of the ice muzzle on his mouth. So he continued monotonously to chew tobacco and to increase the length of his amber beard.

Once in a while the thought reiterated [ree-IT-er-ate-ed] itself that it was very cold and that he had never experienced such cold. As he walked along he rubbed cheekbones and nose with the back of his mittened hand. He did this automatically, now and again changing hands. But rub as he would, the instant he stopped, his cheekbones went numb. His cheeks were sure to be frostbitten; he knew that, and he experienced a pang of regret that he had not devised a nose strap of the sort Bud wore in cold snaps. Such a strap passed across the cheeks, as well, and saved them. But it didn't matter much, after all. What were frosted cheeks? A bit painful, that was all; they were never serious.

Empty as the man's mind was of thoughts, he was keenly observant, and he noticed the changes in the creek, the curves and bends and timber jams, and always he sharply noted where he placed his feet. Once, coming around a bend, he shied abruptly, like a startled horse, curved away from the place where he had been walking, and retreated several paces back along the trail. The creek he knew was frozen clear to the bottom—no creek could contain water in that arctic winter—but he knew also that there were springs that bubbled out from the hillsides and ran along under the snow and on top of the ice of the creek. He knew that the coldest snaps never froze these springs, and he knew likewise their danger. They were traps. They hid pools of water under the snow that might be three inches deep, or three feet. Sometimes a skin of ice half an inch thick covered them, and in turn was covered by the snow. Sometimes there were alternate layers of water and ice skin, so that when one broke through he kept on breaking through for a while, sometimes wetting himself to the waist.

That was why he had shied in such panic. He had felt the give under his feet and heard the crackle of a snow-hidden ice skin. And to get his feet wet in such a temperature meant trouble and danger. At the very least it meant delay, for he would be forced to stop and build a fire, and under its protection to bare his feet while he dried his socks and moccasins. He stood and studied the creek bed and its banks, and decided that the flow of water came from the right. He reflected awhile, rubbing his nose and cheeks, then skirted to the left, stepping gingerly and testing the footing for each step. Once clear of the danger, he took a fresh chew of tobacco and swung along at his four-mile gait.

In the course of the next two hours he came upon several similar traps. Usually the snow above the hidden pools had a sunken, candied appearance that advertised the danger. Once again, however, he had a close call; and once, suspecting danger, he compelled the dog to go on in front. The dog did not want to go. It hung back until the man shoved it forward, and then it went quickly across the white, unbroken surface. Suddenly it broke through, floundered to one side, and got away to firmer footing. It had wet its forefeet and legs, and almost immediately the water that clung to it turned to ice. It made quick efforts to lick the ice off its legs, then dropped down in the snow and began to bite out the ice that had formed between the toes. This was a matter of instinct. To permit the ice to remain would mean sore feet. It did not know this. It merely obeyed the mysterious prompting that arose from the deep crypts of its being. But the man knew, having achieved a judgment on the subject, and he removed the mitten from his right hand and helped tear out the ice particles. He did not expose his fingers more than a minute, and was astonished at the swift numbness that smote them. It certainly was cold. He pulled on the mitten hastily, and beat the hand savagely across his chest.

At twelve o'clock the day was at its brightest. Yet the sun was too far south on its winter journey to clear the horizon. The bulge of the earth intervened between it and Henderson Creek, where the man walked under a clear sky at noon and cast no shadow. At half-past twelve, to the minute, he arrived at the forks of the creek. He was pleased at the speed he had made. If he kept it up, he would certainly be with the boys by six. He unbuttoned his jacket and shirt and drew forth his lunch. The action consumed no more than a quarter of a minute, yet in that brief moment the numbness laid hold of the exposed fingers. He did not put the mitten on, but, instead, struck the fingers a dozen sharp smashes against his leg. Then he sat down on a snow-covered log to eat. The sting that followed upon the striking of his fingers against his leg ceased so quickly that he was startled. He had had no chance to take a bite of biscuit. He struck the fingers repeatedly and returned them to the mitten, baring the other hand for the purpose of eating. He tried to take a mouthful, but the ice muzzle prevented. He had forgotten to build a fire and thaw out. He chuckled at his foolishness, and as he chuckled he noted the numbness creeping into the exposed fingers. Also, he noted that the stinging which had first come to his toes when he sat down was already passing away. He wondered whether the toes were warm or numb. He moved them inside the moccasins and decided that they were numb.

He pulled the mitten on hurriedly and stood up. He was a bit frightened. He stamped up and down until the stinging returned into the feet. It certainly was cold, was his thought. That man from Sulphur Creek had spoken the truth when telling how cold it sometimes got in the country. And he had laughed at him at the time! That showed one must not be too sure of things. There was no mistake about it, it *was* cold. He strode up and down, stamping his feet and threshing his arms, until reassured by the returning warmth. Then he got out matches and proceeded to make a fire. From the undergrowth, where high water of the previous spring had lodged a supply of seasoned twigs, he got his firewood. Working carefully from a small beginning, he soon had a roaring fire, over which he thawed the ice from this face and in the protection of which he ate his biscuits. For the moment, the cold of space was outwitted. The dog took satisfaction in the fire, stretching out close enough for warmth and far enough away to escape being singed.

When the man had finished, he filled his pipe and took his comfortable time over a smoke. Then he pulled on his mittens, settled the earflaps of his cap firmly about his ears, and took the creek trail up the left fork. The dog was disappointed and yearned back toward the fire. This man did not know cold.

Possibly all the generations of his ancestry had been ignorant of cold, of real cold, of cold one hundred and seven degrees below freezing. But the dog knew; all its ancestry knew, and it had inherited the knowledge. And it knew that it was not good to walk abroad in such fearful cold. It was the time to lie snug in a hole in the snow and wait for a curtain of cloud to be drawn across the face of outer space whence this cold came. On the other hand, there was no keen intimacy between the dog and the man. The one was the toil slave of the other, and the only caresses it had ever received were the caresses of the whiplash and of harsh and menacing throat sounds that threatened the whiplash. So the dog made no effort to communicate its apprehension to the man. It was not concerned in the welfare of the man; it was for its own sake that it yearned back toward the fire. But the man whistled, and spoke to it with the sound of whiplashes, and the dog swung in at the man's heels and followed after.

The man took a chew of tobacco and proceeded to start a new amber beard. Also, his moist breath quickly powdered with white his mustache, eyebrows, and lashes. There did not seem to be so many springs on the left fork of the Henderson, and for half an hour the man saw no signs of any. And then it happened. At a place where there were no signs, where the soft, unbroken snow seemed to advertise solidity beneath, the man broke through. It was not deep. He wet himself halfway to the knees before he floundered out to the firm crust.

He was angry, and cursed his luck aloud. He had hoped to get into camp with the boys at six o'clock, and this would delay him an hour, for he would have to build a fire and dry out his footgear. This was imperative at that low temperature—he knew that much; and he turned aside to the bank, which he climbed. On top, tangled in the underbrush about the trunks of several small spruce trees, was a high-water deposit of dry firewood—sticks and twigs, principally, but also larger portions of seasoned branches and fine, dry, last year's grasses. He threw down several large pieces on top of the snow. This served for a foundation and prevented the young flame from drowning itself in the snow it otherwise would melt. The flame he got by touching a match to a small shred of birchbark that he took from his pocket. This burned even more readily than paper. Placing it on the foundation, he fed the young flame, with wisps of dry grass and with the tiniest dry twigs.

He worked slowly and carefully, keenly aware of his danger. Gradually, as the flame grew stronger, he increased the size of the twigs with which he fed it. He squatted in the snow, pulling the twigs out from their entanglement in the brush and feeding them directly to the flame. He knew there must be no failure. When it is seventy-five below zero, a man must not fail in his first attempt to build a fire—that is, if his feet are wet. If his feet are dry, and he fails, he can run along the trail for a half a mile and restore his circulation. But the circulation of wet and freezing feet cannot be restored by running when it is seventy-five below. No matter how fast he runs, the wet feet will freeze the harder.

All this the man knew. The old-timer on Sulphur Creek had told him about it the previous fall, and now he was appreciating the advice. Already all sensation had gone out of his feet. To build the fire, he had been forced to remove his mittens, and the fingers had quickly gone numb. His pace of four miles an hour had kept his heart pumping blood to the surface of his body and to all the extremities. But the instant he stopped, the action of the pump eased down. The cold of space smote the unprotected tip of the planet, and he, being on that unprotected tip, received the full force of the blow. The blood of his body recoiled before it. The blood was alive, like the dog, and like the dog it wanted to hide away and and cover itself up from the fearful cold. So long as he walked four miles an hour, he pumped that blood, willy-nilly, to the surface; but now it ebbed away and sank down into the recesses of his body. The extremities were the first to feel its absence. His wet feet froze the faster, and his exposed fingers numbed the faster, though they had not yet begun to freeze. Nose and cheeks were already freezing, while the skin of all his body chilled as it lost its blood.

But he was safe. Toes and nose and cheeks would be only touched by the frost, for the fire was beginning to burn with strength. He was feeding it with twigs the size of his finger. In another minute he would be able to feed it with branches the size of his wrist, and then he could remove his wet foot-gear, and, while it dried, he could keep his naked feet warm by the fire, rubbing them at first, of course, with snow. The fire was a success. He was safe. He remembered the advice of the old-timer on Sulphur Creek, and smiled. The old-timer had been very serious in laying down the law that no man must travel alone in the Klondike after fifty below. Well, there he was; he had had the accident; he was alone; and he had saved himself. Those old-timers were rather fainthearted, some of them, he thought. All a man had to do was to keep his head, and he was all right. Any man who was a man could travel alone, but it was surprising, the rapidity with which his cheeks and nose were freezing. And he had not thought his fingers could go lifeless in so short a time. Lifeless they were, for he could scarcely make them move together to grip a twig, and they seemed remote from his body and from him. When he touched a twig, he had to look and see whether or not he had hold of it. The wires were pretty well down between him and his finger ends.

All of which counted for little. There was the fire, snapping and crackling and promising life with every dancing flame. He started to untie his moccasins. They were coated with ice; the thick German socks were like sheaths of iron halfway to the knees; and the moccasin strings were like rods of steel all twisted and knotted as by some conflagration [con-flag-RAY-shun]. For a moment he tugged with his numb fingers, then realizing the folly of it, he drew his sheath knife.

But before he could cut the strings, it happened. It was his own fault or, rather, his mistake. He should not have built the fire under the spruce tree. He should have built it in the open. But it had been easier to pull the twigs from the brush and drop them directly on the fire. Now the tree under which he had done this carried a weight of snow on its boughs. No wind had blown for weeks, and each bough was fully freighted. Each time he had pulled a twig he had communicated a slight agitation to the tree—an imperceptible agitation, so far as he was concerned, but an agitation sufficient to bring about the disaster. High up in the tree, one bough capsized its load of snow. This fell on the boughs beneath, capsizing them. This process continued, spreading out and involving the whole tree. It grew like an avalanche, and it descended without warning upon the man and the fire, and the fire was blotted out! Where it had burned was a mantle of fresh and disordered snow.

# Part Two

**Approximate reading time for Part Two:** 15 minutes
**Vocabulary and pronunciation guide:**
　　**flotsam:** floating pieces or cargo from a wrecked ship
　　**spasmodically** [spaz-MOD-ik-al-lee]: with sudden,
　　　　involuntary fits; like a spasm
　　**apathetically** [ap-uh-THET-ik-al-lee]: without emotion;
　　　　unconcerned; listlessly
　　**sidled** [SIDE-uld]: moved sideways
　　**peremptorily** [purr-EMP-tore-uh-lee]: commandingly;
　　　　urgently
　　**poignant** [POYN-yant]: piercing, painful to the feelings
　　**Mercury:** In Roman mythology, Mercury was the messenger to the gods
　　**simile** [SIM-uh-lee]: a figure of speech that uses the
　　　　words "like" or "as" in a comparison

*T*he man was shocked. It was as though he had just heard his own sentence of death. For a moment he sat and stared at the spot where the fire had been. Then he grew very calm. Perhaps the old-timer on Sulphur Creek was right. If he had only had a trail-mate he would have been in no danger now. The trail-mate could have built the fire. Well, it was up to him to build the fire over again, and this second time there must be no failure. Even if he succeeded, he would most likely lose some toes. His feet must be badly frozen by now, and there would be some time before the second fire was ready.

Such were his thoughts, but he did not sit and think them. He was busy all the time they were passing through his mind. He made a new foundation for the fire, this time in the open, where no treacherous tree could blot it out. Next, he gathered dry grasses and tiny twigs from the high-water flotsam. He could not bring his fingers together to pull them out, but he was able to gather them by the handful. In this way he got many rotten twigs and bits of green moss that were undesirable, but it was the best he could do. He worked methodically, even collecting an armful of the larger branches to be used later when the fire gathered strength. And all the while the dog sat and watched, a certain yearning wistfulness in its eyes, for it looked upon him as the fire-provider, and the fire was slow in coming.

When all was ready, the man reached in his pocket for a second piece of birchbark. He knew the bark was there, and, though he could not feel it with his fingers, he could hear its crisp rustling and he fumbled for it. Try as he would, he could not clutch hold of it. And all the time, in his consciousness, was the knowledge that each instant his feet were freezing. This thought tended to put him in a panic, but he fought against it and kept calm. He pulled on his mittens with his teeth, and threshed his arms back and forth, beating his hands with all his might against his sides. He did this sitting down, and he stood up to do it; and all the while the dog sat in the snow, its wolf brush of a tail curled around warmly over its forefeet, its sharp wolf ears pricked forward intently as it watched the man. And the man, as he beat and threshed with his arms and hands, felt a great surge of envy as he regarded the creature that was warm and secure in its natural covering.

After a time he was aware of the first faraway signals of sensation in his beaten fingers. The faint tingling grew stronger till it evolved into a stinging ache that was excruciating, but which the man hailed with satisfaction. He stripped the mitten from his right hand and fetched forth the birchbark. The ex-

posed fingers were quickly going numb again. Next he brought
out his bunch of sulphur matches. But the tremendous cold
had already driven the life out of his fingers. In his effort to
separate one match from the others, the whole bunch fell in
the snow. He tried to pick it out of the snow, but failed. The
dead fingers could neither touch nor clutch. He was very careful. He drove the thought of his freezing feet, and nose, and
cheeks, out of his mind, devoting his whole soul to the
matches. He watched, using the sense of vision in place of that
of touch, and when he saw his fingers on each side of the
bunch, he closed them—that is, he willed to close them, for
the wires were down, and the fingers did not obey. He pulled
the mitten on the right hand, and beat it fiercely against his
knee. Then, with both mittened hands, he scooped the bunch
of matches, along with much snow, into his lap. Yet he was no
better off.

After some manipulation he managed to get the bunch between the heels of his mittened hands. In this fashion he carried it to his mouth. He drew the lower jaw in, curled the
upper lip out of the way, and scraped the bunch with his upper
teeth in order to separate a match. He succeeded in getting
one, which he dropped on his lap. He was no better off. He
could not pick it up. Then he devised a way. He picked it up
in his teeth and scratched it on his leg. Twenty times he
scratched before he succeeded in lighting it. As it flamed he
held it with his teeth to the birchbark. But the burning brim-
stone went up his nostrils and into his lungs, causing him to
cough spasmodically [spaz-MOD-ik-al-lee]. The match fell into
the snow and went out.

The old-timer on Sulphur Creek was right, he thought in the
moment of controlled despair that ensued: after fifty below, a
man should travel with a partner. He beat his hands, but failed
in exciting any sensation. Suddenly he bared both hands, re-
moving the mittens with his teeth. He caught the whole bunch
between the heels of his hands. His arm-muscles not being
frozen enabled him to press the heels of his hands tightly
against the matches. Then he scratched the bunch along his
leg. It flared into flame, seventy sulphur matches at once!
There was no wind to blow them out. He kept his head to one

side to escape the strangling fumes, and held the blazing bunch to the birchbark. As he so held it, he became aware of sensation in his hand. His flesh was burning. He could smell it. Deep down below the surface he could feel it. The sensation developed into pain that grew acute. And still he endured it, holding the flame of the matches clumsily to the bark that would not light readily because his own burning hands were in the way, absorbing most of the flame.

At last, when he could endure no more, he jerked his hands apart. The blazing matches fell sizzling into the snow, but the birchbark was alight. He began laying dry grasses and the tiniest twigs on the flame. He could not pick and choose, for he had to lift the fuel between the heels of his hands. Small pieces of rotten wood and green moss clung to the twigs, and he bit them off as well as he could with his teeth. He cherished the flame carefully and awkwardly. It meant life, and it must not perish. The withdrawal of blood from the surface of his body now made him begin to shiver, and he grew more awkward. A large piece of green moss fell squarely on the little fire. He tried to poke it out with his fingers, but his shivering frame made him poke too far, and he disrupted the nucleus of the little fire, the burning grasses and tiny twigs separating and scattering. He tried to poke them together again, but in spite of the tenseness of the effort, his shivering got away with him, and the twigs were hopelessly scattered. Each twig gushed a puff of smoke and went out. The fire-provider had failed. As he looked apathetically [ap-uh-THET-ik-al-lee] about him, his eyes chanced on the dog, sitting across the ruins of the fire from him, in the snow, making restless, hunching movements, slightly lifting one forefoot and then the other, shifting its weight back and forth on them with wistful eagerness.

The sight of the dog put a wild idea into his head. He remembered the tale of the man, caught in a blizzard, who killed a steer and crawled inside the carcass, and so was saved. He would kill the dog and bury his hands in the warm body until the numbness went out of them. Then he could build another fire. He spoke to the dog, calling it to him; but in his voice was a strange note of fear that frightened the animal, who had never known the man to speak in such a way before. Some-

thing was the matter, and its suspicious nature sensed danger
—it knew not what danger, but somewhere, somehow, in its
brain arose an apprehension of the man. It flattened its ears
down at the sound of the man's voice, and its restless, hunching movements and the liftings and shiftings of its forefeet
became more pronounced; but it would not come to the man.
He got on his hands and knees and crawled toward the dog.
This unusual posture again excited suspicion, and the animal
sidled [SIDE-uld] mincingly away.

The man sat up in the snow for a moment and struggled for
calmness. Then he pulled on his mittens, by means of his
teeth, and got up on his feet. He glanced down at first in order
to assure himself that he was really standing up, for the absence of sensation in his feet left him unrelated to the earth.
His erect position in itself started to drive the webs of suspicion
from the dog's mind; and when he spoke peremptorily [purr-
EMP-tore-uh-lee], with the sound of whiplashes in his voice,
the dog rendered its customary allegiance and came to him. As
it came within reaching distance, the man lost his control. His
arms flashed out to the dog, and he experienced genuine surprise when he discovered that his hands could not clutch, that
there was neither bend nor feeling in the fingers. He had forgotten for the moment that they were frozen and that they
were freezing more and more. All this happened quickly, and
before the animal could get away, he encircled its body with
his arms. He sat down in the snow, and in this fashion held
the dog, while it snarled and whined and struggled.

But it was all he could do, hold its body encircled in his arms
and sit there. He realized that he could not kill the dog. There
was no way to do it. With his helpless hands he could neither
draw nor hold his sheath knife nor throttle the animal. He
released it, and it plunged wildly away, with tail between its
legs, and still snarling. It halted forty feet away and surveyed
him curiously, with ears sharply pricked forward. The man
looked down at his hands in order to locate them, and found
them hanging on the ends of his arms. It struck him as curious
that one should have to use his eyes in order to find out where
his hands were. He began threshing his arms back and forth,
beating the mittened hands against his sides. He did this for

five minutes, violently, and his heart pumped enough blood up to the surface to put a stop to his shivering. But no sensation was aroused in the hands. He had an impression that they hung like weights on the ends of his arms, but when he tried to run the impression down, he could not find it.

A certain fear of death, dull and oppressive, came to him. This fear quickly became poignant [POYN-yant] as he realized that it was no longer a mere matter of freezing his fingers and toes, or of losing his hands and feet, but that it was a matter of life and death with the chances against him. This threw him into a panic, and he turned and ran up the creek bed along the old, dim trail. The dog joined in behind and kept up with him. He ran blindly, without intention, in fear such as he had never known in his life. Slowly, as he ploughed and floundered through the snow, he began to see things again,—the banks of the creek, the stands of timber, the leafless aspens, and the sky. The running made him feel better. He did not shiver. Maybe, if he ran on, his feet would thaw out; and, anyway, if he ran far enough, he would reach camp and the boys. Without doubt he would lose some fingers and toes and some of his face; but the boys would take care of him, and save the rest of him when he got there. And at the same time there was another thought in his mind that said he would never get to the camp and the boys; that it was too many miles away, that the freezing had too great a start on him, and that he would soon be stiff and dead. This thought he kept in the background and refused to consider. Sometimes it pushed itself forward and demanded to be heard, but he thrust it back and strove to think of other things.

It struck him as curious that he could run at all on feet so frozen that he could not feel them when they struck the earth and took the weight of his body. He seemed to himself to skim along above the surface, and to have no connection with the earth. Somewhere he had once seen a winged Mercury, and he wondered if Mercury felt as he felt when skimming over the earth.

His theory of running until he reached camp and the boys had one flaw in it: he lacked the endurance. Several times he stumbled, and finally he tottered, crumpled up, and fell. When he tried to rise, he failed. He must sit and rest, he decided, and next time he would merely walk and keep on going. As he sat and regained his breath, he noted that he was feeling quite warm and comfortable. He was not shivering, and it even seemed that a warm glow had come to his chest and trunk. And yet, when he touched his nose or cheeks, there was no sensation. Running would not thaw them out. Nor would it thaw out his hands and feet. Then the thought came to him that the frozen portions of his body must be extending. He tried to keep this thought down, to forget it, to think of something else; he was aware of the panicky feeling that it caused, and he was afraid of the panic. But the thought asserted itself, and persisted, until it produced a vision of his body totally frozen. This was too much, and he made another wild run along the trail. Once he slowed down to a walk, but the thought of the freezing extending itself made him run again.

And all the time the dog ran with him, at his heels. When he fell down a second time, it curled its tail over its forefeet and sat in front of him, facing him, curiously eager and intent. The warmth and security of the animal angered him, and he cursed it till it flattened down its ears appeasingly. This time the shivering came more quickly upon the man. He was losing in his battle with the frost. It was creeping into his body from all sides. The thought of it drove him on, but he ran no more than a hundred feet, when he staggered and pitched headlong. It was his last panic. When he had recovered his breath and control, he sat up and entertained in his mind the conception of meeting death with dignity. However, the conception did not come to him in such terms. His idea of it was that he had been making a fool of himself, running around like a chicken with its head cut off—such was the simile [SIM-uh-lee] that occurred to him. Well, he was bound to freeze anyway, and he might as well take it decently. With this new-found peace of mind came the first glimmerings of drowsiness. A good idea, he thought, to sleep off to death. It was like taking an anesthetic. Freezing was not so bad as people thought. There were lots worse ways to die.

He pictured the boys finding his body next day. Suddenly he found himself with them, coming along the trail and looking for himself. And, still with them, he came around a turn in the trail and found himself lying in the snow. He did not belong with himself anymore, for even then he was out of himself, standing with the boys and looking at himself in the snow. It certainly was cold, was his thought. When he got back to the States he could tell the folks what real cold was. He drifted on from this to a vision of the old-timer on Sulphur Creek. He could see him quite clearly, warm and comfortable, and smoking a pipe.

"You were right, old hoss; you were right," the man mumbled to the old-timer of Sulphur Creek.

Then the man drowsed off into what seemed to him the most comfortable and satisfying sleep he had ever known. The dog sat facing him and waiting. The brief day drew to a close in a long, slow twilight. There were no signs of a fire to be made, and, besides, never in the dog's experience had it known a man to sit like that in the snow and make no fire. As the twilight drew on, its eager yearning for the fire mastered it, and with a great lifting and shifting of forefeet, it whined softly, then flattened its ears down in anticipation of being scolded by the man. But the man remained silent. Later, the dog whined loudly. And still later it crept close to the man and caught the scent of death. This made the animal bristle and back away. A little longer it delayed, howling under the stars that leaped and danced and shone brightly in the cold sky. Then it turned and trotted up the trail in the direction of the camp it knew, where were the other food-providers and fire-providers.

# Afterword

When I was a boy, my brother and I would, for hours on end, entertain ourselves by playing a card game called "Authors," which I think is still produced today. Through this game alone, I became familiar with the names of the greatest works while I was still in elementary school. How I wish I had become as familiar with the works themselves.

And it is this same wish that I have for your children—not to make them "superbabies" or have them appear so intellectually precocious that their parents can bask in the glow of their children's (undoubtedly inherited) brilliance. Rather, I want to allow children the opportunity to marvel and wonder and pretend *on their own*, without the aid of animated cartoon characters or splashy special effects.

It is entirely possible, if parents and teachers are willing, for children to hear many, perhaps most, of the recognized masterpieces of western literature—novels, short stories, poems, and plays—while they are still in elementary school. What is necessary in order for this to happen, however, is for parents and teachers to do just what I have done for you in these volumes; namely, review each work thoroughly to ensure that it is appropriate for your intended audience, excise (with great care) the parts that impede the telling of the story, and identify the words and names that might cause vocabulary or pronunciation problems.

All this does, I grant you, require a certain amount of time. But it is "quality time" in the truest sense, and I urge you to spend whatever time you can make available in this pursuit. Parents will find a great resource for story suggestions and for correct pronunciations in the teachers at their child's school; believe me, most teachers appreciate very much having any parent ask for their advice. Librarians, both at school and at the public libraries, are also knowledgeable and eager to help.

In preparing these stories for your children and in tapping the resources at your school and library, you are preparing and developing yourself as well, and so the time you invest has a twofold return. Of course, you can always choose to invest your time in other ways and resort to the alternatives, such as Saturday morning monster cartoons, music videos, and comic books. It's strange, though, that in all the interviews that have been conducted with people who claimed to have been "near death" or to have momentarily "seen the other side," not a single person has lamented the fact that he didn't spend more time at the office.